THE Jerusalem BOOK OF QUOTATIONS

A 3,000-YEAR PERSPECTIVE

Jack Friedman

Copyright © Jack E. Friedman
Jerusalem 2007/5767

All rights reserved. No part of this publication may be translated, reproduced, stored in a retrieval system or transmitted, in any form or by any means, electronic, mechanical, photocopying, recording or otherwise, without express written permission from the publishers.

Typesetting and Cover Design by S. Kim Glassman

ISBN: 978-965-229-392-3

Edition: 1 3 5 7 9 8 6 4 2

Gefen Publishing House, Ltd.
6 Hatzvi Street
Jerusalem 94386, Israel
972-2-538-0247
orders@gefenpublishing.com

Gefen Books
600 Broadway
Lynbrook, NY 11563, USA
1-800-477-5257
orders@gefenpublishing.com

www.israelbooks.com

Printed in Israel

Send for our free catalogue

For my sabra wife Dvora
and our children and grandchildren
whose love for Jerusalem
is above our foremost joy

I express grateful appreciation to
the Jewish National and University Library in Jerusalem
and the New York Public Library, whose vast collections of material
on Jerusalem were invaluable resources.

Contents

Introduction vii
Index of Sources... xix

Quotations

   1. Canaanite Period.. 1

   2. Israelite Period... 5

   3. Roman Period 13

   4. Byzantine Period... 25

   5. Early Muslim Period.. 37

   6. Crusader Period and Muslim Reconquest 51

   7. Mameluke Period... 75

   8. Ottoman Period – Up to Nineteenth Century 107

   9. Ottoman Period – Up to 1917 135

 10. British Mandate Period...................................... 189

 11. Israel Period... 197

Topical Index 215
Bibliography of Works Cited.. 249

INTRODUCTION

The Jerusalem Book of Quotations is a work of impressions more than of historical facts. Its primary purpose is to bring together the kaleidoscopic reactions and responses to Jerusalem from the biblical period to our time as recorded by a representative group of those who have been touched by the Holy City: Jews, Christians, Muslims, as well as unbelievers; pilgrims, travelers, conquerors, scholars and statesmen.

The book is a hymn to Jerusalem. But as the impressionistic quotations about the Holy City, its sacred sites and its peoples all too amply demonstrate, it is a hymn whose discordant notes often clash with the ideal of the city as the embodiment of mankind's ethical and spiritual aspirations.

As I made my way through an exhausting, if not exhaustive, collection of accounts, supplementing an interest in Jerusalem's past that has engaged me for several decades, I was reminded of the admonition in Ecclesiastes: "the making of many books is without limit," which I have taken to be a forewarning by the prescient Solomon of the rivers of ink destined to saturate his city.

And I was reminded, more than once, of René de Chateaubriand's lament in the early eighteenth century: "I am certain that whoever has the patience, as I did, to read nearly two hundred modern accounts of the Holy Land [and Jerusalem], the rabbinic collections, and the passages of the ancients on Judea, would still understand nothing."

The challenge the French scholar and visitor to Jerusalem faced was not the scarcity of information in the sources he consulted. It was, rather, the impossibility of constructing from the massive data a cohesive and harmonious image of the Holy City. What he was alluding to was, likely, the competing – if overlapping – approaches to Jerusalem in the three monotheistic faiths.

For Judaism, the frame of reference is the city of Jerusalem, the spiritual center and ancient capital of Israel, mentioned by name some 640 times in the

Bible. The narratives of the Jewish travelers are filled with acts of mourning for the destruction not only of the Temple, but of the Holy City, and with prayers for its redemption.

Christianity and Islam, as well, celebrate the glory of Jerusalem. The former, especially, correlates events in the Bible and in the New Testament (where Jerusalem appears about 140 times) with the landscape of the city. But for Christianity the focus of veneration is on the sites hallowed by the ministry and passion and crucifixion of Jesus and by his presence in Jerusalem and, as well, by visions of the city's transfiguration into the Heavenly Jerusalem. "I passed by no place known to me from the canonical books of Scripture without visiting it," writes the fifteenth-century Dominican priest Felix Fabri.[1] His quest was for the holy spots that yielded indulgences, but his focus is indicative of the particular nature of Christian devotion to the sacredness of Jerusalem.[2]

For Islam, which honors Jerusalem as the third in sanctity after Mecca and Medina, the core of devotion is the Haram-a-Sharif (Temple Mount), centered on the tradition of Mohammed's journey to the site on his winged steed al-Burak, and on the belief that at the end of days the Prophet will judge mankind in the Valley of Jehoshaphat. Jerusalem itself does not appear by name in the Koran.

Muslim internalization of the holiness of Jerusalem was initially circumscribed largely by the Haram-a-Sharif. The renowned tenth-century Muslim historian and geographer al-Muqaddasi suggested that the resplendent Dome of the Rock erected on that site some three hundred years earlier by Caliph Abd al-Malik had been built to counter the influence of the nearby Church of the Sepulcher, lest that imposing Christian shrine "dazzle the minds of Muslims." A more expansive Muslim approach to the city was embodied in the post-Koranic oral traditions in the Hadith, and in the literary genre of writings known as "Merits of Jerusalem," the latter considered by some scholars to have been a Muslim

---

1. *Wanderings*, 2: pt 1, 196.
2. Robert L. Wilken (*The Land Called Holy*, 1992) introduces a territorial dimension to the Christian veneration of Jerusalem. He develops the thesis that Christianity regards the city itself – and the land – as holy, not just the shrines and sites and churches that commemorate the life and acts of Jesus. He points, for example, to the continuing presence of an indigenous Christian population going back to the Byzantine era in the fourth century. The idea of an earthly Christian city, he argues, runs parallel to the apocalyptic vision of a heavenly Jerusalem.

reaction to the Crusades.³ The merits of Jerusalem compositions, which were particularly popular starting in the eleventh century, "generally consisted of…a collection of traditions attributed to the Prophet…in praise of Jerusalem, often with attached rewards for pious acts performed there."⁴

Woven into the seminal relations of the different faiths about Jerusalem, and bolstering their claims of supremacy, were revised depictions of the city and its locales in keeping with their theological predispositions. Thus, Eusebius, the fourth-century biographer of Constantine, contrasts the "New Jerusalem" – symbolized by the recently constructed Church of the Sepulcher – with the site of the destroyed Temple, and applies to the former the title "Holy of Holies."⁵ In other words, Jesus "had taken the place of the Temple and of everything for which it stood."⁶

One scholar, writing of the transposition of Jewish traditions from the Temple Mount to the Church of the Sepulcher beginning in the Byzantine period, describes the phenomenon as "outright confiscation; the rights to ancient, revered traditions about the past were taken over by another religion" – in this case, Christianity.⁷ A more benign interpretation of these shifts, characteristic of a later age, is found in an observation by Mark Twain about Christian travelers in the nineteenth century. Honest as their intentions may have been, these visitors approached Jerusalem "with their verdicts already prepared, and they could no more write dispassionately about it than they could about their own wives and children."⁸

---

3. E.g., Charles D. Matthews, *Palestine: Mohammedan Holy Land* (New Haven: Yale University Press, 1949), xxii.
4. F.E. Peters, *Jerusalem*, 336. On the different approaches of Christianity and Islam to Jerusalem, I cite Zvi Werblowsky: "Whereas in the case of Christianity historic facts (i.e., the life and death of Jesus) created religious facts (e.g., the resurrection and ascension), and both combined to create 'holy places,' the Islamic case is the exact opposite. Beliefs and piety created religious facts [e.g., the nocturnal journey of Mohammed] and these, in turn, produced historic facts…." ("The Meaning of Jerusalem to Jews, Christians, and Muslims," Israel Universities Study Group for Middle Eastern Affairs, 1978, 5–6)
5. John Wilkinson, *Jerusalem Pilgrims before the Crusades*, 176–77.
6. George Adam Smith, *History of Jerusalem*, 2:522.
7. Joshua Prawer, "Christian Attitudes towards Jerusalem," in Prawer, ed., *The History of Jerusalem*, 326.
8. *Innocents Abroad*, 2:243.

From the Christian perspective, the assertion of territorial rights based on a Christian orientation of Jerusalem has been complicated over the centuries by the interdenominational wrangling over possession of sacred space, especially – but not exclusively – in the Church of the Sepulcher. To quote Henry Maundrell, the late-seventeenth-century English traveler, so much "unchristian fury and animosity divides the different sects [in the church], especially the Greeks and Latins, that they have sometimes proceeded to blows and wounds even at the very door of the sepulcher."[9]

In addition to differing faith-driven predispositions, the struggle for "ownership" of the city has also centered on traditions linked to particular sites. The authenticity of these traditions, especially in the early centuries of pilgrimage, was often "measured by standards of faith and prayer rather than of logical proof."[10] As an example, there is the certitude with which the twelfth-century English visitor Saewulf declares that a groove in the Rock on the Temple Mount represents an imprint of the "footsteps" of Jesus, an assertion expressed with equal assurance by the sixteenth-century Muslim historian Mujir al-Din, who attributes the dip in the stone to the footprint of Mohammed.

That the Christian Saewulf and the Muslim Mujir al-Din link the founders of their respective faiths to the shrine that is at the heart of Jerusalem's spiritual significance underscores the role that sectarian perspective has played in the

---

9. The antagonism between Western European and Eastern-rite "native" Christians is evident in the First Crusade. In a "Letter of the Princes" in 1098 after the battle for Antioch, the nobles report to the pope: "We have overcome the Turks and heathens; heretics, however, Greeks and Armenians, Syrians, and Jacobites, we have not been able to overcome." (*The First Crusade: The Chronicle of Fulcher of Chartres*, ed. Edward Peters, 83–84) In the Church of the Sepulcher, an uneasy tension has continued to characterize relations between the two major dispensations. In December 2004 Greek Orthodox and Franciscan priests came to blows after an argument over whether a door in the basilica should be closed during a procession commemorating the fourth-century pilgrimage to Jerusalem of Helena, the mother of the emperor Constantine.
10. Wilkinson, *Jerusalem Pilgrims*, 37. In the words of Edward Gibbon, in the early Byzantine period, the "zeal, perhaps the avarice, of the clergy of Jerusalem cherished and multiplied these beneficial visits [of pilgrims]. They fixed, by unquestionable tradition, the scene of each memorable event." (*History of the Decline and Fall of the Roman Empire*, 2: 480–81).

Introduction

working out of the city's narrative. Simon Goldhill, in his *Temple of Jerusalem*,[11] provides a more sweeping illustration of the effect of partisan allegiance. Discussing the Roman destruction of the Temple in 70 CE, Goldhill notes that according to Josephus (*Wars of the Jews*, 6.4) Titus opposed the burning of the sanctuary. Although a Jew, Josephus was writing "under the patronage of Titus himself, and he knew how to praise the Roman by celebrating his clemency."[12] By contrast, the fourth-century church historian Sulpicius Severus reports that Titus ordered the sacking of the Temple despite the importunities of his generals because Severus was "keen to show that those emperors who did not adopt Christianity were the evil enemies of the newly successful religion."[13]

The accretion of site-linked traditions frequently evoked expressions of incredulity among later visitors. George Sandys, whose 1610 journey to Jerusalem was one of the first by an English Protestant after the Reformation, insisted that his account would "deliver the Reader from many erring reports of the too credulous devote, and too too vain-glorious." What he was doing in effect, in the earthy metaphor of Christianus Adrichomius's *Briefe Description of Hierusalem* (1595) which served Sandys as a source, was attempting to "[sweep] the streetes and corners of [Jerusalem] with the broome of truth." Sandys's (and Adrichomius's) target was the Roman Catholic scheme of Jerusalem, which continued to be propounded by the Franciscans who controlled the access of Western Christians to the Holy Land.

Saewulf's twelfth-century visit took place at a time when the Temple Mount had been incorporated into the Christian narrative, implicitly advancing Christian rights to Jerusalem. In the earlier Byzantine era, the chief importance of the Temple Mount was that it lay in ruins, in keeping with Jesus' prophecy that the Temple would be destroyed.[14] The detailed plan of Jerusalem in the sixth-century Madaba map does not even identify the Temple Mount. During the Latin kingdom, however, the site achieved a degree of Christian sanctity as the Crusaders mounted a large gold cross atop the Dome of the Rock ("Templum Domini") and constructed an altar in the al-Aksa Mosque ("Templum

---

11. Cambridge: Harvard University Press, 2005.
12. Goldhill, *The Temple of Jerusalem*, 17.
13. Ibid. See the quotation from Severus in this book.
14. Meir Ben-Dov, *In the Shadow of the Temple*, 25.

Solomonis"). It became the home of (and gave its name to) the newly formed Order of the Knights Templars.[15]

Christianity's newfound identification with the Temple Mount was short-lived, as the reconquering Muslims under Saladin in 1187 ejected the symbols of the Christian presence. Other assertions of possession of the mount and its environs – and their implications for rights to Jerusalem – have had more enduring consequences. Notable is the presumed spot where al-Burak, the steed of Mohammed, was tethered during the Prophet's ascent to the heavens. Early Muslim writers fix the location "under the corner of the [Aksa] Mosque," or to the right of the Dome of Gabriel.[16] Since the nineteenth century the tradition of al-Burak has been linked to Barclay's Gate in the Western Wall. This was a period when that shrine was assuming increasing importance as the focus of Jewish spiritual and, later, national aspirations.

The uncertain itinerary of al-Burak suggests another way in which claims for predominance in Jerusalem have been reinforced over time: the shift of traditions from one locale to another. The whereabouts of Adam illustrate the point. As recorded in the Midrash, Jewish lore reports his creation from the soil of Moriah, the Temple Mount. That, as the Midrash notes, is also where Abraham was commanded by God to offer up his son Isaac. By the sixth century, *The Breviary of Jerusalem*, a handbook for pilgrims, locates these primal occurrences in the Church of the Sepulcher. "There Adam was formed. There Abraham offered his son Isaac in the very place where our Lord was crucified."

A later Christian pilgrim, Daniel the Abbot, observes in the twelfth century that the skull of Adam lies beneath the rock on which the crucifixion was enacted, a transfer of a portion of our common father's mortal remains from the Tomb of

---

15. Goldhill (*The Temple of Jerusalem*, 107–8) argues that there is an intriguing dichotomy in Christianity's attitude toward the history and theology of the Temple. "On the one hand, Christians celebrated the destruction of the Temple as the triumph of Christianity over Judaism…. On the other hand, Christians elevate the Temple as an image of spiritual order. The Temple becomes Christ, the community of Christians, the Christian's body and even a model for the Church. The new Temple is fundamental to Christianity, and finding how the Temple is to be remade is a defining Christian activity."
16. Ibn Abd Rabbih (Le Strange, *History of Jerusalem under the Moslems*, 82); Ibn Khusru [Khusraw], *An Account of Jerusalem*, 15.

the Patriarchs in Hebron where Jewish sources place them.[17] Calvary, says Felix Fabri, was a place "worthy of honor from ancient times before the crucifixion of Christ."[18]

In a broader context of religious polemic in the service of exclusionary intent, the Crusader leader Richard Lion-Heart sends a message to the Muslim conqueror Saladin in 1191 laying out the conditions for a peace agreement. As quoted by Baha ad-Din Ibn Shaddad, Richard proclaims, "Jerusalem is for us an object of worship that we could not give up even if there were only one of us left." To which Saladin responds, "Jerusalem is ours as much as yours; indeed it is even more sacred to us than it is to you, for it is the place from which our Prophet accomplished his nocturnal journey and the place where our community will gather [on the Day of Judgment]."[19]

Religious – more properly, political – fiat was similarly at work in the destruction of the Franciscan chapel on Mount Zion in the fifteenth century. As recounted by Fabri, when the Mameluke sultan Barshay (1422–37) was informed of the tradition that King David was buried on that hill he declared, "we Saracens [Muslims] also count David as holy, even as Christians and Jews do…. Wherefore, neither Christians nor Jews shall have that place, but we will take it for ourselves." In placing the imprint of Islam on Mount Zion, the sultan was, of course, acting no differently than had the Crusaders in their transformation of the Dome of the Rock into a Christian enclave.[20]

The contention for territorial preeminence, fed by justifications rooted in religious history and traditions, has of course continued unabated, as demonstrated by the quotations from more recent periods. The Jews must not be enabled to pave the path adjacent to the Western Wall, declares an Islamic religious rul-

---

17. The shifts in the locales by no means occur in a linear chronological fashion. Saewulf cites the opinion of Augustine that Adam is buried in Hebron.
18. *Wanderings* 1:pt 2, 367.
19. *an-Nawadir as-Sultaniyya*…[Sultanly anecdotes]; quoted in Gabrieli, *Arab Historians of the Crusades*, 226.
20. Willful displacement of the opponent was not necessarily related to places. Mark Twain expresses wonderment that none of the Renaissance artists "ever put into the face of the Madonna that indescribable something which proclaims the Jewess…." (*Innocents Abroad* 1:194).

ing in 1840,[21] because "it adjoins the wall of the Haram-a-Sharif and also the spot where al-Burak was tethered." In a more embracing pronouncement, William Thomson, an American missionary and author of one of the nineteenth century's most popular accounts of the Holy Land, insists that Jerusalem is "the common property of the whole Christian world." The Jews, too, in the wake of the burgeoning Zionist movement, mingle their dirges for Jerusalem destroyed with reassertions of their ancient rights to the city. Here is David Ben-Gurion, responding to the United Nations plan in 1949 to internationalize Jerusalem: "We will not countenance a UN effort to tear Jerusalem from the State of Israel – it is the eternal capital of the Jewish people."

In this period one occasionally encounters a more universalistic, less sectarian, view of Jerusalem: "the theater of the most…stupendous events…in the annals of the world," in the words of J.T. Barclay, the nineteenth-century American missionary and researcher. It is also a time that gives abundant expression to the skeptical reactions of a new class of visitor, the urbane – likely Protestant – traveler seeking not spiritual fulfillment but the satisfaction of curiosity. "We…[were] shown…some nails of the true cross [and] a fragment of the cross itself," says Twain after a visit to the Cathedral of Notre Dame. "We had already seen a large part of the true cross in a church in the Azores." But even the cynically disposed American humorist cannot fail to be moved at the traditional site of the crucifixion. The visitor "fully believes that he is looking upon the very spot where the Savior gave up his life."

The most distinctive shift from the mid-nineteenth-century onward has been the application of scholarship and scientific inquiry in the service of a more rational understanding of the Holy City and its past, a development exemplified by the founding in 1865 of the Palestine Exploration Fund in England to study the biblical history of the country "in accordance with scientific principles."[22] But despite the attempts to distinguish "between the real and the ideal, between fact and imagination,"[23] the struggle for "Whose Jerusalem?" has continued unabated.

---

21. *Islamic Pious Foundations in Jerusalem* (see Sherif Pasha).
22. David M. Jacobson, "Search for the Holy Temple," *Eretz Magazine* (May–June 1997): 28.
23. Franklin Walker, *Irreverent Pilgrims: Melville, Browne and Mark Twain in the Holy Land* (Seattle: University of Washington Press, 1974), 32.

Introduction

   At first glance, it may seem possible to soften, if not mute, the disharmony in the perceptions of Jerusalem by looking at this complex city as a "tapestry in time." The phrase is that of Samuel Heilman, a contemporary social researcher and student of Jerusalem. This striking metaphor suggests that the fluidity of time might enable us to capture a harmonious snapshot of Jerusalem by selecting a particular point in its history. Go back before the common era and we are looking, in discrete chapters, at the stronghold of the Jebusites, or the city of the kings of Judah and the prophets, or the Hasmoneans, or the emerging Roman Empire and the birth of Christianity. Refocus the movable tapestry and our portrait is of Rome, its dominance fading as it gives way to the Byzantine Empire, the early Muslim conquest, the Crusades and, eventually, to the Ottoman Empire and, in our period, to the British Mandate and the revival of Jewish sovereignty.

   However, even a time-fixed configuration cannot avoid the disharmony reflected in our sources. Take the Roman period: Simon Bar Kochba daringly inscribing "for the freedom of Jerusalem" on coins, even as Hadrian, in the words of the fourth-century church historian Philostorgius, renames the city "Aelia…in order to banish and exclude thence the Jewish race, that they may not find in the name…a pretext for claiming it as their country."

   A final observation. In addition to demonstrating the dissonance that characterizes the perceptions of Jerusalem, the quotations also – a point that needs to be made – give voice to the wellspring of reverence and love for the city and its sacred precincts that runs through most of the reports. But far too often the narratives, and the quotations, leave little room for the point of view of the other. "Walk around Zion," says the Psalmist (48.13), "circle it, count its towers, take note of its ramparts, go through its citadels, that you may recount it to a future age." Of the majority of authors in this book, pilgrims and travelers and others who have written of the city from afar, each in his own way went round Jerusalem's towers and recorded his conclusions – conclusions which, however, rest on competing dispensational beliefs and traditions. Thus, the reader seeking enlightenment and harmony in the aggregate of the quotations would in the end, like Chateaubriand, still understand nothing.

   In the dust of the curb abutting the parking space outside my home at the edge of Jerusalem's Rehavia neighborhood I often observe columns of small reddish ants moving purposefully in opposing directions. "Go to the ant and grow wise," we are advised in Proverbs (6:6). From my house, I look out at the adjacent Valley of the Cross, named for the massive bulk of the sixth-century monastery that guards the spot where according to Christian tradition the wood of the cross was grown.[24] On a hill above the monastery sits the wide box-like shape of the Knesset, symbol of Israel reborn, and in a dell below is an incongruous assemblage of structures belonging to several scout troops. A painted sign atop one of the buildings reads Modi'in, city of birth of the heroes of the Hanukkah story.

Small groves of olive trees make their homes in the valley, descendants of the stock that once grew thickly in the vicinity, leading George Sandys to speculate that the wood of the cross came not from the palm, "but rather, if any, the Olive, of which that place hath store."[25] When the olives are ripe, Arabs in small family groups gather under the trees and beat the branches with long poles to release the fruit, which lands on cloths spread out below.

Like the collection of authors assembled in the book – and like the zealous ants in my parking alcove – the Christians, Jews and Arabs in the valley move in their divergent directions. Despite the latent tension and the volatility, one cannot deny the existence of a sense of accommodation that makes this arrangement possible.

But even such accommodation, reluctant and grudging as it may be, seems to be at variance with the exclusivistic assertions that resonate in many of the quotations. Nevertheless, without intending to become embroiled in the cacophonous debates over the status of Jerusalem, I would argue that the present situation demonstrates that accommodation can be a reality. In the long history of Jerusalem, this is one of those rare periods when Jews, Christians, Muslims, and those without denominational affiliation can find unimpeded fulfillment in the pursuit of their unique patrimonies in this sacred place.

No less a partisan of theologically sanctioned possession than Friar Fabri declared that "Christians would care little about the Saracens' [over]bearing rule in Jerusalem, provided only that we were allowed freedom to pass in and out of the Lord's sepulcher without fear and without vexations and extortions." But, alas,

---

24. The enterprising Greek Orthodox clerics who control the shrine not long ago affixed a plaque to the monastery's exterior wall attributing its construction to Helena, the mother of Constantine, in the fourth century.
25. *Relation of a Journey*, 144.

"since Christians and Saracens cannot agree about this matter, unhappy Jerusalem has suffered…and will hereafter suffer." Fabri would have had little cause to cavil about the current state of affairs.

I would maintain that the facts support this conclusion, even as I acknowledge my relationship to Jerusalem as a believing Israeli and American Jew. And I would hope that those whose ties spring from other influences will share my conviction that this Holy City, nourished by the universal broadness of spirit of the faith that gave meaning to Jerusalem, will one day yield its promise as a city of peace for all nations. "Rejoice with Jerusalem and be glad for her, all you who love her" (Isaiah 66:10).

January 2007

Notes on the Text

With some exceptions, spellings in the quotations have been modernized, and American usage has been employed (e.g., Sepulcher, not Sepulchre).

Regarding the use of parentheses ( ), and square brackets [ ]: the former indicates a word or phrase that appears in the original but out of sequence, the latter an insertion to clarify the context of the citation. Years in parentheses below the author's name indicate date of visit to Jerusalem.

Many of the authors cited have appeared in numerous editions under the hands of different translators and editors. My primary objective in selecting texts has been to provide authoritative and accurate expressions of what the authors wrote. In some cases, because of a lack of accessibility, I have depended on older editions of these writings.

For quotations from scripture, I used primarily the following editions: for the (Jewish) Bible, the Jewish Publication Society *Tanakh: The Holy Scriptures; The New JPS Translation According to the Traditional Hebrew Text*, 1985; for the New Testament, the translation of the London Trinitarian Society (no date); and for the Koran, *A Contemporary Translation* by Ahmed Ali, 2nd revised ed., Princeton University Press, 1990.

All quotations are identified by source in the quotations. Full bibliographical references are in the list of works cited.

General References for Further Reading
(See works cited for full bibliographical information)

Adler, Elkan, ed., *Jewish Travellers*, 1966.
Gabrieli, Francesco., *Arab Historians of the Crusades*, 1984.
Hammer, Reuven., *The Jerusalem Anthology*, 1995.
Hillenbrand, Carole., *The Crusades: Islamic Perspectives*, 2000.
Millgram, Stanley, *Jerusalem Curiosities*, 1990.
Naor, Mordecai, *City of Hope: Jerusalem from Biblical to Modern Times*, 1997.
Peters, Edward, ed., *The First Crusade*, 1998.
Peters, F. E., *Jerusalem*, 1985.
Rosovsky, Nitza, ed., *City of the Great King*, 1996.
Schur, Nathan, *Twenty Centuries of Christian Pilgrimage to the Holy Land*, 1992.
Wilkinson, John, *Jerusalem Pilgrims before the Crusades*, 1973.

Index of Sources

A
Abd al-Malik (caliph) 39
Adomnan 39
Adrichomius, Christianus 109
Agnon, S.Y. 199
'Ali of Herat 53
Allenby, General Edmund 191
Anonymous (Jewish pilgrim inscription) 27
Anonymous (letter from Jerusalem) 40
Anonymous ("A Song Mad[e] by F.B.P.") 109
Anonymous ("weeping in Zion") 40
Anonymous Pilgrims 53
Antoninus Martyr 27
Aristeas 7
Arnold von Harff 77
Augustine, Saint 27
Avigad, Nahman 199

B
Baedeker, Karl 137
Baha ad-Din Ibn Shaddad 68
Balfour, Arthur James 191
Bar Kochba, Simon 15
Barclay, J.T. 137
Bartlett, W.H. 139
Begin, Menachem 199
Bellow, Saul 200

xix

Belon, Pierre 109
Ben-Dov, Meir 200
Benedict 41
Ben-Gurion, David 191, 202
Benjamin of Tudela 53
Berger, Philippe 142
Bernard the Monk 41
Bible 3, 7
Biddulph, William 110
Blake, William 142
Blyden, Edward Wilmont 143
Bordeaux Pilgrim 28
Breviary; or, Short Description of Jerusalem 28
British Secretary of State for the Colonies 192
Buckingham, James Silk 144
Bunyan, John 111
Burchard of Mount Zion 78
Butler, Samuel 144
Byron, George Gordon 144

C   Calvin, John 111
Casola, Pietro 78
Chateaubriand, François-René de 145
Chaucer, Geoffrey 79
Chelebi, Evliye 111
Chelo, Isaac ben Joseph 80
Chesterton, G.K. 192
Chronicon Paschale 29
Churchill, Winston 193, 203
Cicero 15
The City of Jerusalem 55

Index of Sources

"Civita Cattolica" 147
Clarke, Daniel Edward 147
Clinton, Bill 203
Columbus, Christopher 80
"Commemoratorium on the Churches in Jerusalem" 41
Conder, Claude Reignier 148
Curtis, George W. 149
Curzon, Robert 149

D
Daniel the Abbot 55
Dayan, Moshe 203
The Deeds of the Franks (Gesta Francorum) 56
Dio Cassius 15
Diodorus Siculus 15
Disraeli, Benjamin 150

E
Eban, Abba 204
Eberhard of Wurtermberg, Count 112
Egeria 29
Elijah of Ferrara 81
Elliott, Charles W. 150
Epiphanius the Monk 42
Eucherius 30
Eusebius 30
"Execration Texts" 3

F
Fabri, Friar Felix 81
Farhi, Estori 86
Finn, James 151
Fitzimmons, Friar Simon 87
Fra Niccolo of Poggibonsi 99

Freese, Jacob 150
Fulcher of Chartres 57
Fuller, Thomas 112

G Gedaliah of Siemiatycze 113
Gibbon, Edward 114
Ginsberg, Asher Hirsch (Ahad HaAm) 151
Godfrey de Bouillon 58
Goren, Rabbi Shlomo 204
Gregory VIII, Pope 59
Gregory of Nyssa 31
Gur, Mordecai 204

H ha-Kohen, Joseph 119
Halevi, Judah 59
Harawi, Abu al-Hasan al- 60
Hareven, Shulamith 204
Harizi, Judah al- 60
Hecataeus of Adbera 11
Heilman, Samuel 205
Heine, Heinrich 151
Herbert, George 114
Herzl, Theodor 152
Heschel, Abraham Joshua 205
Heywood, Thomas 115
Hirschberg, A.S. 153
Horn, Father Elzear 115

I Ibn 'Abd Rabbih 42
Ibn al-Athir 60
Ibn al-Firkah al-Fazari 89

Index of Sources

Ibn al-Qalanisi 61
Ibn az-Zaki 62
Ibn Battuta 88
Ibn Ezra 61
Ibn Ishaq 42
Ibn Khusru (Khusraw), Nasir 43
Ibn Taymiyya 90
Ibn Wasil, Jamal ad-Din 62
Idrisi, al- 62
Imad ad-Din 63
Imber, Naftali Herz 153
"In the Footsteps of the Master" 91
"Itinerary of a Certain Englishman" 91

J

Jacob, Rabbi, messenger of Rabbi Jechiel of Paris 92
Jacobus de Voragine 93
Jerome, Saint 32
John of Wurzburg 65
"Joseph" (Narkis Street Baptist Congregation) 205
Josephus Flavius 16
Jowett, William 153
Julian (emperor) 33

K

Kaleel, Mousa J. 154
Karo, Rabbi Joseph 118
Kenyon, Kathleen 206
Kernohan, R.D. 207
Kinglake, Alexander William 154
Kipling, Rudyard 193
Kollek, Teddy 208
Kook, Rabbi Abraham Isaac 193

	Koran	45
	Kumsi, Daniel ben Moshe al-	45
L	Lamartine, Alphonse-Marie-Louis de	155
	Le Strange, Guy	155
	Lear, Edward	155
	Lewis, Bernard	209
	"Life of Constantine"	45
	Lincoln, Abraham	156
	Lithgow, William	119
	Lloyd George, David	194
	Ludolph von Suchem	93
	Luther, Martin	120
M	Maccabees, Book of	11
	Macleod, Norman	156
	Maimonides	66
	Mandeville, Sir John	94
	Manning, Reverend Samuel	156
	Margoliouth, David Samuel	158
	Martineau, Harriet	158
	Marx, Karl	159
	Mason, John	120
	Mas'udi	47
	Matathias (Maccabee)	11
	Maundrell, Henry	120
	Melville, Herman	160
	Menahem Mendel of Kamieniec, Rabbi	162
	Meshullam, Rabbi, ben Rabbi Menahem of Volterra	94
	Michener, James	209
	Midrash	17

Index of Sources

Millgram, Abraham E. 209
Milton, John 123
Montefiore, Sir Moses and Lady Judith 162
Morris, Robert 163
Moryson, Fynes 124
Moses ben Elijah the Karaite, Rabbi 126
Moses of Basola, Rabbi 125
Mujir al-Din 96
Muqaddasi, al- 47
Muqatil b. Sulayman 48
Muthir al Ghiram 97

N

Nahmanides 98
Napoleon, Bonaparte 110
Narkiss, General Uzi 210
Netanyahu, Benjamin 210
New Testament 18
Noah, Mordecai Emanuel 163
Nuseibeh, Wajeen Yacob 210

O

Obadiah of Bertinoro, Rabbi 101
Oesterreicher, Msgr. John M 210
Ogier VIII d'Anglure, Seigneur 102
Oliphant, Laurence 164
Omar (Caliph) 49
Origen 19
Oz, Amos 211

P

Pascha, John 126
Pausanias 20
Petachia of Ratisbon, Rabbi 66

Petrarch, Francesco ... 103
Philostorgius ... 33
Photius ... 49
Piacenza Pilgrim ... 33
Pierotti, Ermete ... 164
Pliny the Elder ... 20
Pococke, Richard ... 126
Poryat (Praeger), Moses ben Israel of Prague ... 127
Procopius ... 34

Q
Quarles, Francis ... 128

R
Rabin, Yitzhak ... 211
Raymond d'Aguilers ... 67
Richard Lion-Heart ... 67
Robinson, Edward ... 165
Roosevelt, Theodore ... 166
Rossi, David de ... 128

S
Saewulf ... 68
Said, Edward ... 211
Saladin ... 69
Samuel ben Samson, Rabbi ... 70
Sanderson, John ... 128
Sandys, George ... 129
Santo Brasca ... 77
Schwarz, Joseph ... 167
Seetzen, Ulrich ... 167
Shakespeare, William ... 130
Sheehan, Vincent ... 194
Shemer, Naomi ... 211

Index of Sources

Sherif Pasha 168
Shipler, David K. 212
Simon (Maccabee) 11
Smith, George Adam 169
Sophronius 35
Sozomen 35
Stanley, Arthur P. 169
Stephens, John Lloyd 171
Storme, Albert 212
Storrs, Sir Ronald 194
Strabo 20
Suleiman the Magnificent 130
Sulpicius Severus 36
Suriano, Francesco 103

T

Tacitus 20
Talmud 21
Tasso, Torquato 131
Taylor, Bayard 175
Thackeray, William Makepeace 175
Theoderich 70
Theodosius 36
Thomson, William McClure 176
Timberlake, Henry 131
Toynbee, Arnold 195
Tudebode, Peter 71
Twain, Mark 179
Tymme, Thomas 132
Tyndale, William 132

U
Urban II, Pope 71
Usuma bin Munqidh 71

V
Vespasian 23
Volney, Count Constantin 132

W
Warburton, Eliot 182
Warner, Charles Dudley 183
Warren, Charles 185
Weizmann, Chaim 185
Wey, William 105
Whittier, John Greenleaf 186
Wiesel, Elie 212
Wilde, William Robert 186
Wilkinson, Rev. John 212
William of Tyre 72
Willibald, Saint 49
Wilson, Charles W. 187
Winthrop, John 134

Y
Yakut 73
Yehoshua, A.B. 213
Yerushalmi, Moses 134
Yitzchok, Rabbi Levi of Berditchev 119

Z
Zamakshari, al- 73
Zuta, H.A. and L. Sukenik 195

#1
Canaanite Period
UP TO TWELFTH CENTURY BCE

"Execration Texts"

INSCRIBED ON CLAY BOWLS OR FIGURINES, CIRCA 1900 BCE

"Recorded historical information about Jerusalem dates back only four thousand years, beginning about one thousand years after the city's establishment: Jerusalem is first clearly mentioned in the Egyptian Execration Texts."*
    –Ben-Dov, *Historical Atlas*, 22–23

*Bearing images of enemies, these inscribed bowls or figurines were broken to ensure that the enemies would be vanquished. The name of Jerusalem also appears in the fourteenth-century BCE El-Amarna letters.

Bible

"Melchizedek, king of Salem, brought out bread and wine."
    –Genesis 14:18*

*Cf. Psalms 76:3: "Then his dwelling was in Salem."

"Thus said the Lord God to Jerusalem: By origin and birth you are from the land of the Canaanites – your father was an Amorite and your mother a Hittite."*
    –Ezekiel 16:3

*In this prophecy Ezekiel rebukes Israel for its transgressions.

#2 Israelite Period
UP TO 63 BCE

- King David's conquest of Jerusalem from the Jebusites
- First Temple (King Solomon)
- Babylonian destruction and exile
- Return from Persia
- Second Temple (Ezra and Nehemiah)
- Greek conquest and Hasmoneans
- Start of Roman domination

Aristeas

SECOND-CENTURY BCE JEWISH-HELLENISTIC WRITER; OFFICIAL IN COURT OF PTOLEMY II, KING OF EGYPT 285–246 BCE

"When we arrived in the land of the Jews, we saw the city situated in the middle of the whole of Judea on the top of a mountain of considerable altitude. On the summit the temple had been built in all its splendor."
—Letter of Aristeas, Alexandria; quoted in Naor, *City of Hope*, 29*

*The letter, which purports to describe the events surrounding the translation of the Bible known as the Septuagint, is considered "more a romance than a historical account" of that occasion. ("Aristeas," *Encyclopedia Judaica*, 1972).

Bible

"David captured the stronghold of Zion; it is now the City of David."
—2 Samuel 5:7

"Thereupon David went and brought up the Ark of God…to the City of David."
—2 Samuel 6:12

"And it came to pass in the four hundred and eightieth year after the children of Israel were come out of the land of Egypt, in the fourth year of Solomon's reign over Israel…that he began to build the house of the Lord."
—1 Kings 6:1

"I will protect and save this city for My sake,

And for the sake of My servant David."
—2 Kings 19:34

"And in the fifth month, on the seventh day, the nineteenth year of king Nebuchadnezzar king of Babylon, Nebuzaradan, the chief of the guards, an officer of the king of Babylon, came to Jerusalem. And he burned the House of the

Lord, the king's palace, and all the houses of Jerusalem...."
—2 Kings 25:8–9

"I will restore your magistrates as of old,

And your counselors as of yore.

After that you will be called

City of Righteousness, Faithful City."
—Isaiah 1:26

"And the many peoples shall go and say:

'Come, let us go up to the Mount of the Lord,

To the House of the God of Jacob;

That He may instruct us in His ways,

And that we may walk in His paths.'

For instruction shall come forth from Zion,

The word of the Lord from Jerusalem."
—Isaiah 2:3

"Ah, Ariel, Ariel,*
City where David camped."
—Isaiah 29:1

*A poetic name of Jerusalem.

"And the ransomed of the Lord shall return,

And come with shouting to Zion,

Crowned with joy everlasting."
—Isaiah 35:14

"For the sake of Zion I will not be silent,

For the sake of Jerusalem I will not be still...."
—Isaiah 62:1

"Rejoice with Jerusalem and be glad for her,

All you who love her."
—Isaiah 66:10

"And go out to the Valley of ben Hinnom – at the entrance of the Harsith* Gate – and proclaim there the words which I will speak to you.... [They]

have filled this place with the blood of the innocents. They have built shrines to Baal, to put their children to the fire as burnt offerings to Baal…. Assuredly, a time is coming…when this place shall no longer be called Topheth or Valley of Ben-hinnom, but Valley of Slaughter."
—Jeremiah 19:2–6

*=discarded pottery shards?

"Thus said the Lord God: I set this Jerusalem in the midst of nations, with countries round about her."
—Ezekiel 5:5

"Let the nations rouse themselves and march up

To the Valley of Jehoshaphat;

For there will I sit in judgment

Over all the nations roundabout."
—Joel 4:12

"For instruction shall come forth from Zion,

The word of the Lord from Jerusalem."
—Micah 4:2

"There shall yet be old men and women in the squares of Jerusalem…. And the squares of the city shall be crowded with boys and girls playing…."
—Zechariah 8:4–5

"Walk around Zion,

circle it; count its towers…"
—Psalms 48:13

"I rejoiced when they said to me,

'We are going to the House of the Lord.'

Our feet stood inside your gates, O Jerusalem,

Jerusalem built up, a city knit together…."
—Psalms 122:1–2

"Pray for the well-being of Jerusalem:

May those who love you be at peace."
—Psalms 122:6

"By the waters of Babylon,

there we sat,

sat and wept

as we thought of Zion."
—Psalms 137:1

"How can we sing a song of the Lord on alien soil?

If I forget you, O Jerusalem, let my right hand wither;

let my tongue stick to my palate if I cease to think of you,

if I do not keep Jerusalem in memory even at my happiest hour."
—Psalms 137:4–5

"Alas!

Lonely sits the city

Once great with people!

She that was great among nations

Is become like a widow."

. . . .

"Bitterly she weeps in the night,

Her cheek wet with tears.

There is none to comfort her

Of all her friends."
—Lamentations 1:1–2

"Thus said King Cyrus of Persia. The Lord God of Heaven has given me all the kingdoms of the earth and has charged me with building Him a house in Jerusalem…. Anyone of you of all His people…let him go up to Jerusalem…and build the House of the Lord God of Israel…."
—Ezra 1:2–3; see also 2 Chronicles 36:23

"I went out by night by the Valley Gate to the Jackal's well and to the Dung Gate;* and I inspected the walls of Jerusalem which were broken down and its gates which had been destroyed by fire."
—Nehemiah 2:3

*Not the present Dung Gate (See Vilnay, *Jerusalem: The Old City*, 45–46).

"The basket-carriers were burdened, doing work with one hand while the other held a weapon. As for the builders, each had his sword girded at his side as he was building."
—Nehemiah 4:11–12

Hecataeus of Adbera

CA. 300 BCE; PHILOSOPHER AND GRAMMARIAN, SAID TO BE AUTHOR OF HISTORY OF THE JEWS CITED OFTEN BY JOSEPHUS

"There is not a single statue or votive offering [in the Temple], no trace of a plant, in the form of a sacred grove or the like."
—Josephus, *Against Apion*, bk. 1 quoted in Stern, ed., *Greek and Latin Authors* 1:39

Book of Maccabees

"King Antiochus sent an elderly Athenian to force the Jews to abandon their ancestral customs and no longer regulate their lives according to the laws of God. He was also commissioned to pollute the Temple at Jerusalem and dedicate it to Olympian Zeus...."
—2 Maccabees 6:1–2; translation of Peters, *Jerusalem*, 54

Matathias (Maccabee)

"Wretched am I, why was I born to behold

The dissolution of my people and the destruction of the holy city,

To sit idly by while it is given into the hands of its enemies,

The sanctuary into the hands of foreigners?"
—1 Maccabees 2:7; translation of Hammer, *Jerusalem Anthology*, 79

Simon (Maccabee)

"We have not taken foreign land, nor ruled over foreign possessions, but only the inheritance of our ancestors which at one time had been unjustly conquered by our enemies."*
—1 Maccabees 15:33; my translation

*Simon, the last of the Maccabean brothers, responding to the representative of Antiochus after the Hasmoneans had defeated the Seleucids and restored Jewish rule in Jerusalem and the land.

#3
Roman Period
UP TO 324 CE

- Rise of Christianity
- Destruction of Second Temple and Jerusalem
- Bar Kochba Rebellion
- Hadrian and Aelia Capitolina

Simon Bar Kochba

LED REBELLION AGAINST ROMAN RULE, 132–35 CE

"For the freedom of Jerusalem"
—Inscription on coin minted during the rebellion

Cicero

106–43 BCE; ROMAN ORATOR, POLITICIAN AND PHILOSOPHER

"Even while Jerusalem was still standing and the Jews were at peace with us, the practice of their sacred rites was at variance with the glory of our empire, the dignity of our name, the customs of our ancestors."
—"The Speech in Defense of Lucius Flaccus," *Cicero* [Loeb Classical Library] vol. 10, 441

Dio Cassius

CA. 160–230 CE

"They never had any statue of him [God] even in Jerusalem itself, but [believe] him to be unnamable and invisible…."
—*Roman History* 37.17

"Thus was Jerusalem destroyed on the very day of Saturn, the day which even now the Jews reverence most."
—Ibid., 65.7

"At Jerusalem [Hadrian] founded a city in place of the one which had been razed to the ground, naming it Aelia Capitolina, and on the site of the temple of the god he raised a new temple to Jupiter."
—Ibid., 69.12

Diodorus Siculus

CA. 80–20 BCE; ROMAN HISTORIAN

"Now the majority of his friends advised the king [Antiochus VII (Sidetes)] to take the city by storm and to wipe out completely the race of Jews…."
—Diodorus 34.1

Josephus Flavius

37–95? CE; JEWISH HISTORIAN, EYEWITNESS TO END OF SECOND TEMPLE

"And now it was that the king of Babylon sent Nebuzaradan...to Jerusalem, to pillage the temple... and to lay the city even with the ground, and to transplant the people into Babylon."
—*Antiquities of the Jews* 10.8

"...Pompey went into it [the Temple]...and saw all that which it was unlawful for any other men to see but only for the high priests."
—Ibid., 14.4

"These* were for largeness, beauty, and strength beyond all that were in the habitable earth.... [Herod] built these...to gratify his own private affections, and dedicated these towers to the memory of those three persons who had been the dearest to him...."
—*Wars of the Jews* 5.4

*The towers Herod built on the site of the present Citadel of David, which he named Hippicus, Phasael, and Mariamme.

"Now as these towers [Hippicus, Phasael, Mariamme] were themselves in the north side of the wall, [Herod] had a palace inwardly thereto adjoined, which exceeds all my ability to describe it.... [It] was entirely walled about to the height of thirty cubits...."
—Ibid.

(Titus): "I do not force you [the Jews] to defile...your sanctuary [the Temple].... I will endeavor to preserve...your holy house, whether you will or not."*
—Ibid., 6.2

*Cf. Sulpicius Severus, below.

"All the [conquering Roman] soldiers had such vast quantities of the spoils which they had gotten by plunder, that in Syria a pound weight of gold was sold for half its former value."
—Ibid., 6.6

"Thus was Jerusalem taken in the second year of the reign of Vespasian on the eighth

of the month of Gorpiaeus [September 26, 70 BCE]."
—Ibid., 6.10

"…Caesar gave orders that [the army] should now demolish the entire city and temple, but should leave…standing [the towers] of the greatest eminency…[Phasael], and Hippicus, and Mariamme;* and so much of the wall as enclosed the city on the west side. This wall was spared, in order to afford a camp for such as were to lie in garrison…."
—Ibid., 7.1

*The three towers built by Herod on the site of the present Citadel of David.

Midrash

"The Land of Israel is in the center of the world; Jerusalem is in the center of the Land of Israel; the Holy Temple is in the center of Jerusalem; the Holy of Holies is in the center of the Holy Temple; the Holy Ark is in the center of the Holy of Holies; and the Foundation Stone [the holy Rock] from which the world was established is before the Holy Ark."
—*Midrash Tanhuma*, Kedoshim 10*

* Except where noted, all translations from Midrash are mine.

"When he [Vespasian] conquered [Jerusalem], he divided its four walls between four commanders [for destruction], and it was Pengar who got the western gate…and from heaven they decreed that it should not be destroyed. Why? Because the Presence of God (*Shekhinah*) is in the west…. Pengar did not destroy his [wall]. Vespasian…[asked]: 'Why did you not destroy your section?' [Pengar] answered: …had I destroyed it nobody would ever have known what you had destroyed. Now, people will see and say, 'Look at Vespasian's power! What [a strong city] he destroyed.' Vespasian said to him, 'You have spoken well, but because you did not obey my order, you will go up to the summit and throw yourself

down.... Pengar went up and threw himself down and he died."
—*Midrash Rabbah Lamentations* 1:31, translated by D. Delson, in Peters, *Jerusalem*, 226

God "considered all cities and found no city wherein the Temple might be built, other than Jerusalem."
—*Midrash Rabbah*, Leviticus 13:2

"Jerusalem has seventy names."
—*Midrash Rabbah*, Bamidbar 14:12

"If one prays in Jerusalem it is as if one were praying before the Throne of Glory, for the very gate of heaven is located there, as it is said [Genesis 28:17]: 'that is the gateway to heaven.'"
—*Midrash Psalms* 91:7

"Adam was created from the soil of Moriah, and he lived there...."
—Ibid., 92:6

"[T]he gate of Gan Eden is near Mount Moriah."
—Ibid.

New Testament

JERUSALEM IS MENTIONED SOME 140 TIMES IN THE NEW TESTAMENT; OUR SELECTIONS ILLUSTRATE THE LINKS BETWEEN THE ORIGINS OF CHRISTIANITY AND THE CITY

"And when they [Jesus and the disciples] drew near to Jerusalem, and were come to Bethpage, unto the Mount of Olives...."
—Matthew 21:1

"And Jesus entered into Jerusalem, and into the temple...."
—Mark 11:11

"And they came to a place which was called Gethsemane, and [Jesus] said to his disciples, sit you here while I shall pray."*
—Mark 14:32

*Cf. Luke 22.39–41: "And he came out, and went, as was his wont, to the Mount of Olives; and his

disciples also followed him....
And he was withdrawn from
them about a stone's cast, and
prayed...."

"And when they were come to
the place which is called Calvary,
there they crucified him...."
—Luke 23:33

"You are come unto Mount Zion,
and...the heavenly Jerusalem"
—Hebrews 12:22

"Later on Jesus went up to
Jerusalem for one of the Jewish
festivals. Now at the Sheep Pool
in Jerusalem there is a place with
five colonnades. Its name in the
language of the Jews is Bethesda."
—John 5:1–2

"[F]or there are the two
covenants; the one from the
mount Sinai, which gendereth
to [engenders] bondage, which
is Agar. For this Agar is
mount Sinai...and answereth
to Jerusalem which now
is, and is in bondage with
her children. But Jerusalem
which is above is free...."
—Galatians 4:24–26

"For here we have no continuing
city, but we seek one to come."
—Epistle to the Hebrews, 13:14

"And I John saw the
holy city, new Jerusalem,
coming...out of heaven...."
—Revelation 21:2

Origen

185?–254? CE; CHRISTIAN
THEOLOGIAN, RESIDENT
OF CAESAREA

"[T]he body of Adam, the
first human being, was buried
where Christ was crucified."
—Commentary on Matthew 27:32–33;
quoted in Wilken,
The Land Called Holy, 94

"Therefore that city where Jesus
suffered these indignities had
to be utterly destroyed."*
—*Contra Celsum*, 199

*Origen continues: "The Jewish nation had to be destroyed, and God's invitation to blessedness transferred to others, I mean the Christians...."

Pausanias

SECOND CENTURY CE; GREEK TRAVELER AND GEOGRAPHER

"The Hebrews have a grave, that of Helen[e] [of Adiabene]... which the Roman Emperor razed to the ground. There is a contrivance in the grave whereby the door, which like all the grave is of stone, does not open until the year brings back the same day and the same hour. Then the mechanism, unaided, opens the door...."
—Quoted in Stern, ed., *Greek and Latin Authors* 2:196

Pliny the Elder

23–79 CE; ROMAN NATURALIST

"...the district that formerly contained Jerusalem, by far the most famous city of the East and not of Judea only."
—*Natural History* 5.15

Strabo

63? BCE–21? CE; GREEK GEOGRAPHER AND HISTORIAN

"[I]t is said that Jerusalem, the metropolis of the Judeans, is visible from [Jaffa]."
—*Geography* bk. 16, 2.34

"Pompey seized the city, it is said, after watching for the day of fasting,* when the Judeans were abstaining from all work...."
—Ibid., 2.40

*Probably a reference to the Sabbath, which Strabo, like other ancient writers, thought was a fast day (Stern, ed., *Greek & Latin Authors*, 1:307n.).

Tacitus

CA. 55–120 CE; ROMAN HISTORIAN

"The first Roman to subdue the Jews and set foot in their temple by right of conquest was Gnaeus Pompey:* thereafter it was a matter of common knowledge that there were no representations of the gods within, but that the place

was empty and the secret
shrine contained nothing."
—*History* 5.9

*In 63 BCE.

"Caligula* ordered the Jews to set up his statue in their temple...."
—Ibid.

*12–41 CE.

"The founders of the city had foreseen that there would be many wars because the ways of their people differed so from those of the neighbors...."
—Ibid., 5.12

Talmud

"Because of the fragrance of the incense, brides in Jerusalem did not have to perfume themselves."
—*Yoma* 39b

"He who has not seen Jerusalem in her splendor has not seen a desirable city in his life."
—*Sukkah* 51b

Cf. Baba Batra 4a: "Whoever has not seen the [Temple] of Herod, has never seen a beautiful building in his life."

"I [the Almighty] shall enter heavenly Jerusalem only after I have entered the Jerusalem on earth."
—*Taanit* 5a

"Four things befell our fathers on the Seventeenth of Tammuz and five on the Ninth of Av. On the Seventeenth of Tammuz the tables [of the Ten Commandments] were broken, and the Whole-Offering ceased, and the city [of Jerusalem] was breached, and Apostomus... burnt [the Scrolls of] the Law, and an idol was set up in the sanctuary. On the Ninth of Av it was decreed against our fathers that they should not enter the Land of Israel...and the Temple was destroyed the first and second time, and Beth Tor [Bethar]...and the city was ploughed up."
—*Taanit* 26a

"Ten measures of beauty were bestowed upon the world: nine upon Jerusalem and one on the rest of the world."*
—*Kiddushin* 49b

*Cf. *Avot d'Rabbi Natan* B, 48.

"Whoever mourns for Zion will merit to witness its rejoicing, as it says: 'Rejoice for joy with her, all you who mourn for her' (Isaiah 66:10)."
—*Baba Batra* 60b

"The sages have…ordained thus: A man may whitewash his house, but he should leave a small area unfinished [in remembrance of Jerusalem.]"
—*Baba Batra* 60b

"Once [Rabbi Akiva and three fellow Sages] were coming up to Jerusalem. When they reached Mount Scopus, they rent their garments. When they came to the Temple Mount they saw a fox emerging from the Holy of Holies, and they started to weep. But Rabbi Akiva smiled. His companions said to him, 'Why are you smiling?' He replied, 'Why are you weeping?' They said, 'A place about which it is written: A stranger who comes close shall be put to death (Numbers 1:51), and now foxes are walking about there – should we not weep?' 'That is why I am smiling,' Rabbi Akiva replied, reminding them that the Prophets had foretold both the destruction of Jerusalem and its restoration. 'Now that the prophecy of its desolation has been fulfilled,' he said, 'I know that its restoration will also come to pass.'"
—*Makkot* 24b

"No man ever said, 'The place is too confined for me to lodge in Jerusalem.'"
—*Avot* 5:5

"The Temple Mount was five hundred cubits by five hundred…. All who entered the Temple Mount entered by the right and went around that way. They exited by the left. If, however, something had

happened, the person would enter and go around to the left. 'Why do you go around to the left?' 'Because I am a mourner.' 'May He who dwells in this House comfort you....'"
—*Middot* 2:2

"There is no beauty like the beauty of Jerusalem."
—*Avot d'Rabbi Natan* A 28

"Ten measures of wisdom were bestowed upon the world; nine upon Jerusalem and one on the rest of the world."
—*Ibid.*, B 48

"The world is like a human eye. The white is like the ocean which surrounds the earth. The pupil is like the earth. The opening in the pupil is like Jerusalem. The reflection in the opening is like the Temple...."
—*Derech Eretz Zuta* 9

Vespasian
9–79 CE; ROMAN EMPEROR, 69–79 CE, FATHER OF TITUS AND DOMITIAN

"Judaea Capta"*
—Coin issued by Vespasian and Titus and Domitian to mark downfall of Jerusalem in 70 CE; in Mazar, *The Mountain of the Lord*, 235

*"Captive Judea."

#4
Byzantine Period
UP TO 638 CE

- Constantine and Helena
- Jerusalem a Christian city
- Justinian, ruled 527–65
- Persian conquest (Chosroes), 614–27

Anonymous

CA. FOURTH CENTURY

"And you will see and your heart
will rejoice and their bones
like an herb [will flourish]...."
—Jewish pilgrim inscription on
Western Wall,* below Robinson's
Arch; variant of Isaiah 66:14

*Ben-Dov, *Western Wall*, 223–34,
dates it to the fourth–eighth
centuries.

Antoninus Martyr

SPANISH PILGRIM; ACCOUNT
WRITTEN CA. 560–570 CE

"[I]n the same valley [below the
Mount of Olives] is a basilica
of the Blessed Mary...in
which is shown a sepulcher,
from which they say [she]
was taken up into heaven."*
—*Of the Holy Places Visited*, Palestine
Pilgrims' Text Society, 2:14

*This may be the first expression
of the belief of Mary's
Assumption in the pilgrim
literature. (Wilkinson, *Jerusalem
Pilgrims*,158, credits the Piacenza
Pilgrim with the distinction.)

"This wood of the cross was of
nut. When the holy cross is
brought forth from its chamber
into the atrium of the church
to be adored, at that same hour
a star appears in heaven, and
comes above the place where
the cross is placed. While the
cross is being worshipped,
the star stands above it...."
—Ibid., 2:17

"Thence we come to the Basilica
of the Holy [Mount] Zion,
where are many wonders,
among which is the cornerstone
mentioned in Scripture, which
was rejected by the builders."*
—Ibid., 2:19

*Psalms 118:22.

St. Augustine

354–430 CE

"[A]nd my fellow-citizens
in that eternal [heavenly]
Jerusalem which Thy pilgrim
people sigheth after...."
—*Confessions*, bk. 9

"...I beseech Thee by our King, and by our pure and holy country, Jerusalem...."
—Ibid., bk. 10

"[R]emembering Jerusalem, with heart lifted up towards it, Jerusalem my country, Jerusalem my mother...."
—Ibid., bk. 12

Bordeaux Pilgrim
(333 CE)

"There are two statues of Hadrian [on the ruins of the Temple Mount], and, not far from the statues there is a perforated stone to which the Jews come every year and anoint it, bewail themselves with groans, rend their garments, and so depart."*
—Anonymous Pilgrim of Bordeaux, "Jerusalem"

*This is the first surviving description of a pilgrimage.

"This spring [the Gihon] runs [into the Pool of Siloam] for six days and six nights, but on the seventh day, which is the Sabbath, it does not run at all...."
—Ibid.

"On the left hand (of the "house of Pontius Pilate") is the little hill of golgotha [where] at present, by the command of the Emperor Constantine, has been built a basilica, that is to say, a church of wondrous beauty [The Church of the Sepulcher]...."
—Ibid.

Breviary; or, Short History of Jerusalem
EARLY SIXTH CENTURY

"[H]ere [in the Church of the Sepulcher] is the horn with which David and Solomon were anointed.... Here Adam was formed...; here Abraham offered his own son Isaac...."
—*Breviary*, Palestine Pilgrims' Text Society, 2:14

"In the midst of this church [on Mount Zion] is the crown of thorns which Jesus received."
—Ibid., 2:16

Chronicon Paschale

SEVENTH CENTURY; ANONYMOUS

Eudocia* "founded many buildings in Jerusalem, and restored the entire wall of Jerusalem."
—*Chronicon Paschale*, 75

*Wife of Byzantine emperor Theodosius II; resident in Jerusalem from ca. 450.

"In this year [614]…Jerusalem… was captured by the Persians, and in it were slain many thousands of clerics, monks, and virgin nuns. The Lord's tomb was burnt and the far-famed temples of God, and, in short, all the precious things were destroyed. The venerated wood of the Cross…was taken by the Persians…."*
—Ibid., 156

*The Byzantine emperor Heraclius is said to have recovered the relic and returned it to Jerusalem in 630.

Egeria

CHRISTIAN PILGRIM
(CA. 380 CE)

"Now at daybreak because it is the Lord's Day [Sunday] everyone proceeds to the greater church, built by Constantine, which is situated in Golgotha behind the Cross…."*
—*The Pilgrimage of Etheria [Egeria]*, 50

*Egeria is referring to the two main parts of the Church of the Sepulcher, Calvary (Golgotha) – the "greater church" – and the Resurrection (Anastasis), which were not connected in Constantine's construction. The Crusaders built a roof linking the two parts.

"The deacons stand round the table,* and a silver-gilt casket is brought in [in] which is the holy wood of the Cross…. When [the Cross] has been put upon

the table, the bishop…holds the extremities of the sacred wood…while the deacons who stand around guard it. It is guarded because the custom is that the people…kiss the sacred wood…. And because…some one is said to have bitten off and stolen a portion of [the relic]…."
—Ibid., 75

*During the ceremony of the Veneration of the Cross.

Eucherius

BISHOP OF LYONS
(SECOND OR THIRD DECADE OF FIFTH CENTURY)

"[T]he fountain of Siloam gushes forth, not running continuously, but on certain days and hours welling through caverns in the rock…."
—"Letter…to Faustinus the Priest," in *The Epitome of Eucherius…*, Palestine Pilgrims' Text Society, 2:10

"[O]n the east of the Temple is Geenon [Gehenna], [which is] the valley of Josaphat [Jehoshaphat]…."*
—Ibid.

*See Eusebius note, below.

On the Mount of Olives "are two very famous churches, one… built on the very place where we are told that the Lord talked with His disciples, the other on the place from which He is said to have ascended to heaven."*
—Ibid.

* Cf. Theodosius.

Eusebius

264?–340 CE, CHURCH HISTORIAN, BIOGRAPHER OF CONSTANTINE, NATIVE OF PALESTINE

"From that time on,* the entire race [of Jews] has been forbidden to set foot anywhere in…Jerusalem, under the terms and ordinances of a law of Hadrian…. It was colonized by an alien race and the Roman city which subsequently arose changed its name in honor of Aelius Hadrianus…[to] Aelia."
—*Church History* 4.6

*After Hadrian's subjugation of the Jews. Cf. Philostorgius.

"Aceldama.... Field of Blood...pointed out even until today in Aelia...."
—*Onomasticon*, 29*

*In this work, which is dated between 313 and 325, Eusebius uses the pre-Constantinian Roman name of Jerusalem (see Taylor's introduction, *Onomasticon*, 3).

Gehenna "lies alongside the wall of Jerusalem to the east."*
—Ibid., 43

*I.e., the Valley of Jehoshaphat. Eusebius may be the source for the location of Gehenna in Jehoshaphat, an identification echoed in later Christian and Muslim accounts.

"This sacred cave [the tomb of Jesus] certain impious and godless persons had thought to remove entirely from the eyes of men, supposing in their folly that they should be able effectually to obscure the truth.... Calling on the divine aid [Constantine] gave orders that the place should be thoroughly purified...."
—*Life of the Blessed Emperor Constantine* 3.26

"Then indeed did this most holy cave present a faithful similitude of [Jesus'] return to life, in that, after lying buried in darkness, it again emerged to light, and afforded to all who came to witness the sight, a clear and visible proof of the wonders of which that spot had once been the scene, a testimony to the resurrection of the Savior clearer than any voice could give."
—Ibid., 3.28

"[O]n the very spot which witnessed the Savior's sufferings, a new Jerusalem was constructed, over against the one so celebrated of old, which, since the foul stain of guilt brought on it by the murder of the Lord, had experienced the last extremity of desolation...."
—Ibid., 3.33

Gregory of Nyssa

CA. 334–395 CE; BISHOP OF NYSSA IN CAPPADOCIA, ECCLESIASTICAL WRITER (CA. 380 CE)

"When the Lord invites the blessed to their inheritance in the kingdom of heaven,

He does not include a pilgrimage to Jerusalem among their good deeds...."
—"On Pilgrimages," in *Ascetic and Moral Treatises*

"[I]f the Divine grace was more abundant about Jerusalem than elsewhere, sin would not be so much the fashion amongst those that live there...."
—Ibid.

St. Jerome

CA. 347–419 CE; RESIDENT OF PALESTINE FROM 385; AUTHOR OF THE VULGATE TRANSLATION OF THE BIBLE

"As Judea is exalted above all other provinces, so is this city exalted above all Judea."

....

"[I]n the city are so many places of prayer that a day would not be sufficient to go round them all."
—Epistle 46 [to Marcella]*

*In this epistle, dated 386, Jerome seeks to persuade Marcella to join him in the Holy Land. In the two following quotations, he argues that one's presence at the Jerusalem shrines is not necessary for true worship.

"Access to the courts of heaven is as easy from Britain as it is from Jerusalem; for the 'kingdom of God is within you.'"
—Epistle 58 [to Paulinus]

"'O God, the heathen have come into your inheritance; thy holy temple have they defiled; they have made Jerusalem an orchard.'"*
—Epistle 127 [to Marcella], *Select Letters of St. Jerome*, 463

*Psalms 79:1. Jerome is not mourning the Roman destruction of Jerusalem but the sack of Rome in 410 by the Goths.

"Jerusalem is now made a place of resort from all parts of the world, and there is such a throng of pilgrims of both sexes that all temptation, which in some degree you might avoid elsewhere, is here collected together."
—Epistles; quoted in Tuchman, *Bible and Sword*, 24

"Right to this present day those faithless people who

killed the servant of God and even, most terribly, the Son of God himself, are banned from entering Jerusalem except for weeping.... That mob of wretches congregates, and while the manger of the Lord sparkles, the Church of His Resurrection flows, and the banner of His Cross shines forth from the Mount of Olives, those miserable people groan over the ruins of their Temple...."

–On Zephania 1.16; quoted in Peters, *Jerusalem*, 144

Julian

331–63 CE; ROMAN EMPEROR 361–63 CE, CALLED THE "APOSTATE"

"[The Jews] should...offer their suppliant prayers on behalf of my imperial office to Mighty God....This you ought to do, in order that, when I have successfully concluded the war with Persia, I may rebuild by my own efforts the sacred city of Jerusalem, which for so may years you have longed to see inhabited, and may bring settlers there, and, together with you, may glorify the Most High God therein."

–"Ad Comuniatatem Iudaecorum [To the community of the Jews]"; ed. Bidez and Cumont; quoted in Stern, ed., *Greek and Latin Authors* 2:561

Philostorgius

BORN CA. 368; CHURCH HISTORIAN

"The Roman emperor Hadrian, who was called Aelius, named the city Aelia, after himself, in order entirely to banish and exclude thence the Jewish race, that they may not find in the name of the city a pretext for claiming it as their country."*

–*Ecclesiastical History*, translated by Edward Walford, 1855, 7.11, http://www.vitaphone.org/history/philostorgius.html

*Cf. Eusebius.

Piacenza Pilgrim

(CA. 570 CE); ANONYMOUS TRAVELER

In the "valley of Gethsemane" [Jehoshaphat] is the "basilica of

Saint Mary…the place at which she was taken up from this life."
— *The Piacenza Pilgrim;* quoted in Wilkinson, *Jerusalem Pilgrims,* 83

"In this church [on Mount Zion] is the column at which the Lord was scourged…."*
— Ibid., 84

*In contrast to the historical City of David – the "stronghold of Zion" (e.g., 2 Samuel 5:7) – on the spur south of the Temple Mount, Christian writers as early as the fourth century "consistently applied the name 'Sion' to the loftier spur immediately to the west, which for Josephus was familiar as part of the Upper City." (Wilkinson, *Jerusalem Pilgrims,* 171)

"(Jesus) had a well-shaped foot, small and delicate…with a handsome face, curly hair, and a beautiful hand with long fingers, as you can see from a picture which is there in the Praetorium [residence of Pontius Pilate]."
— Ibid.

"[A]bove Siloam is a hanging basilica beneath which the water of Siloam rises."
— Ibid.

Procopius

SIXTH CENTURY; GREEK HISTORIAN, NATIVE OF PALESTINE

"In Jerusalem the Emperor Justinian dedicated to the Mother of God a shrine with which no other can be compared. This is called by the natives the "New [Nea] Church."*
— *Buildings* 5.6

*Completed in 543; destroyed by an earthquake ca. 746.

"The [Nea] church required… columns whose appearance would not fall short of the beauty of the building…. God revealed a natural supply of stone perfectly suited to this purpose in the nearby hills…."*
— Ibid.

*See Ben-Dov, below. Based on an examination of the excavated site after 1967, he argues that the pillars had been removed by Justinian's builders from the porticoes of the nearby ruins of the Temple Mount. See also Le Strange, *History of Jerusalem under the Moslems*, 10.

Justinian "quickly sent everything to the sanctuaries of the Christians in Jerusalem."*
–*History* 4.11

*The reference is to the treasures of Solomon's Temple originally taken to Rome by Titus in 70 CE and captured by the Vandals in their sack of Rome in 455 before being retaken by Justinian. Ben-Dov (*In the Shadow of the Temple*, 240) asserts: "The story [of the treasure's return to Jerusalem] seems designed to legitimize the presence in the Nea Church of what the Byzantines took to be implements from the Temple."

Sophronius

560–638 CE; PATRIARCH OF JERUSALEM, 634–38 CE

"Deceitfully the Mede
Came from terrible Persia
Pillaging cities and villages
Waging war against the
ruler of Edom [Rome]

"Advancing on the Holy Land,
The malevolent one came
To destroy the city of
God, Jerusalem."*
–"On the Capture [of Jerusalem] by the Persians"; quoted in Wilken, *The Land Called Holy*, 229

*The reference is to the Persian conquest in 614 led by Chosroes.

Sozomen

FIFTH CENTURY; GREEK CHURCH HISTORIAN, NATIVE OF PALESTINE

"The venerated wood [of the Cross] having thus been identified, the greater portion of it was deposited in a silver case, in which it is still preserved in Jerusalem; but the empress [Helena] sent part of it to her son Constantine, together with the nails by which the body of Christ had been fastened...."*
–*Church History* 2.1; quoted in Peters, *Jerusalem*, 139

*See anonymous "Life of Constantine," below.

Sulpicius Severus

LATE FOURTH CENTURY; CHURCH HISTORIAN

"It is said that Titus summoned his council, and...consulted it whether he should overthrow a sanctuary of such workmanship, since it seemed to many that a sacred building, one more remarkable than any other human work, should not be destroyed.... On the other hand, others, and Titus himself, expressed the opinion that the Temple should be destroyed...in order that the religion of the Jews and Christians should be more completely exterminated. For those religions, though opposed to one another, derive from the same founders...and the extirpation of the root would easily cause the offspring to perish."*
 —*Chronica* 2, 30.3; quoted in Stern, ed., *Greek and Latin Authors* 2:64

*Some scholars suggest that Sulpicius's statement here derives from Tacitus (Stern, ed., *Greek and Latin Authors* 2:66).

Theodosius

SIXTH CENTURY; EUROPEAN PILGRIM, IDENTITY UNKNOWN

"[T]here [on the Mount of Olives] are built four and twenty churches."
 —*Topography of the Holy Land*, Palestine Pilgrims' Text Society, 2:10

"[T]he place of Calvary, where Abraham offered up his son *for a burnt-offering*...."
 —Ibid.

#5
Early Muslim Period
UP TO 1099
- Umayyad, Abbasid, Fatimid dynasties

Abd al-Malik ibn Marwan

646–705 CE; UMAYYAD CALIPH, BUILT DOME OF THE ROCK IN 691 CE

"The Messiah who is Jesus, son of Mary, was only an apostle of God…."*

—Koran 4:171

"It does not behoove God to have a son."*

—Koran 19:35

"God has not begotten a son, nor is there any god beside Him…"*

—Koran 23:91

*Among Koranic verses inscribed by Abd al-Malik in the Dome of the Rock (See Angelika Neuwirth, "The Spiritual Meaning of Jerusalem in Islam," in Rosovsky, *City of the Great King*, 491 n78; Millgram, *Jerusalem Curiosities*, 29).

Adomnan

IRISH SAINT WHO TRANSCRIBED THE TRAVELOGUE DICTATED TO HIM BY ARCULF, BISHOP OF GAUL, WHO VISITED THE HOLY LAND SOMETIME BETWEEN 679 AND 688 CE

"On the spot where the Temple once stood, near the eastern wall, the Saracens have now erected a square house of prayer, in a rough manner, by raising beams and planks upon some remains of old ruins…."

—Arculf, "Travels"; quoted in Wright, *Early Travels*, 1–2

"The church of the Holy Sepulcher is very large and round, encompassed with three walls…containing three altars…. It is supported by twelve stone columns…and it has eight doors…four fronting the north-east, and four to the south-east."

—Ibid., 2

"[B]etween the Martyrdom and the Golgotha, is a seat, in which is the cup of our Lord, concealed in a little shrine….* In it also is the sponge which was held up to our Lord's mouth. The soldier's

lance, with which he pierced our Lord's side…is also kept in the portico of the Martyrdom…."
—Ibid., 3

*"[This is] the Holy Grail of later legend. But the legend seems to have originated outside a Christian context, and does not assume a Christian form till the twelfth century" (Wilkinson, *Jerusalem Pilgrims*, 97n).

"Arculf saw…a lofty column…in the middle of the city, which at mid-day at the summer solstice, casts no shadow, which shows that this is the center of the earth."*
—Ibid.

*Cf. Moryson, below.

"On Mount Zion, Arculf saw a square church, which included the site of our Lord's Supper, the place where the Holy Ghost descended upon the apostles, the marble column to which our Lord was bound when he was scourged, and the spot where the Virgin Mary died. Here also is shown the site of the martyrdom of St. Stephen."
—Ibid., 5

"On the highest point of Mount Olivet, where our Lord ascended into heaven, is a large round church…. On the ground, in the midst of it, are to be seen the last prints in the dust of our Lord's feet, and the roof appears open above, where he ascended; and although the earth is daily carried away by believers, yet still it remains as before, and retains the same impression of the feet."
—Ibid.

Anonymous
BEFORE TENTH CENTURY

"How long will there be weeping in Zion and lamentation in Jerusalem? Have Mercy on Zion and build anew the walls of Jerusalem."
—Quoted in Carmi, ed., *Penguin Handbook of Hebrew Verse*, 204

Anonymous
END OF TENTH CENTURY

"[T]here is a synagogue on the Mount of Olives to which our

#5 Early Muslim Period

Jewish confreres gather during the month of Tishri. There they weep upon [the] stones [at the site of the Temple Mount], roll in its dust, encircle its walls, and pray.... Here we worship on holy days facing the Lord's Temple, especially on Hoshana Rabba."
—Letter from Jerusalem; quoted in Peters, *Jerusalem*, 234

Benedict
CHRISTIAN CHRONICLER; ACCOUNT WRITTEN CA. 1000

"Then Charles [Charlemagne] came to the Most Holy Tomb of Our Lord and Savior Jesus Christ, which is also the place of the Resurrection. He adorned the holy place with gold and jewels, and he also placed on it a large gold standard."*
—*Chronicle*; quoted in Peters, *Jerusalem*, 217

*There is no evidence of Charlemagne's visit to Jerusalem (Peters, *Jerusalem*, 217).

Bernard the Monk
ALSO KNOWN AS BERNARD THE WISE, TRAVELOGUE WRITTEN CA. 870 CE

On Easter morning, when the "office [is] over they go on singing *Kyrie eleison* till an angel comes and kindles light in the lamps which hang above the sepulcher. The patriarch passes some of this light to the bishops and the rest of the people, and thus each one has light where he is standing."*
—*A Journey to the Holy Places and Babylon*; quoted in Wilkinson, 142

*This is the first descriptive account of the ceremony of the Holy Fire (Wilkinson, *Jerusalem Pilgrims*, 142n). Bernard's travelogue is the last full account of a Christian pilgrimage before the Crusades (Barclay, *City of the Great King*, 343; Wilkinson, ibid., 13).

"Commemoratorium on the Churches in Jerusalem"
WRITTEN AS A REPORT TO CHARLEMAGNE, CA. 808 CE

"The Church of St. Mary* which was [thrown] down by the

earthquake and engulfed by the earth has side walls thirty-nine *dexteri* long and a facade thirty-five *dexteri* wide; inside it is thirty-two wide and fifty long...."
–quoted in Wilkinson, *Jerusalem Pilgrims*, 137

*The reference is to the Nea Church, dedicated by Justinian in 543, which some later writers identified with the al-Aksa Mosque (e.g., Horn, *Ichnographiae*, 209n). After the Six-Day War in 1967, its remains were uncovered near the Jewish Quarter (see Ben-Dov, below).

Epiphanius the Monk

PURPORTED AUTHOR OF GUIDEBOOK COMPLETED BETWEEN 750 AND 800 CE

"And at the west gate of the Holy City is the Tower of David, in which he sat in the dust and wrote the Psalter."
–"The Holy City and the Holy Places"; quoted in Wilkinson, Jerusalem *Pilgrims*, 117

Ibn 'Abd Rabbih

POET AND LITERARY SCHOLAR, ACCOUNT WRITTEN 913

The Dome of the Chain, "where during the times of the children of Israel, there hung down the chain that gave judgment (of truth and lying) between them."
–Quoted in Le Strange, *History of Jerusalem under the Moslems*, 71

"Under the corner of the (Aksa) Mosque is the spot where the Prophet tied up his steed, Al Burak."
–Ibid., 83

Ibn Ishaq

DIED CA. 773 CE; AUTHOR OF EARLIEST SURVIVING BIOGRAPHY OF MOHAMMED

"The apostle of Allah [Mohammed], accompanied by Gabriel, was transported to Jerusalem, where he found Abraham and Moses and other prophets."
–"Night Journey," in *Sirat Rasoul Allah*

"Seventeen months after the apostle arrived in Medina, the *kiblah* was changed from Jerusalem to Mecca.... [Mohammed said] Allah said, 'Turn your face to the holy mosque [the Kaaba at Mecca]; and wherever you are, turn your face to that.'"
—"The *Kiblah*," in *Sirat Rasoul Allah*

Nasir Ibn Khusru (Khusraw)

1004–CA. 1088;
MUSLIM TRAVELER
(1047)

"The people of Sham [Syria] and that quarter call Jerusalem 'Kuds,' and such as the inhabitants of those climes as are unable to go to Mecca at that season [Ramadan] tarry at Jerusalem... till they have celebrated the 'Id-i-Kurban according to immemorial custom."
—*An Account of Jerusalem*, 1*

*This account is the last by a Muslim writer before the Crusades (Le Strange, *History of Jerusalem under the Moslems*, 45).

"That valley [of Hinnom] is the Valley of Hell."
—Ibid., 3

"The common people...assert, that every one who approaches the brink of the valley [of Hinnom] hears the cries of the inmates of hell...; but for my own part I heard nothing going on there."
—Ibid.

"[I]t is on account of the 'sakhrah' stone [the Rock]...that the [al-Aksa] Mosque has been erected on that very spot. This 'sakhrah' stone is that which the Almighty God commanded Moses...to make the 'kiblah'.... [T]hither were they accustomed to turn their faces in prayer, till such time as the Almighty commanded [Mohammed] that the 'ka'bah' [in Mecca] should be the site of the 'kiblah.'"
—Ibid., 4

"[T]his is the very cradle [on the Rock on the Haram-a-Sharif] in which Jesus during

his infancy lay and conversed with various persons."
—Ibid., 7

"[I]t is even said that this Mosque [The Dome of the Rock] was the very birthplace of Jesus."
—Ibid.

"This is the [mosque] to which God brought Mustafa [Mohammed] on the night of his ascension from Mecca, and from hence he went up to Heaven, according to the words contained in the Koran: 'Praised be he who transported his servant at night from the Mesjidu-l-haram [Mecca] to the Mesjidu-l-aska.'"
—Ibid., 8

"It is said that the ark of the tabernacle, spoken of by Almighty God in the Koran as carried by angels, is deposited there [in the Dome of the Rock]."
—Ibid., 12

"I have heard that Abraham and Isaac while yet a child, went there, and that these are the marks of their feet."
—Ibid., 14

"[E]very prayer offered up in Jerusalem is as acceptable as 25,000 others; while every one uttered at Medina…is accounted equal to 50,000, and every one offered up at Mecca to 100,000."
—Ibid., 15

"They say that on the night of [Mohammed's] ascension the 'Burak' [Mohammed's steed] was brought to this spot [Dome of Gabriel], for our Prophet…to mount on."
—Ibid.

"In the courtyard of the Mosque [The Dome of the Rock]…there is a spot where a diminutive Mosque of hewn stone stands…. Close to the enclosure there is a stone…and they say that it was Solomon's throne. They also told me that

#5 Early Muslim Period

Solomon…sat down there while the Mosque was being built."
—Ibid., 18

"The Christian infidels have a church at Jerusalem [Church of the Sepulcher], which they style 'Beytu-l-makamah,' and consider extremely holy."*
—Ibid., 21

*Le Strange, *History of Jerusalem under the Muslims*, 125, has "Bai'at al Kumamah" (cf. Mas'udi).

"This Ruler [of Egypt, al-Hakim]…directed the church to be pillaged, desolated, and destroyed, and for a long time it lay in ruins…."
—Ibid., 22

Koran

"We shall turn you to a *Kiblah* that will please you.

So turn towards the Holy Mosque [Mecca],

and turn towards it wherever you be."
—2:144

Daniel ben Moshe al-Kumsi

NINTH CENTURY; KARAITE*

"Jews, why do you not do as other nations, to come [to Jerusalem] to pray…"
—Quoted in Yaari, *Igrot Eretz Yisrael*, 58

*The Karaites are a schismatic sect that rejects Judaism's oral law and interprets the Bible literally; they had a separate community in Jerusalem.

"If you do not come [to Jerusalem] because you covet and are obsessed with your merchandise, then [at least] send five men from each city with enough [money] to support them, so that we can become a united group to supplicate our Lord continuously in the mountains of Jerusalem…."
—Ibid., 59

"Life of Constantine"

ANONYMOUS, CA. 820 CE

Bishop Macarius and Helena "fasted and prayed continuously:

and instantly the Lord…revealed the place of his holy Tomb…at the very place where had been erected a temple and statue of the unclean she-devil Aphrodite."
—"Life of Constantine"; quoted in Wilkinson, *Jerusalem Pilgrims*, 202

"With much fear and joy…Helena lifted up the…Wood of the venerable Cross: part of it she took…to keep for herself, and was eager to send them to her son…Constantine, in Byzantium (which she did); and the rest she laid up in a silver box, and handed over to the godly Macarius, the Archbishop of…Jerusalem…."*
—Ibid.

*Cf. Sozomen, above.

In "Jerusalem [Helena] founded a church [the Church of the Sepulcher] where the life-giving Wood of the…Cross was found, and called it 'Saint Constantine' after her son's name."
—Ibid., 203

On Mount Zion, "Helena…mother of Constantine founded a long and broad and immense church…. To the left of the diaconicon [vestry] [is] the Tomb of the holy Prophet David…."*
—Ibid., 204

*This is the first Christian mention of King David's tomb on Mount Zion (Wilkinson, *Jerusalem Pilgrims*, 204)

"Holy Empress Helena…founded also many other churches of God in those holy places; at the Pit of the prophet Jeremiah, at the spring of Siloam, at the Potter's Field…."*
—Ibid., 204

*This is the "earliest known statement of the belief…that…Helena was personally responsible for building almost all the churches in the country" (Wilkinson, *Jerusalem Pilgrims*, 202).

#5 Early Muslim Period

Mas'udi
DIED 956 CE; MUSLIM HISTORIAN AND GEOGRAPHER, ACCOUNT WRITTEN 943 CE

"It was Solomon who first built the Holy House, which same is now the Aksa Mosque.... When he had completed the building thereof, he set about building a house for his own use. This last is the place that, in our own day, is called the Kanisah al Kumanah* [the Church of the Resurrection]."
   –Quoted in Le Strange, *History of Jerusalem under the Moslems*, 123

*"The 'Church of the Sweepings' or 'of the Dunghill' – Kumanah being a designed corruption of Kavamah [kiyama], the name given to the church by the Eastern Christians, this being the Arabic equivalent of Anastasia – 'the Resurrection'" (Le Strange, *History of Jerusalem under the Moslems*, 122). See also Gabrieli, *Arab Historians of the Crusades*, 148n.

al-Muqaddasi
BORN 945–46 CE; MUSLIM HISTORIAN AND GEOGRAPHER, NATIVE OF JERUSALEM, ACCOUNT WRITTEN 985 CE

"[I]s it not evident how Caliph Abd al-Malik, noting the greatness of the Dome of the Kumamah [Holy Sepulcher] and its magnificence, was moved lest it should dazzle the minds of Muslims and hence erected, above the Rock, the Dome which is now seen there."
   –*Description of Syria and Palestine*, Palestine Pilgrims' Text Society, 3:22–23

"In Jerusalem are all manner of learned men and doctors, and for this reason the heart of every man of intelligence yearns towards her."
   –Ibid., 3:35

"...Jerusalem [is] the pleasantest of all places in the way of climate...the cold there does not injure, and the heat is not noxious."
   –Ibid., 3:36

"[I]s not this to be the plain of marshalling on the Day of Judgment.... Verily Mecca and Medina have their superiority by reason of the Ka'abah and the Prophet...but verily, on the Day of Judgment both [cities] will come to Jerusalem...."
—Ibid., 3:36–37

"This mosque [al-Aksa] is even more beautiful than that of Damascus, for during the building of it they had for a rival and as a comparison the great church [of the Holy Sepulcher] belonging to the Christians of Jerusalem, and they built this to be more beautiful than that other."
—Ibid., 3:41

Muqatil b. Sulayman
DIED 768 CE; AUTHOR OF COMMENTARY ON THE KORAN

"The first land which Allah blessed is the land of Bayt al-Maqdis."

"The rock which is in Bayt al-Maqdis is the center of the entire world."

"Allah, may He Be Exalted and Praised, forgave the children of Israel their sins in Bayt al-Maqdis."

"Jesus, may he rest in peace, was born in Bayt al-Maqdis."
—from traditions in Praise [or: on the Merits] of Jerusalem in Muqatil's commentary on the Koran; quoted in Prawer, ed., *The History of Jerusalem*, 383*

*Muqatil is one of the earliest sources of Muslim writings in praise of Jerusalem. These works were especially widespread beginning in the eleventh century; according to some scholars their popularity reflected Muslim reaction to the Crusades (Peters, *Jerusalem*, 336).

Omar

CA. 581–644; SECOND CALIPH, LEADER OF MUSLIM CONQUEST OF JERUSALEM IN 638 CE

"No Jewish person shall be allowed to dwell in Iliya [Aelia=Jerusalem] with them [the city's Christian inhabitants]."*
 —From agreement of surrender issued by Omar to city's residents; quoted in Moshe Gil, "The Political History of Jerusalem," in Prawer, ed., *The History of Jerusalem*, 8

*Gil ("The Jewish Community," in Prawer, ed., *The History of Jerusalem*, 170) notes that in fact within a few years the Muslims acceded to Jewish requests for permission to resettle in Jerusalem.

Photius

820–893 CE; PATRIARCH OF CONSTANTINOPLE 858–867 AND 877–886 CE, SAINT IN EASTERN CATHOLIC AND EASTERN ORTHODOX CHURCHES

"…Helena, when she visited Jerusalem and cleared that holy place of the piles of rubbish and filth there, extended the buildings and the city wall. She started at a point on the ancient wall overlooking the saving Tomb, extended the perimeter, and enclosed the lifegiving Tomb within the enlarged circuit."
 —Question 107 to Amphilochius; quoted in Wilkinson, *Jerusalem Pilgrims*, 146

St. Willibald

CA. 700–787; FIRST ENGLISH PILGRIM TO LEAVE AN ACCOUNT (CA. 723)

"St. Mary departed this life in the middle of Jerusalem at the place called Holy [Mount] Zion."
 —From the *Life of Willibald* by the nun Hugeburc, ca. 780; quoted in Wilkinson, *Jerusalem Pilgrims*, 131

#6 Crusader Period and Muslim Reconquest
UP TO 1260

- Crusader conquest in 1099 (Godfrey of Buillon)
- Muslim reconquest in 1187 (Saladin and Ayyubid dynasty)
- Frederick II, German emperor and king of Jerusalem

'Ali of Herat

TWELFTH CENTURY;
MUSLIM TRAVELER
(1173)

"To the East of the Dome of the Rock is...the Dome of the Chain; it is here Solomon, the son of David, administered justice."
 —Quoted in Le Strange, *History of Jerusalem under the Moslems*, 53

"The Church of the Kumanah* [Resurrection] is one of the most wonderful buildings of the world."
 —Ibid., 127–28

*See note to Mas'udi, above.

Anonymous Pilgrims

ELEVENTH AND TWELFTH CENTURIES

"Above the Lord's sepulcher brightly burns a lamp...which goes out by itself every year at the ninth hour on Good Friday, and again lights itself on Easter Day, at the hour of Christ's resurrection."
 —Aubrey Stewart, trans., *Anonymous Pilgrims*, 16

"The Templars are most excellent soldiers. They wear white mantles with a red cross, and when they go to the wars a standard of two colors called *balzaus* is borne before them.... When they think fit to make war and the trumpet has sounded, they sing in chorus the Psalm of David, 'Not unto us, O Lord'... [Psalms 115], kneeling on the blood and necks of the enemy...."
 —Ibid., 29–30

"The Hospitallers bear a white cross on their mantles and are good knights, who, besides their service in the field, take care of the sick and the needy. They live under a rule and discipline of their own."
 —Ibid., 30

Benjamin of Tudela

JEWISH TRAVELER WHOSE
ITINERARY TOOK HIM TO MOST
OF THE KNOWN WORLD
(1163)

Jerusalem "contains a dyeing-house, for which the Jews pay a small rent annually to the

king, on condition that besides the Jews no other dyers be allowed in Jerusalem. There are about 200* Jews who dwell under the Tower of David...."
—*Itinerary*, 22

*Another manuscript lists four Jews.

"The city also contains two buildings, from one of which – the hospital [of the Knights Hospitallers] – there issue forth four hundred knights; and therein all the sick...are lodged.... The other building is called the Temple of Solomon [al-Aksa]; it is the palace built by Solomon the king of Israel. Three hundred knights [Templars] are quartered there...."
—Ibid.

"[O]ur ancient Temple [is] now called Templum Domini.* Upon the site of the sanctuary Omar ben al-Khatab erected an edifice with a very large and magnificent cupola.... In front of that place is the Western Wall, which is one of the walls of the Holy of Holies. This is called the Gate of Mercy [sic], and thither come all the Jews to pray.... In Jerusalem, attached to the palace which belonged to Solomon, are the stables built by him...."
—Ibid., 23

*The reference is to the Dome of the Rock.

"In front of Jerusalem is Mount Zion, on which there is no building except a place of worship belonging to the Christians."
—Ibid., 24

"On Mount Zion are the sepulchers of the House of David, and the sepulchers of the kings that ruled after him. The exact place cannot be identified...."
—Ibid.

The City of Jerusalem
ANONYMOUS, CA. 1220

"Jerusalem…is no longer in the place where it stood when Jesus Christ was…crucified…. When Jesus Christ was on the earth the city of Jerusalem was on Mount Zion, but it is no longer there."
— *The City of Jerusalem*, 1–2

"At this place where the Tomb is the church is quite round, and it is open from above without any covering; and within the monument is the Stone of the Sepulcher. And the monument is vaulted over."
—Ibid., 8–9

"Here [in the Church of the Sepulcher] there is a chapel called St. Helena, where [she] found the cross, the nails, the hammer and the crown."
—Ibid., 10

"[T]he upright beam of the cross was found [near] the Temple…for it was brought from Lebanon with the timber for the Temple, [but] they could find no place where it fitted, being either too long or too short."
—Ibid., 22

"When Jesus Christ was put upon the cross…the head of Adam was within [this] wood, and when the blood…flowed from his wounds, the head of Adam came forth…and received the blood, which is the reason why on all the crucifixes which they make in…Jerusalem, at the foot of the cross is a head in remembrance of Adam's head."
—Ibid.

Daniel the Abbot
THE FIRST RUSSIAN PILGRIM KNOWN BY NAME (1106)

"Beneath this rock lies the skull of the first man, Adam. At the time of our Lord's crucifixion… the veil of the Temple rent, and the rock crave asunder, and the rock above Adam's skull opened, and the blood and water which flowed from Christ's side ran down through the

fissures upon the skull, thus washing away the sins of men."
— *The Pilgrimage of the Russian Abbot Daniel*, chap. 11

From Calvary "is 200 fathoms to the tower and house of David, where...the holy prophet...wrote his Psalter."
—Ibid., chap. 14

"...I have seen with my own sinful eyes how that Holy Light* descends upon the redeeming Tomb of our Lord.... Many pilgrims relate incorrectly the details about the descent.... Some say that the Holy Ghost descends in the form of a dove, others that it is lightning from heaven which kindles the lamps. This is all untrue...but the Divine grace comes down unseen from heaven, and lights the lamps...."
—Ibid., chap.96

*On Holy Friday.

The Deeds of the Franks (Gesta Francorum)

UNKNOWN AUTHOR, PARTICIPANT IN THE CRUSADER CONQUEST OF JERUSALEM, 1099

"On Wednesday and Thursday we launched a fierce attack on the city, both by day and night, from all sides, but before we attacked our bishops and priests preached to us, and told us to go in procession round Jerusalem to the glory of God, and to pray and give alms and fast, as faithful men should do."
—*Deeds*, 90

"Next morning [the Crusaders] went cautiously up on to the Temple [the Dome of the Rock] roof and attacked the Saracens, both men and women, cutting off their heads with drawn swords."
—Ibid., 92

"Not far off is Golgotha...where Christ the Son of God was crucified, and where the first Adam was buried, and

where Abraham offered
his sacrifice to God."
—Ibid., 98

"This is the valley (of Jehoshaphat) in which the Lord will come to judge the world."
—Ibid., 99

"This line,* copied from the Sepulcher of the Lord…and multiplied fifteen times, indicates the height of Christ. On the day on which you see it, you shall not suffer sudden death.

"The second line,* multiplied nine times, indicates the breadth of Christ's Body, and it gives the same protection against sudden death on the day on which it has once been seen."
—Ibid., 103

*The lines appear in the manuscript of the *Deeds*. Hill, editor of the *Deeds*, calculates a height of 6 ft. 4 in. and width of 2 ft. 11 in.

Fulcher of Chartres
BORN 1059; EYEWITNESS TO CONQUEST OF JERUSALEM IN 1099

"The Church of the Lord's Sepulcher…round in form, was never covered…."*
—*A History of the Expedition to Jerusalem*; quoted in Peters, ed., *First Crusade*, 88

*This was before the Crusaders brought the parts of the church under one roof.

The "present position [of the rock in the Dome of the Rock] is under the altar where the priest performs the rituals."
—Ibid., 89

"On the top of Solomon's Temple [al-Aksa Mosque], to which [the defending Muslims] had climbed in fleeing, many were shot to death with arrows and cast down headlong from the roof. Within this Temple about ten thousand were beheaded…..* They did not spare the women and children."
—Ibid., 91

*Cf. Ibn al-Athir, below.

"After they had discovered the cleverness of the Saracens, it was an extraordinary thing to see our squires and poorer people split the bellies of those dead Saracens, so they might pick out *besants* [gold coins] from their intestines, which they had swallowed down their horrible gullets while alive. After several days, they made a great heap of their bodies and burned them to ashes, and in these ashes they found the gold more easily."
—Ibid.

"Then [after the conquest of Jerusalem], going to the Sepulcher of the Lord and His glorious Temple, the clerics and also the laity, singing a new song unto the Lord in a…voice of exaltation…visited the Holy Place as they had so long desired to do."
—Ibid., 92

"[T]he Temple of Solomon is large and wonderful, but it is not the one Solomon built. This one, because of our poverty, could not be maintained in the condition in which we found it. Wherefore it is already in large part destroyed."
—*A History of the Expedition to Jerusalem*; quoted in Peters, *Jerusalem*, 314–15

Godfrey de Buillon

FIRST CRUSADER RULER OF JERUSALEM, 1099–1100

"I will not wear a crown of gold where my Master wore a crown of thorns."*
—Quoted in Chesterton, *The New Jerusalem*, 236

*Another version: "How can a man born of woman bear the title 'King of Jerusalem,' where only one person, Christ the Lord, has reigned?" (Ben-Dov, *Historical Atlas*, 197–98). Fabri (*Wanderings*, 1:2, 355–56) writes that even Godfrey's successor, Baldwin I, who was crowned as king of Jerusalem, "wore a crown not of gold but of thorns…on days of solemn state, even when other kings were present…."

Pope Gregory VIII

CA. 1100–1187; DIED AFTER TWO MONTHS IN OFFICE

"'O God, the heathen came into your inheritance, the Holy Temple have they defiled, they have laid Jerusalem in heaps....'"*
—Quoted by G. H. Campbell, *The Knights Templars* [London: Duckworth, 1937], 108; quoted in Ben-Ami, *Social Change in a Hostile Environment*, 177

*Reaction to Saladin's reconquest in 1187.

Judah Halevi

CA. 1075–1141; JEWISH SCHOLAR AND POET

"My heart is in the East, and I am in the uttermost west"
—"My Heart Is in the East," *The Selected Poems of Judah Halevi*, 2

"Zion! Will you not ask if peace be with your captives

That seek your peace...the remnant of your flocks?"
—"Ode to Zion," ibid., 3

"Sweet would it be unto my soul to walk naked and barefoot

Upon the desolate ruins where your holiest dwellings were."
—Ibid.

"And who shall grant me, on the wings of eagles,

To rise and seek thee through the years,

Until I mingle with thy dust beloved,

The waters of my tears?"
—"On the Way to Jerusalem," ibid., 157

"Spain is my country and Jerusalem, my destiny."
—Letter by Judah Halevi; quoted in Naor, *City of Hope*, 137

Abu al-Hasan al-Harawi

TWELFTH CENTURY; IN JERUSALEM DURING CRUSADER OCCUPATION (1173)

"For the Christians the tomb [of Jesus] is situated there which they call the tomb of the Resurrection [kiyama] because they locate in this place the resurrection of the Messiah; in reality the site was Refuse [kumanah], the place of refuse because the sweepings of the area were thrown there; it was a place outside the city.... And God alone knows the truth."*
—Quoted in Hillenbrand, *The Crusades*, 317

*See note to Mas'udi, above.

Judah al-Harizi

1165–1225; SPANISH JEWISH POET (1217)

"When did Jews return here?

When the city fell under Arab sway.*

But why had the Christians driven us away?

They claim we shamelessly killed their God, who did then disown us...."
—*Tahkemoni*, Gate 28

*The reference is to Saladin's reconquest of the city in 1187.

"[Saladin] told the city's dwellers young and old, Speak unto Jerusalem's heart: let all the sons of Ephraim [the Jews] who dwell apart...speed like the hart! From every corner, come; build you your home!"
—Ibid.

"And now in God's holy court idols resort, images grimace and make sport."
—Ibid., Gate 47

Ibn al-Athir

1160–1233; MUSLIM HISTORIAN, EYEWITNESS TO THE LATER CRUSADES

"In the Masjid al-Aksa, the Franks slaughtered more than

70,000 people,* among them a large number of Imams and Muslim scholars."
—*Kamil at-Tawarikh*; quoted in Gabrieli, *Arab Historians of the Crusades*, 11

*During the Crusader conquest in 1099. See Fulcher, above.

"The Franks stripped the Dome of the Rock of more than forty silver candelabra, each of them weighing 3,600 drams, and a great silver lamp weighing forty-four Syrian pounds...."
—Ibid.

Ibn Ezra

CA. 1089–1164; JEWISH SCHOLAR

"Salem is Jerusalem."
—Gloss on Genesis 14:18

Ibn al-Qalanisi

CA. 1073–1160; SYRIAN HISTORIAN, EARLIEST ARAB CHRONICLER TO WRITE ABOUT THE CRUSADES

"It is told in the history al-Hakim bi-amri'llah* that in [1007–1008] he ordered the destruction of the Church of al-Kumanah [the Church of the Sepulcher] in Jerusalem, a church that had considerable importance for the Christians and which they venerated."
—Quoted in Peters, *Jerusalem*, 258

*Fatimid caliph of Egypt (996–1021).

"The Jews [in Jerusalem] assembled in the synagogue, and the Franks burned it over their heads."*
—*Damascus Chronicle*, 48

*The reference is to the Crusader conquest of Jerusalem, 1099. Hillenbrand, *The Crusades*, 66, quotes Ibn Taghribirdi: "They collected the Jews in the church [synagogue] and burnt it down with them in it."

The Christians "hang their lamps on the altar, and then by a trick they cause fire to appear in the balsam oil in their lamps, since this oil has the property of igniting with the oil of jasmine and it produces a flame of remarkable whiteness and brilliance...."
—Quoted in Peters, *Jerusalem*, 259

Jamal ad-Din Ibn Wasil

1207–98; AYYUBID OFFICIAL AND CHRONICLER

"I entered Jerusalem, and I saw priests and monks in charge of the Sacred Rock.... I saw on it bottles of wine for the ceremony of the mass. I entered the Aksa mosque and in it a bell was suspended."*
—Quoted in Hillenbrand, *The Crusades*, 291

*Ibn Wasil is writing about the brief Christian reoccupation of Jerusalem (1229–440) under an agreement during the Sixth Crusade between the Ayyubid sultan of Egypt and Frederick II of Germany.

Ibn az-Zaki

CADI OF DAMASCUS IN 1187

God "is pleased with your conduct...inasmuch as He has rendered it easy for your hands to recover this strayed camel [Jerusalem] from the possession of a misguided people, and bring it back to the fold of Islam...."*
—Quoted in Ben-Ami, *Social Change in a Hostile Environment*, 177

*Sermon in al-Aksa Mosque, 1187, in presence of Saladin, after defeat of Crusaders.

"What a wonderful coincidence! God allowed the Muslims to [re]take the city as a celebration of the anniversary of their Prophet's Night Journey."*
—Quoted in Hillenbrand, *The Crusaders*, 189

*See Imad ad-Din, below.

al-Idrisi

1099–1166; MUSLIM SICILIAN GEOGRAPHER

"[Y]ou come to the holy house built by Solomon, the son of David. This, in the time of the Jews, was a mosque (or house

of prayer), to which pilgrimage was made; but it was taken out of their hands, and they were driven from thence. And when the days of Islam came, under the kings of the Muslims, the spot came once more to be venerated as the Masjid al Aksa."
—Quoted in Le Strange, *History of Jerusalem under the Moslems*, 28

"The Dome (of the Rock) has four Gates. The Western Gate has opposite to it an Altar, whereon the Children of Israel were wont to offer up their sacrifices."
—Ibid., 51

Imad ad-Din
1125–1201; SECRETARY TO SALADIN

"When the Muslims entered the city…some of them climbed to the top of the cupola [of the Dome of the Rock] to take down the cross. When they reached the top a great cry went up from the city and from outside the walls, the Muslims crying the Allah akbar in their joy, the Franks groaning in consternation and grief.…"*
—history of Muslim reconquest of Jerusalem; quoted in Gabrieli, *Arab Historians of the Crusades*, 144

*The cross was "dragged through the streets…and melted down in David's Tower" (Benvenisti, *The Crusades in the Holy Land*, 70):

"The Templars had built their living-quarters against al-Aksa, with storerooms and latrines and other necessary offices taking part of the area of al-Aksa."
—Ibid.

"By a striking coincidence the date of the conquest of Jerusalem* was the anniversary of the Prophet's ascension to heaven."**
—Ibid., 160

*October 2, 1187.

**"[A]ware of the profound impact which his victorious entry into Jerusalem would make, Saladin waited to take possession of the city until…the anniversary" (Hillenbrand, *The Crusades*, 189).

"When Saladin accepted the surrender of Jerusalem, he ordered the mihrab* [in al Aksa] to be uncovered.... The Templars had built a wall before it, reducing it to a granary and, it was said, a latrine.... East of the *kiblah* they had built a big house and another church. Saladin had the two structures removed.... The Koran was raised to the throne and the Testaments cast down.... The mists dissolved, the true directions came into view, the sacred verses were read...and the clappers silenced...the muezzins were there and not the priests, corruption and shame ceased...."
—Ibid., 164

*The niche indicating the direction of prayer.

"As for the Rock, the Franks built over it a church and an altar...."
—Ibid., 168

"The Franks had cut pieces from the Rock, some of which they had carried to Constantinople and Sicily and sold...."
—Ibid., 170–71

"The Oratory of David...was in a fortified stronghold. It was set up high in a commanding position and was used by the governor... Saladin [established there] a prayer leader, muezzins, and guards...The place where this fortress was built had been the house of David and Solomon... where people went to find them."
—Ibid., 173–74

"Some [of Saladin's officials] advised him to demolish [the Church of the Sepulcher]... making it impossible to visit.... But the majority said: 'Demolishing...it would serve no purpose.... For it is not the building...but the home of the Cross that is the object of worship. The various Christian races would still be making the pilgrimage here....'"*
—Ibid., 174–75

*Saladin did not destroy the church.

John of Wurzburg

GERMAN THEOLOGIAN, BELIEVED TO HAVE SERVED AS BISHOP OF WURZBURG (CA. 1160 OR 1170, DURING THE PERIOD OF CRUSADER RULE)

The [Dome of the Rock] is "covered on the outside with lead, on the summit of which the figure of the Holy Cross has been placed by the Christians...."
—John of Wurzburg, 18

"Close to [al-Aksa Mosque]* the Knights Templars have many spacious and connected buildings, and also the foundations of a new and large church which is not yet finished."
—Ibid., 21

*John refers to it in the Crusader designation as the "Palace [Temple] of Solomon."

The blood of Jesus on the Cross "flowed to the lower parts [of the Crucifixion site], wherein Adam is said to have been buried.... But this baptism of Adam means nothing more than that Adam was redeemed by the blood of Christ, since the Scripture tells us that he was buried at Hebron."
—Ibid., 32

"In the street which leads from the Gate of David [Jaffa Gate] down the hill toward the Temple...near the tower of David, is a convent of Armenian monks, built in honor of St. Sabas.... In this same quarter...there is a large church built in honor of St. James the Great, inhabited by Armenian monks...."*
—Ibid., 45

*The Armenian Quarter has been in its present location since the seventh century (Ben-Dov, *Man and Stone*, 222).

Mary's "blessed body is not there,* because we are told that when...the sepulcher was visited...the body was not found there. From this there has arisen a pious belief that not only her soul, but also her body, was raised...by her Son into heaven, which Jerome seems to hint at doubtfully...."
—Ibid., 52

*In the Church of St. Mary on Mount Zion.

Maimonides

1135–1204; PREEMINENT JEWISH PHILOSOPHER AND CODIFIER OF JEWISH LAW (ARRIVED IN HOLY LAND IN 1165)

"The place where David and Solomon built [the Temple] was the site where Abraham built the altar upon which he offered up Isaac, where Noah built when he left the Ark, where Cain and Abel offered [their sacrifices], and where Adam offered a sacrifice, at the site where he was created."
—*Hilchot Beit Hab'chira* [Laws of the Temple] 2:1

"There was a stone in the Holy of Holies, at its western wall, upon which the Ark rested. In front of it stood the jar of manna and the staff of Aaron. When Solomon built the Temple, knowing that it was destined to be destroyed, he built underneath, in deep and winding tunnels, a place in which to hide the Ark. It was King Josiah who commanded the Ark be hidden in the place which Solomon had prepared...."
—Ibid., 4:1

"[T]he sanctity of Jerusalem has never lapsed."
—Ibid., 6:16

"Even though the Sanctuary is today in ruins...we are obliged to reverence it in the same manner as when it was standing.... For even though it is in ruins, its sanctity endures."
—Ibid., 7:7

Rabbi Petachia of Ratisbon

JEWISH TRAVELER; ACCOUNT AS TRANSCRIBED BY RABBI JUDAH THE PIOUS BAR SAMUEL (1170–87)

"The only Jew [in Jerusalem] is Rabbi Abraham, the dyer, and he pays a heavy tax to the king to be permitted to remain there."
—Quoted in Adler, *Jewish Travellers*, 88

"The Tower of David still exists."
—Ibid., 90

"At Jerusalem there is a gate… Gate of Mercy. [It] is piled up with stone and lime. No Jew is permitted to go there, and still less a Gentile. One day the Gentiles wished to remove the rubbish and open the gate, but the whole land of Israel shook and there was a tumult in the city until they abstained. There is a tradition among the Jews that the Divine glory appeared through this gate and through it would return. It is exactly opposite the Mount of Olives."
—Ibid.

Raymond d'Aguilers

ELEVENTH–TWELFTH CENTURY; EYEWITNESS TO CRUSADER CONQUEST OF JERUSALEM, 1099; ACCOUNT WRITTEN BEFORE 1105

"There is a fountain at the foot of Mount Zion, which is called the Pool of Siloam. Indeed, it is a large spring, but the water flows forth only once in three days, and the natives say that formerly it emptied itself only on Saturdays; the rest of the week it remained stagnant."
—Quoted in Peters, ed., *The First Crusade*, 251

"The bishops and clergy replied [to suggestion that a king be named]: 'You ought not to choose a king where the Lord suffered and was crowned. For if a David, degenerate in faith and virtue, should say in his heart, "I sit upon the throne of David and hold his kingdom," the Lord would probably destroy him….'"
—Ibid., 253

"[I]n the Temple and porch of Solomon men rode in blood up to their knees and bridle reins. Indeed, it was a just and splendid judgment of God that this place should be filled with the blood of the unbelievers, since it had suffered so long from their blasphemies."
—Ibid., 260

Richard Lion-Heart

1157–99; A LEADER OF THE THIRD CRUSADE

"The points at issue are Jerusalem, the Cross, and the land. Jerusalem is for us an object of worship that we could

not give up even if there were only one of us left.... The Cross, which is for you simply a piece of wood with no value, is for us of enormous importance."*
—Quoted by Baha ad-Din Ibn Shaddad, biographer of Saladin, in Gabrieli, *Arab Historians of the Crusades*, 225

*Richard expressing conditions for peace with Muslims in 1191. See Saladin below.

"Fair Lord God, I pray Thee, suffer me not to behold Thy Holy City, since I cannot deliver it from the hands of Thine enemies."*
—Quoted by Joinville, "Chronicles," in Joinville and Villehardouin, *Memoirs of the Crusades*, 275

*Expressed by Richard on hilltop overlooking Jerusalem in 1192, after realization he could not take the city. "The English king refused to gaze upon the city he could not take, and covered his eyes with his shield" (Benvenisti, *The Crusades in the Holy Land*, 46).

Saewulf
TWELFTH CENTURY; ANGLO-SAXON PILGRIM
(1192)

"[O]n that road [to Jerusalem], not only the poor and weak, but the rich and strong, are surrounded with perils; many are cut off by the Saracens, but more by heat and thirst; many perish by the want of drink, but more by too much drinking."
—*Travels*; in Wright, *Early Travels*, 36

"The entrance to the city of Jerusalem is from the west, under the citadel of king David, by the gate which is called the gate of David."
—Ibid.

"Below is the place called Golgotha, where Adam is said to have been raised to life by the blood of our Lord which fell upon him.... But in the Sentences of St Augustine, we read that he was buried in Hebron...."
—Ibid., 38

"At the head of the church…not far from the place of Calvary, is the place called Compas, which our Lord…himself signified and measured with his own hand as the middle of the world…."*

—Ibid.

*Cf. Moryson, below.

"There are still seen in the rock [on the Temple Mount] the footsteps of our Lord…."

—Ibid., 40

"About a stone's throw from that place [site of the Ascension] is the spot where, according to the Assyrians,* our Lord wrote the Lord's Prayer in Hebrew, with his own fingers on marble; and there a very beautiful church was built, but it has since been entirely destroyed by the Pagans…."

—Ibid., 42

*Syrian Christians.

"The church of the Holy Cross, about a mile west of Jerusalem, in the place where the holy cross was cut out…has been similarly laid waste by the Pagans; but the destruction fell chiefly on the surrounding buildings and the cells of the monks, the church itself not having suffered so much."

—Ibid., 43

Saladin

1137?–1193; KURDISH MUSLIM GENERAL AND WARRIOR, FOUNDER OF AYYUBID DYNASTY

"If God gives us the grace to drive His enemies from Jerusalem what happiness will be ours! What blessings shall we owe to Him if He chooses to assist us! For Jerusalem has been in enemy hands for ninety-one years."

—Quoted by 'Imad ad-Din, author of a history of the fall of Jerusalem to the Muslims, in Gabrieli, *Arab Historians of the Crusades*, 151

"Jerusalem is the city that David founded and advised Solomon to build…."

—Ibid., 153

"Jerusalem is ours as much as yours; indeed it is even more sacred to us than it is to you, for it is the place from which our Prophet accomplished his nocturnal journey and the place where our community will gather [on the Day of Judgment]. Do not imagine that we can renounce it or vacillate on this point."*
—Quoted by Baha ad-Din Ibn Shaddad, biographer of Saladin, in Gabrieli, *Arab Historians of the Crusades*, 226

*Response to Richard Lion-Heart in 1191 regarding conditions for peace with the Christians; see Richard Lion-Heart above.

Rabbi Samuel ben Samson

MEMBER OF GROUP OF SOME 300 FRENCH AND ENGLISH JEWS WHO JOURNEYED TO JERUSALEM (1211)

"We arrived at Jerusalem from the western side. Upon beholding it, we rent our garments, as is appropriate. Overwhelmed by emotion, we wept bitterly."
—Quoted in Yaari, *Igrot Eretz Yisrael*, 78

"[W]e went to the Mount of Olives, where the red heifer was burnt."
—Ibid.

Theoderich

TWELFTH CENTURY; CHRISTIAN PILGRIM (1172)

"This building [al-Aksa Mosque], with all its appurtenances, has passed into the hands of the Knights Templars who dwell in it and all the other buildings connected with it…and are ever on the watch to guard and protect the country.

"On the other side of the palace [al-Aksa]…the Templars have erected a new building…. Moreover, they are laying the foundations of a new church of wonderful size and workmanship in this place…."
—*Guide to the Holy Land*, 30

Peter Tudebode

ELEVENTH CENTURY; FRENCH PRIEST, PART OF THE FIRST CRUSADE, EYEWITNESS TO CRUSADER CONQUEST OF JERUSALEM, 1099

"[T]he Christians [Crusader forces]…came to the monastery of the Blessed Mary in the Valley of Jehosaphat, from which her most holy body was snatched up to heaven."
—*Historia de Hierosolymitano Itinere*; quoted in Peters, ed., *The First Crusade*, 247

"[A]ll of Jerusalem was clogged with cadavers. The Saracen survivors pulled out the corpses of the fellows to the gate exits, corded them up in mounds like houses, and put them to the torch. Has anyone ever seen or heard of such a holocaust of infidels?"
—Ibid., 249

Pope Urban II

CA. 1042–1099

"Enter upon the road to the Holy Sepulcher; wrest that land from the wicked race, and subject it to yourselves. That land which as the Scripture says 'floweth with milk and honey,' was given by God unto the possession of the children of Israel."
—Proclamation of Urban at Council of Clermont in 1095 as recorded by Robert of Rheims; quoted in Peters, ed., *First Crusade*, 28*

*Neither Robert of Rheims nor the three other contemporary chroniclers who report the speech profess to give a precise verbal account of what Urban said (Runciman, *History of the Crusades*, 1:107).

"[U]ndertake this journey for the remission of your sins."
—Ibid.

Usuma bin Munqidh

1095–1188; MUSLIM AUTHOR FROM SYRIA

"When I was in Jerusalem I used to go to the Masjid al-Aksa, beside which is a small oratory which the Franks have made into a church."
—Autobiography; quoted in Gabrieli, *Arab Historians of the Crusades*, 79–80

William of Tyre
CA. 1130–85; CRUSADER HISTORIAN, NATIVE OF PALESTINE, LATIN ARCHBISHOP OF TYRE

"This first-born son of Satan falsely declared that he was a prophet sent by God and thereby led astray the lands of the East, especially Arabia. The poisonous seed which he sowed so permeated the provinces that his successors employed sword and violence, instead of preaching and exhortation, to compel the people, however reluctant, to embrace the erroneous tenets of the prophet...."
—*History of Deeds* 1:60

"Chosroes*...took the Holy City...and carried away with him to Persia the Cross of the Lord."
—Ibid., 1:61

*Persian ruler, in 614.

"The Holy City, beloved of God, was subjected to the domination of unbelieving enemies, because of our sins."
—Ibid., 1:63

"The good will between Harun [al-Rashid] and the Christians [of Jerusalem] rested on an admirable treaty which the devout Emperor Charles [Charlemagne]...brought about.... The gracious favor of that potentate [Harun] was a source of much comfort to the faithful...."
—Ibid., 1:64

"Everywhere was frightful carnage, everywhere lay heaps of severed heads, so that soon it was impossible to pass or to go from one place to another except over the bodies of the slain."*
—Ibid., 1:370

*He is describing the Crusader conquest of Jerusalem.

"Jerusalem was taken in the year of the Incarnation of the Lord 1099 on Friday, July 15, about the ninth hour of the day....* Pope Urban II was presiding over the Holy Roman Church and Henry IV was administering the empire of the Romans. King Philip was reigning in France, and Alexius was wielding the

scepter over the Greeks. Guiding and directing all was the merciful hand of the Lord...."
—Ibid., 1:378

*"It was on that day...that the first man was created and the second was delivered over to death for the salvation of the first" (*History of Deeds*, 369–70).

"The Gentiles [Jews and Muslims] who were living there at the time the city was taken by force had perished by the sword...; and if any had by chance escaped, they were not permitted to remain in the city. For to allow anyone not belonging to the Christian faith to live in so venerated a place seemed like a sacrilege...."
—Ibid., 1:507

The Knights Templars "are called Brethren of the Soldiery of the Temple because...they had their residence in the royal palace near the Temple of the Lord [the Dome of the Rock]."
—Ibid., 1:526

Yakut

THIRTEENTH CENTURY; MUSLIM SCHOLAR AND GEOGRAPHER

"There is here [in the Church of the Sepulcher] the tomb which the Christians call Al Kayamah (the Anastasis) because of their belief that the Resurrection of the Messiah took place here. In point of fact, however, the name is Kumanah,* not Kayamah, for the place was the Dunghill of the inhabitants of the city, and stood anciently without the town, being the place where they cut off malefactors' hands, and where they crucified thieves."
—Quoted in Le Strange, *History of Jerusalem under the Moslems*, 128–29

*See note to Mas'udi, above.

al-Zamakshari

DIED 1144; MUSLIM COMMENTATOR ON THE KORAN

"There is disagreement regarding the place from which the Night Journey originated ['to the distant shrine'] [Koran 17:1]. Some say it was the holy mosque [of Mecca] itself. This is likely.... In the same night...Mohammed

was [also] raised up to heaven [Koran 53:4–10], that is, his Ascension took its departure from Jerusalem…'the distant shrine…': This is Jerusalem. At that time no mosque existed farther away [from Mecca] than the one at Jerusalem."
–Quoted in Peters, *Jerusalem*, 182–83

#7
Mameluke Period
UP TO 1515

Arnold von Harff

CA. 1471–1505; GERMAN KNIGHT
(CA. 1495–98)

"We...came to St. Anne's House, which the Christians in former times made into a beautiful church, but now the heathen have turned it into their praying house or mosque, so that Christians cannot enter."
– *The Pilgrimage of Arnold von Harff*; quoted in Peters, *Jerusalem*, 355

"We came to the Temple of Solomon [al-Aksa Mosque].... By means of gifts and other friendly help, I was taken by a Mamluk into this Temple. But no Christian or Jew is suffered to enter there or draw near, since they say and maintain that we are base dogs and not worthy to go to the holy places on pain of death...."
–Ibid., 406

The Muslims "have also their cemetery outside the [Golden] gate toward the Vale of Jehoshaphat.... Therefore they guard the gate closely against Christians and Jews, whom they regard as more filthy than dogs, lest they should tread upon their graves."
–Ibid., 411

"Within Jerusalem live many Jews, among them certain learned doctors of Christian teaching, born in Lombardy, and two Christian monks who...fell away from the Christian faith to the Jewish sect...."
–Ibid., 477

Santo Brasca

ITALIAN PILGRIM
(1480)

"[A] man should undertake the [pilgrimage] voyage solely with the intention of...contemplating and adoring the most Holy Mysteries...in order that Jesus may graciously pardon his sins; and not...from ambition, or to be able to boast 'I have been there,' or 'I have seen that,' ...."
–Quoted in Newett, ed., *Canon Pietro Casola's Pilgrimage*, 10

The pilgrim "should carry with him two bags – one right full of patience, the other containing two hundred Venetian ducats…."*
—Ibid., 10

*Newett adds (13): "To these two bags of money and patience [Pietro Casola] added…on his own account, a bag of faith."

Burchard of Mount Zion

THIRTEENTH CENTURY;
DOMINICAN MONK
FROM GERMANY
(CA. 1275)

"The city now stands where it has always stood, for since the Temple of the Lord stands within the city walls it would be foolish, no, altogether impossible, to move it to another place because of the walls wherewith it is fenced on all sides…."*
—*Burchard of Mount Zion*, Palestine Pilgrims' Text Society, 12:66

*This account, written ca. 1280, is notable for its accurate description of the topography of Jerusalem.

"[T]here are many [Christian] holy places in the city which stir men to devotion, so…that one day does not suffice for visiting them all."
—Ibid., 75

Pietro Casola

1427–1507; ITALIAN PRIEST
AND SCHOLAR
(1494)

"The city has one beautiful building; that is its Mosque [Dome of the Rock]. Neither Christian nor Jew can enter there."
—Quoted in Newett, ed., *Canon Pietro Casola's Pilgrimage*, 251

"Many people say that this Mosque [Dome of the Rock] is the Temple built by Solomon. But I cannot believe it…because the Holy Scripture relates that Nebuchadnezzar caused the Temple of Solomon to be thrown to the ground."
—Ibid., 252

"Now the observant friars of St. Francis live there [Mount Zion], and they have a very well kept convent, and…if it were not for the prohibition of the Moors…they would make it much more beautiful."
—Ibid., 254

"[T]he castle of the Pisans [Tower of David], seen from outside it appears to be strong. In my opinion no care is taken of it. I never saw a guard there…."
—Ibid., 255

"In Jerusalem, I was never able to see a beautiful woman…they go about with their faces covered by a black veil."
—Ibid., 257

"You must know that although the Sepulcher is governed by the Friars of Mount Zion and by other sects of Christians… nevertheless they cannot go in and out at pleasure, but must do so at the pleasure of that dog who always keeps the keys.

He is the Moor who auctions the tolls on the pilgrims and on those who wish to visit the Sepulcher even at other times."
—Ibid., 259

In the "Chapel of our Lady [on Mount Zion]…a large piece of the Cross of Christ is honored."
—Ibid.

"It is very commonly said that Saint Helena…caused this wonderful temple [the Church of the Sepulcher] to be built, nor do we read anywhere that it was built by anyone else."
—Ibid., 278

Geoffrey Chaucer

CA. 1340–1400; FATHER OF ENGLISH LITERATURE

"And she [the Wife of Bath] had thrice been to Jerusalem"
—Prologue, *Canterbury Tales*

"May Jesu in mercy send

Me wit to guide your way...

Upon that perfect,
glorious pilgrimage

Called the celestial, to Jerusalem."
—The Parson's Prologue,
Canterbury Tales

Isaac ben Joseph Chelo

SPANISH JEWISH KABBALIST
(1334)

"On Mount Zion there stood formerly the fortress of Zion which King David...took from the Jebusites and called with his name."*
—*The Roads from Jerusalem*; quoted in Adler, *Jewish Travellers*, 130

*See note to Piacenza Pilgrim, above, re Mount Zion.

"The Jewish community in Jerusalem...is quite numerous. It is composed of fathers of families from all parts of the world, principally from France.... They live here in happiness and tranquility...for the royal authority is just and great....

Among the different members of the holy congregation...are many who are engaged in handicrafts such as dyers, tailors, shoemakers, etc. Others carry on a rich commerce in all sorts of things.... Some are devoted to science, such as medicine, astronomy, and mathematics. But the greater number of their learned men are working day and night at the study of the Holy Law...."
—Ibid., 133

Christopher Columbus

1451–1506; MARITIME
EXPLORER CREDITED WITH
DISCOVERY OF NEW WORLD

"Before the end of the world, all prophecies have to be fulfilled, the Gospels need to be diffused all over the world and the Holy City of Jerusalem has to be given back to the Christian Church."*
—Quoted in Prawer, *World of the Crusaders*, 147

*Written after the discovery of the New World.

"I propose to Your Majesties* that all the profit to be derived from my enterprise should be used for the recovery of Jerusalem."
—Ibid., 152

*Ferdinand and Isabella.

Elijah of Ferrara

JEWISH TRAVELER FROM ITALY
(1434)

"The Jews [in Jerusalem] ply their trades side by side with the Ishmaelites, and no jealousy between them results…."
—Quoted in Adler, *Jewish Travellers*, 153

Friar Felix Fabri

CA. 1441–1502; GERMAN DOMINICAN FRIAR
(1480; 1483–84)

"When we were come to the gate which is called the Gate of David [Jaffa Gate]…we passed through it with bowed heads, for by the act of so passing we received plenary indulgences."
—*Wanderings*, vol. 1, pt. 1, 282

"[F]or the celebration of the Mass [on Mount Zion]…the sacristan beat a wooden board, because [the churches] have no bells of any kind, nor are they suffered to have them by the infidels, but give notice of divine service by beating wooden boards…."
—Ibid., 287–88

"No one should think visiting the places to be a light task; there is the intense heat of the sun, the walking from place to place, kneeling, and prostration: above all, there is the strain that everyone puts on himself in striving with all his might to rouse himself to earnest piety and comprehension of what is shown to him in the holy places, and to devout prayer and meditation, all of which cannot be done without great fatigue…."
—Ibid., 299

"When [Sultan Barsbay, 1422–37] was told that David and other kings…of his seed were buried there [on Mount Zion], he said: 'We Saracens also count David

as holy, even as the Christians
and Jews do, and we believe the
Bible as they do. Wherefore,
neither the Christians nor Jews
shall have that place, but we
will take it for ourselves."*
—Ibid., 303

*In 1452–53, the Franciscans lost to the Muslims possession of their place beneath the Cenacle on Mount Zion identified as the tomb of David.

"Before the door on either side
thereof [were marble benches]
upon which these men [Muslim
guards] sat with their faces
turned away. They were men
of fine presence, well stricken
in years…wearing long beards,
and of solemn manners.… We
went by them with shame
and blushing, because it is a
great confusion that Christ's
faithful worshipers should be
let into the Christ's Church
by Christ's blasphemers.…"
—Ibid., pt. 2, 341

"We went up one by one, and
touched the sacred pillar [at
which Jesus was scourged] with
our hands, passing them through
an iron grating. Here, also, we
received plenary indulgences."
—Ibid., 349

"We put our arms and our
heads into the hole* to the
very bottom: and…received
plenary indulgences."
—Ibid., 365

*The socket of the Cross.

"Adam, our first parent, died
here [rock of Calvary];

Abraham was blessed
here by Melchizedek;*

Isaac was brought hither by
his father to be sacrificed,

The brazen serpent
was set up here;

The Lord Jesus was
crucified and died here."
—Ibid., 366

*"In the temple which he [Melchizedek] had built" (*Wanderings*, vol. 2, pt. 1, 221).

"[B]y the side of the great
hospital [of the Knights

Hospitallers] the Saracens have built a tall and costly tower [a minaret]...and close to the tower they have built a mosque, facing the Church of the Holy Sepulcher."
—Ibid., 395

"After having read these [Gospel] accounts, a man who sees the ancient tombs in the Holy Land easily understands what the Lord's sepulcher must have been like; but it cannot possibly now be like what it was then, because of the Church that has been built above it, and because of the decoration....

"Some say that under the marble slabs the rock of the monument and the Holy Sepulcher still exists entire.... Others say that no man knows for certain or can affirm that the true rock is or is not under the slabs. Others plainly assert that there has not been a piece as large as a grain of millet left there of the true stone.

"The devout and quiet pilgrim should grasp this fact, that whether the cave as it stands at the present day be the true and entire monument...matters very little...because the main fact... abides there...that this was the place of the most holy burial and resurrection of Christ...."
—Ibid., 400, 411, 415

"At the present day all the Christians who are in Jerusalem assemble in the church on Easter Eve, and the Greeks shut their priest into the Lord's monument with an unlighted candle, which he brings forth lighted, with a loud cry, and from which all the lamps are lighted. But it is not lighted by a miracle, but artificially, albeit the ignorant mob raises its cries to heaven, praising God, as though a miracle had been wrought, and so they noise it among the people and even among the Saracens."
—Ibid., 422

"The Church of the Holy Sepulcher is more beautiful than all the other churches in the world from the variety of the nations who praise God therein, yet it is rendered hideous and

shocking by the abominable errors of those who enter it."*
—Ibid., 430

*The reference is to other Christian denominations who are guilty of "various deadly errors in the essentials of the faith."

"[F]rom this place [Church of the Assumption in Valley of Jehoshaphat] the glorious Virgin ascended into heaven...."
—Ibid., 466

"In the midst of this church [Church of the Ascension, on the Mount of Olives] there stands a great chapel...wherein is the exceeding holy place of the footprints of the Lord Jesus Christ, which he left stamped into the rock when he ascended from that place into heaven."
—Ibid., 484

"The valley of Hinnom is the same as the valley of Jehoshaphat."*
—Ibid., 491

*I.e., on the eastern side of the city. In Jewish tradition the valley is west of the city.

"[S]ometimes it has happened, and does still happen, that pilgrims pile up stones for themselves in that valley [of Jehoshaphat], wishing before the day of judgment to secure a place for themselves whereon they may sit on the day of judgment."
—Ibid., 492

"[T]he very spot where grew the tree of the holy cross...called Church of the Holy Cross."*
—Ibid., vol. 2, pt. 1, 1

*Fabri cites another tradition, linking the wood of the cross to a beam placed by Solomon in the "sheep pool of Bethesda" (1: pt.2, 456, 522)

"They say that Solomon had a garden in this place [Monastery of the Cross] also, and that sometimes he would drive hither from Jerusalem in his golden chariot to enjoy it."
—Ibid., 2

"Certain nobles were led by vanity to write their names, with the symbols of their birth and peerage, on the walls [of the Church of the Sepulcher]…and painted their coats of arms thereon…. Some of them carved their names with iron chisels and mallets on the pillars and marble slabs…."
—Ibid., 85–86

"The Jews and Saracens say that these under ground [vaulted] chambers [under the Temple Mount] were the stables of Solomon's horses…. [But it is not to be] believed that Solomon kept beasts in that most noble house…whereunto the stalling of horses would have been irreverent…."
—Ibid., 129

At the juncture of the east and south walls of the Temple Mount is "a stone which seems to have been part of a marble column…partly contained within the wall. The Saracens have a fable…that on the day of Judgment, when all men are gathered together in the Valley of Jehoshaphat, Mohammed will come and take his seat…to judge the world."
—Ibid., 130

"I rose early…and having said matins, I stole out of the convent alone and rambled off to the holy places…. In each of these places I picked up pebbles, marked them, and put them into a bag…. Moreover, I gathered up some of the thorns which grow in the hedges on the side of the Mount of Olives…and Mount Zion, and I bound twigs of them together and wound them into a crown of thorns wherewith I believe the Lord Jesus was crowned."
—Ibid., 214

"Above the Fish Gate, or Merchants' Gate [Jaffa Gate], [Hadrian] set up a sow or pig carved in marble for the confusion of the Jews, that none of them might presume to enter there."
—Ibid., 237

"I can boldly declare that had this temple [the Dome of the Rock] not been built, the Christians never would have lost Jerusalem and their own church;* for the Saracens are so jealously fond of this temple of theirs, that while it stands the Christians can have no peace in Jerusalem; wherefore it would have been better to tear it up from its foundations than to dedicate it to the name of Christ, as has often been done."
—Ibid., 241–42

*Fabri is referring to the Crusader conversion of the site to Christian worship.

"At this present day the Christians would care little about the Saracens' bearing rule in Jerusalem, provided only that we were allowed freedom to pass in and out of our temple of the Lord's sepulcher without fear and without vexations and extortions. Neither would the Saracens mind if the Christians were lords of the Holy City, if we would render up the temple to them. But since Christians and Saracens cannot agree about this matter, unhappy Jerusalem has suffered…and will hereafter suffer…beyond any other city in the world."
—Ibid., 262

"In their frenzy,* [the Muslim conquerors] burst open the bars and doors of the Church of the Lord's Resurrection…profaned the altars, broke the glass windows, and tore down the carven images from the walls."
—Ibid., 342

*During the reconquest of Jerusalem from the Crusaders in 1187.

Estori Farhi

1280–CA. 1355; RABBINIC SCHOLAR AND EARLIEST JEWISH GEOGRAPHER OF THE HOLY LAND (1312–19)

"The roads of Zion are in mourning, its streets desolate, and its sites not determined with any degree of certainty. The town is presently higher than Mount Moriah, because it has been so frequently destroyed and rebuilt on the same site,

so that remains of old vaulted roofs are found under the houses, and serve as foundations for more recent buildings."
—Quoted in Holtz, *The Holy City*, 130

"And the Gentile who is not of your people Israel is master of the House [Temple]

And none who belong to the House [the priests] are present there.

In Your ever-faithful kindness, my God, establish the House as of old,

Bring salvation to your chosen people."
—"Prayer at the Gate of Mercy," *Kaftor VaPerach* 1:114

"Mount Zion is the city of David, the royal residence, and the Millo."*
—Ibid., 1:116

*See note to Piacenza Pilgrim, above, re Mount Zion.

Friar Simon Fitzimmons

ANGLO-IRISH
FRANCISCAN PILGRIM
(1322–23)

In the Church of St. Denis in Belvieu, "we saw one nail of those with which the Lord was affixed to the tree of the cross...."
—*Itineraries*; quoted in Hoade, *Western Pilgrims*, 4

In the chapel of the kings of France in Paris "are most precious relics, to wit, the crown of thorns of Christ...a big and glorious cross of the wood of the holy life-giving cross, two nails with which the Lord was nailed to the cross, [and] the lance, so it is said...with which His side was opened...."
—Ibid., 5

"[W]e came to a monastery [the Monastery of the Cross], in which abide schismatic monks, the Cumani [Georgian monks], in whose church beneath the high altar is the

place where was cut the most precious wood of the Cross...."
—Ibid., 43

To the north of the "hole in which the cross of Christ was fixed" the "head of Adam was found...."
—Ibid., 45

"[F]rom the Sepulcher [tomb of Jesus] to the east, within the entrance to the choir [is] the round hole, in which Christ placed his finger, saying 'This is the center of the world....'"*
—Ibid., 45

*Cf. Moryson.

Ibn Battuta

MUSLIM VOYAGER
(1335)

"We...reached Jerusalem...third in excellence after the two shrines of Mecca and Medina...."
—*Travels in Asia and Africa*,* 55

*Ibn Battuta's accounts of his extensive travels are an important source of Islamic social and cultural history of the period

"The greater part [of the Dome of the Rock] is covered with gold so that the eyes of one who gazes on its beauties are dazzled by its brilliance...."
—Ibid., 56

"[T]he Valley of Jahannam [Gehenna] [is located] to the east of the town...."
—Ibid., 56

"Among the grace-bestowing sanctuaries of Jerusalem is a building [the Church of the Ascension]...to the east of the town...said to mark the place whence Jesus ascended to heaven."
—Ibid., 56–57

"All who come on pilgrimage to visit [the Church of the Sepulcher] pay a stipulated tax to the Muslims, and suffer very unwillingly various humiliations."
—Ibid., 57

Ibn al-Firkah al-Fazari

DIED 1329; MUSLIM SCHOLAR AND RELIGIOUS LEADER IN DAMASCUS

"O Apostle of Allah, which mosque was stationed in the earth first? He said, The Sacred Mosque of Mecca. I said, then which one? He said, The Mosque al-Aksa. I said, How much time intervened? He said, Forty years."

– *The Book of Arousing Souls*; quoted in Matthews, *Palestine: Mohammedan Holy Land*, 3.*

*The work is a notable example of the genre of the "Merits of Jerusalem" books that appeared at the beginning of the eleventh century (Peters, *Jerusalem*, 336).

"So the commencement of the Mosque al-Aksa was before Shem."

–Ibid., 4

"And a prayer in the Sacred Mosque [of Mecca] is worth a hundred thousand prayers, and a prayer in my mosque [in Medina] is worth a thousand prayers, and a prayer in the Mosque al-Aksa is worth ten thousand prayers."*

–Ibid.

*This is one of a number of traditions reported by al-Firkah (and others) about the comparative benefits of prayer at the three sites.

"We* came to the south side of the mosque, and he tied up there his mount."

–Ibid., 8

*The angel Gabriel and Mohammed during the latter's nocturnal journey to Jerusalem mounted on al-Burak.

"On the authority of Abu Hureirah it is related: the Apostle of Allah said that whoever prays in Jerusalem, all his guilt is forgiven him."

–Ibid., 10

"All the rivers and the clouds and the winds come from under the Rock of Jerusalem."

–Ibid., 15

"Allah hath not sent a prophet to the earth since the descent of Adam (from Paradise) who hath not set as his point to face in prayer the Rock of Jerusalem [i.e., the *kiblah*]. Our Prophet prayed thus for sixteen months."
—Ibid., 18

"And verily, the valley to the rear [of the eastern wall of the city] is the Valley of Gehenna [Hinnom]."
—Ibid., 19

"Zamzam [in Mecca] and the spring of Siloam in Jerusalem are each a spring of Paradise."
—Ibid., 23

"The Apostle of Allah said, The Koran was sent down to me in three places, Mecca, Medina, and Syria – which means Jerusalem...."
—Ibid., 27

"Noah presented his offering* on the Rock of Jerusalem."
—Ibid., 32

*After the Flood. See Genesis 8:20.

Ibn Taymiyya
1263–1328; MUSLIM LAWYER AND SCHOLAR

The Ka'ba (in Mecca) "was the *kiblah* of Abraham and other prophets. One who today regards the rock [on the Haram-a-Sharif] as the *kiblah* and prays toward it is a renegade apostate who must repent. Either he seeks repentance or he is killed."
—"In Support of Pious Visits to Jerusalem"; quoted in Peters, *Jerusalem*, 376

"In Jerusalem, there is not a place one calls truly sacred...."
—Ibid., 377

"[K]nowledgeable people among the Companions [of Mohammed] and their successors...did not glorify the Rock. Its being the *kiblah*

was abrogated just as Saturday being a festival according to the law of Moses…was. It was replaced in the law of Mohammed…by Friday."
—Ibid., 377

"In the Footsteps of the Master"

BY AN ANONYMOUS DISCIPLE OF RABBI OBADIAH OF BERTINORO (1495)

"Nearby is a building like a tower called the Pillar of Absalom. It is half hidden by stones which have been thrown at it, because there stood the building of Absalom who rebelled against his father."
—"In the Footsteps of the Master," in Wilhelm, ed., Roads to Zion, 26

"[T]he burial place of the prophet Samuel of Ramah [at Nebi Samuel]…is on top of the mountain and there is a fine synagogue there…."
—Ibid., 26

"Itinerary of a Certain Englishman"

ANONYMOUS ACCOUNT (1344–45)

"We descended from Calvary to the place of Golgotha, where [the Greek friars] showed us the cleft stone and the small hole in which they said the head of Adam was found."
—Itinerary, in Hoade, Western Pilgrims, 67

"[T]he Saracens [Muslims], like executioners, were present with their sticks, having already opened the doors of the church: and having opened the door of the Sepulcher…."*
—Ibid.

*The Muslims had "not only the key of the church, but also that of the Tomb" (Hoade, 67n).

"Under the church [of the Last Supper] in a vault are the monuments of Kings David and Solomon."
—Ibid., 69

"We went farther in the valley [of Kidron], having to the left many habitations of the Jews, who are potters, and who have no houses except in the caves in the rocks, where they live as the wild beasts."
—Ibid., 71

"[T]here is a fort encompassed by high walls, in which there is a church of the Greeks [Georgians], and in a chapel, to the side of the church, on the pavement, there is a hole, wherein grew the wood of the cross on which hung the Savior of the world…."
—Ibid., 76

Rabbi Jacob, the Messenger of Rabbi Jechiel of Paris

JOURNEYED TO THE HOLY LAND (AND IRAQ) TO RAISE FUNDS FOR A YESHIVA IN PARIS
(1238–44)

"When we reach Zophim [Mount Scopus], we see Jerusalem and make one rent in our garments, and when we reach Jerusalem we go on one of the ruins and look at the Temple Mount and the wall of the Court of Women, and the Court of Israel, the site of the Altar, and the site of the Temple, and the Sanctuary, and we make a second rent in our garments for the Temple."
—Adler, *Jewish Travellers*, 117

"Round the *Eben Shethiah*,* the Ishmaelite Kings have built a very beautiful building for a house of prayer and erected on the top a very fine cupola. The building is on the site of the Holy of Holies and the Sanctuary.… The Muslims gather there on their holy days in crowds and dance around it in procession as the Israelites used to do on the seventh day of the festival, if we may compare holy things with profane."
—Ibid., 118–19

*The Foundation Stone; i.e., the Rock on the Temple Mount.

Jacobus de Voragine

DIED 1298; LEADER OF
THE DOMINICAN ORDER,
ARCHBISHOP OF GENOA

"[T]radition holds that the Cross of Christ was fashioned of four different woods, namely the wood of the palm-tree…the cypress…the olive, and…the cedar…each of these forming one of the four parts of the cross.…"
—*Golden Legend*, 270

Helena "brought back to her son Constantine a part of the Cross…[and also] gave her son the nails…four in number."
—Ibid., 275

Ludolph von Suchem

FOURTEENTH CENTURY;
GERMAN PILGRIM
(1336–41)

"In Jerusalem stand the Lord's Temple and Solomon's Temple.…"*
—*Description of the Holy Land*, Palestine Pilgrims' Text Society, 12:98

*Von Suchem is referring to the Dome of the Rock and al-Aksa Mosque. As he notes, the Muslims call the Dome "'the holy Rock,' not 'the Temple'.…"

"A little way to the north of this Temple [the Dome of the Rock] there is a church on the spot where the Blessed Virgin Mary was born, and on that same spot St. Anne and St. Joachim her husband lie buried…. Out of this church…the Saracens have now made a church of their own. Yet all the story of Anne and Joachim and the Blessed Mary's birth remains nobly painted on the front of the church. This painting in my time used to be…explained to the Christians by an old Saracen woman…. She…declared that the picture of Joachim stood for Mohammed, and the painting of the trees for paradise, where Mohammed kissed girls.…"
—Ibid., 12:100–101

"It was on this mount that of old stood the city of David*…. Upon this Mount Zion…there once was built an exceedingly fair

monastery called the Convent of St. Mary.... In this monastery there now dwell [Franciscan] Minorite brethren...."
—Ibid., 12:101–102

*See note to Piacenza Pilgrim, above.

"[T]he Saracens have as much respect for Christ's sepulcher as Christians have for a Jewish synagogue."
—Ibid., 12:105

Sir John Mandeville

AUTHOR OF ACCOUNT OF PURPORTED TRAVELS TO JERUSALEM AND OTHER PLACES (1322)

"[I]t is not long since [the tomb of Jesus] was all open, that men might kiss it and touch it. But because pilgrims...labored to break the stone in pieces or in powder, therefore the sultan has caused a wall to be made round the sepulcher, that no man may touch it."
—*The Book of Sir John Mandeville*, 1322–1356, in Wright, *Early Travels*, 166

Rabbi Meshullam ben Rabbi Menahem of Volterra

JEWISH TRAVELER FROM ITALY (1481)

"[W]hen I saw [Jerusalem's] ruins, I rent my garments a hand breadth, and in the bitterness of my heart recited the appropriate prayer...."
—Adler, *Jewish Travellers*, 189

"...Jerusalem has no walls except a little on one side where I entered, and although through our sins it is all in ruins there are ten thousand Muslim householders and about two hundred and fifty Jewish householders."
—Ibid., 189

"On the east side [of the Temple Mount] are the Gates of Mercy...and on the sides are Muslim graves...."
—Ibid.

"[E]very year when the Jews go to Synagogue on the eve of the Ninth of Ab all the lamps in the Temple Court [Temple

Mount] go out of their own accord and cannot be kindled again, and the Muslims know when it is the Ninth of Ab, which they observe somewhat like the Jews because of this."
—Ibid., 190

"The temple area is on Mount Moriah in the place where our father Abraham bound his son Isaac for sacrifice...."
—Ibid., 191

"[E]ven the Muslim[s] throw a stone on his ["Absalom's"] grave because he rebelled against his father, and at the side there is a very great heap of stones, and every year the heap is removed."
—Ibid., 192

"On the southern side [of the Temple Mount] is Mount Zion, that is the city of David, and above it, near to David's tomb... is a church of the Franciscans."
—Ibid.

"[A]ll around Jerusalem there are many caves and in them are buried many pious and saintly people without number, but we do not know who they are except those marked...and we see that the Muslims also honor all these places and that they have the same traditions about them as we.... The Muslims have many a time sought to have these graves closed up and to have them dedicated as *wakf* in their hands...."
—Ibid., 193–94

The leaders of the Jews "go every year with the congregation behind them to Mount Zion on the ninth of Ab to mourn and weep, and thence they descend to the valley of Jehoshaphat and go upon the Mount of Olivet, when they see the whole of the Temple area and mourn for the destruction of the Temple."
—Ibid., 196

Mujir al-Din

END OF FIFTEENTH CENTURY;
MUSLIM HISTORIAN,
NATIVE OF JERUSALEM

"The practice [of the Descent of the Holy Fire] is still going on…in the Kumanah [Church of the Sepulcher], and the day is called 'the Saturday of the Light.' There occur under the very eyes of the Muslims a number of hateful things which are not right to hear or look upon. Making public manifestation of their infidel faith, the Christians cry out in a loud voice 'Hasten to the religion of the Cross.'"
—*Histoire de Jérusalem et d'Hébron*;
quoted in Peters, *Jerusalem*, 261

"According to Khalid ibn Ma'dan, the Prophet said…:'Let anyone who has visited Jerusalem go to the Prayer Niche of David and bathe himself in the fountain of Siloam, since it comes from Paradise; let him abstain from going into the churches and buying anything there, since a sin committed at Jerusalem is the equivalent of a thousand sins, and a good work there is the equal to a thousand good works."
—Ibid., 374

"As for the view of Jerusalem from afar, filled with brilliance and beauty, it is one of the famous wonders. The most attractive view is that which one enjoys from the eastern side, from the Mount of Olives."
—Ibid., 390

"The principal quarters of Jerusalem are as follows:…The Maghrebi Quarter.…The Sharaf Quarter.…The Quarter of Alam.…The Quarter of the People of al-Salt.…The Jewish Quarter.…The Quarter of the Feather.…The Quarter of Zion inside the walls.… The Dawiyya Quarter.…The Quarter of the Banu Harith.…"
—Ibid., 392–93

"During the reign of al-Malik al-Zahir [1438–1453 CE]…the sultan [ordered] the destruction of all new constructions built…on Zion, and the seizure of the tomb of David from the Christians.… The bones of the monks buried near the tomb of David were exhumed. These

events took place on July 10, 1452, which was a festival day."
—Ibid., 420

In 1452, "the new buildings at Bethlehem and the Kumanah [Church of the Sepulcher] were torn down. The wooden balustrade recently put up in the Kumanah was ripped out and taken amidst shouts of 'God is Great!' to the Aksa Mosque."
—Ibid.

"When Omar* came to Jerusalem, he followed (David's) example, praying in the same place, which was also called the Mihrab of Omar, because there he first prayed on the day of the conquest of Jerusalem. But it was originally the Mihrab of David."
—*Histoire de Jérusalem et d'Hébron*; quoted in Barclay, *City of the Great King*, 379

*Second caliph, leader of Muslim conquest of Jerusalem in 638.

"On the south side [of the Rock] is the footprint of the prophet, which was there impressed when he mounted the celestial beast Burak, for the nocturnal journey."
—Ibid., 383

I "was astounded to see the rock detached on all sides, and not joined to the earth."
—Ibid.

"The Castle [the Tower of David]…formerly called the Mihrab of David, who dwelt there…has a great tower named of David, and built by Solomon."
—Ibid., 399

Muthir al Ghiram

ANONYMOUS ACCOUNT OF MUSLIM ARRIVAL IN THE CITY AFTER SALADIN'S RECONQUEST OF THE CITY, COMPOSED 1351

"And [the Christian] Patriarch [of Jerusalem] took us [Omar] to the Church [of the Sepulcher] which goes by the name of the Kumanah,* and said he: 'This is David's Mosque.' And Omar looked around and pondered,

then he answered....'Thou liest, for the Apostle described to me the Mosque of David, and by his description this is not it.'"
   –Quoted in Le Strange, *History of Jerusalem under the Moslems*, 61

*See note to Mas'udi, above.

Nahmanides (Rabbi Moshe ben Nachman)

1194–1270; SPANISH JEWISH TALMUDIC SCHOLAR (ARRIVED IN JERUSALEM 1267)

"Great is the desolation.... Jerusalem is more ravaged than the rest of the country. And yet, despite the destruction, it is very good."
   –Letter to his son, in Yaari, *Igrot Eretz Yisrael*, 85

Jerusalem "has almost 2,000 inhabitants, among them about 300 Christians, survivors of the sword of the sultan. There are no Jews in the city, for since the arrival of the Tartars [Mongols], some fled, others died by the sword. [The exception] is two brothers, dyers by trade.... A minyan gathers in their home on the Sabbath...since many visitors come [from abroad]...to see the Sanctuary and mourn over it."
   –Ibid.

"[H]e who merits to see Jerusalem in her ruins will merit to see her rebuilt and repaired when the Divine Presence returns to her."
   –Ibid.

"My heart and eyes will dwell with [my children left behind] forever.... But [this] loss...is compensated by my present joy of a day passed within thy courts, O Jerusalem! visiting the ruins of the Temple and crying over the ruined sanctuary; where it is granted me to caress your stones, to fondle your dust, and to weep over your ruins. I wept bitterly, but I found joy in my tears. I tore my garments, but I felt solace in it."
   –Entry of Nahmanides into Jerusalem, in Yaari, *Masa'ot Eretz Yisrael*, 77

Fra Niccolo of Poggibonsi

ITALIAN FRANCISCAN PILGRIM
(1346–50)

"Lo! the most holy, the most royal, and most noble, and magnificent above all the cities of the world, you, Jerusalem."
–*Voyage*, 9

The Sepulcher "is a holy tomb.... [W]hoever here will pray with devotion, all his sins are forgiven."
–Ibid., 15

"I want to relate how this chapel [of the tomb of Jesus] is guarded, that is, locked. As said, it has three doors: two are sealed and locked so that they never open; the other door...opens and is well furnished with key and seal.... And these seals and keys are held by Saracens, other than those who hold the keys to the door of the church; and they open the chapel...and allow one to stand within for the space of three Our Fathers; and then they throw him out and lock [the door again]."
–Ibid., 16

The "castle [Tower of David]... is not as when built by David, because it is in ruins, and has been rebuilt three times. All around is a moat...."*
–Ibid., 29

*The moat, still to be seen, was built by the Crusaders.

In St. Savior's Church on Mount Zion, the "stone table of the...altar was that which by the angels was placed at the exit of the Holy Sepulcher, when Jesus Christ...was there placed in the tomb, and the angels took it from the Sepulcher and placed it where it now is...."
–Ibid., 30

"[H]ere [on Mount Zion] you find a chapel, where Christ appeared to the Apostles, eight days after the resurrection.... And there Jesus Christ had the holy Supper with the Apostles...."
–Ibid., 34

"[T]he valley of Jehoshaphat, wherein the world will be judged."
—Ibid., 36

[Gethsemane is] the "garden… where Christ was arrested, and where he prayed to the Father."
—Ibid., 44

The Golden Gate "is very large, and consists of two gates, one beside the other. Between the two gates is a wall of two feet in width and a vaulted arch."
—Ibid., 45–46

"The Templum Domini [Dome of the Rock] is very beautiful exteriorly…with a round dome like a hat…. How it is within, I know not, because the cursed Saracens have made of it a mosque…."
—Ibid., 46–47

"There is the Church of St. Anne, where was born the Virgin Mary, for there were the dwellings of Joachim."
—Ibid., 47

"And going straight, half way on the road from Jerusalem to Bethlehem is a beautiful monastery, by name of St. Elias."
—Ibid., 50

"In the center of the church [the Monastery of the Cross] there is a wall with a door, on which is painted St. Abraham, and how here sprang up the tree of the Holy Cross. Beneath the altar is a deep hole, and in the middle of it grew the wood, from which was made one part of the Holy Cross…. [T]he cross of Christ was of four woods…. The upright…was the wood which Seth the son of Adam…brought from Paradise…. The second… for the arms…was of cypress…. The third…was of cedar…. The fourth was of olive…."
—Ibid., 57

"It is said that as soon as Adam, for his sin, was cast

out from paradise he was forthwith in Jerusalem...."
—Ibid., 58

Rabbi Obadiah of Bertinoro

CA. 1450–BEFORE 1516; ITALIAN RABBI, AUTHOR OF COMMENTARY ON THE MISHNA (MIGRATED IN 1487)

"About three quarters of a mile from Jerusalem, at a place where the mountain is ascended by steps, we beheld the famous city of our delight, and here we rent our garments, as was our duty. A little farther on, the sanctuary, the desolate house of our splendor, became visible, and at the sight of it we again made rents in our garments."
—Letters, in Adler, *Jewish Travellers*, 234

"Jerusalem is for the most part desolate and in ruins.... [I]t is not surrounded by walls.... As for Jews, about 70 families of the poorest class have remained; one who has bread for a year is called rich. Among the Jewish population there are many forsaken widows from Germany, Spain, Portugal, and other countries, so that there are seven women to one man...."
—Ibid., 234–35

"At one time [the Jews] had more houses, but these are now heaps of rubbish and cannot be rebuilt, for the law of the land is that a Jew may not rebuild his ruined house without permission, and the permission often costs more than the whole house is worth."
—Ibid., 236

"No Jew may enter the enclosure of the temple. Although sometimes the Arabs are anxious to admit carpenters and goldsmiths to perform work there, nobody will go in, for we have all been defiled (by touching bodies of the dead)."
—Ibid., 239

"The waters of Siloam flow underground in the valley of Jehoshaphat. Siloam is not exactly a stream, but rather a

spring which rises up every morning till about noon, then falls and flows under the mountain to a place near which there is now a large ruin."
—Ibid., 240–41

"On Mount Zion, near the Sepulcher of the Kings, the Franciscans have a large church."
—Ibid., 243

"All possible winds blow in Jerusalem. It is said that every wind before going where it listeth comes to Jerusalem to prostrate itself before the Lord. Blessed be He that knoweth the truth."
—Ibid., 243

"The Mount of Olives is lofty and barren; scarcely an olive tree is to be found on it."
—Letters; quoted in Hammer, ed., *Jewish Anthology*, 167

Seigneur Ogier VIII d'Anglure

FRENCH NOBLEMAN
AND PILGRIM
(1395–96)

"And these indulgences [at the holy sites] were granted by Saint Sylvester, the Pope, at the prayer and request of Saint Helen[a] and of her son Saint Constantine, the emperor of Constantinople."
—*Holy Jerusalem Voyage*, 23

In a "chapel attached to the Church of Notre Dame [on Mount Zion]…are the tombs of David…and Solomon…and within the chapel is a crypt in which David wrote the Psalter."
—Ibid., 30

"[T]here is a very beautiful church conducted by Greek Monks, which…is called Holy Cross. Beneath the great altar… is the spot where one of the arms of the cross grew – that is, the log from which the crosspiece of the holy true cross…was made."
—Ibid., 38

"…Jerusalem is a very great and beautiful city, however filthily and vilely maintained by the Saracens…."
—Ibid., 41

"[T]he holy city is at present not enclosed [by walls] at all, except by the houses that have been built over the ditches…though at the Jaffa Gate there is a strong castle…."
—Ibid.

Francesco Petrarch

1304–74; ITALIAN POET AND HUMANIST

"Then we come to Zion and the Mount of Olives, then also to the place from which he ascended to heaven and where it is believed he will return on the day of judgment…."
—*Itinerary to the Sepulcher* 16.4*

*The *Itinerary* is addressed to an acquaintance planning a pilgrimage to the Holy Land, a journey Petrarch did not undertake.

Francesco Suriano

FIFTEENTH–SIXTEENTH CENTURY; VENETIAN MERCHANT, FRANCISCAN GUARDIAN (1481–84, 1493–1515)

"This is the city so beloved by God."
—*Treatise on the Holy Land*, 42

The Knights of St. John, "commonly known as the Hospitallers…were like to the Maccabees, having God on their side."
—Ibid., 45

"This said round church has two main domes. One stands over the Holy Sepulcher and this is in the center of the church. But the second is to the west."
—Ibid., 46

"The door of the Church of the Holy Sepulcher is always locked and sealed, the key being held by the Saracens…so that any Christian who wishes to enter, must pay the tribute."
—Ibid., 48

"The said fire* does not descend in truth…though all the nations, save us Friars, feign this falsehood to be true."
—Ibid., 48

*The reference is to the Holy Fire ceremony on Easter of the Greek Christians.

"[T]he Greeks [are] our worst and atrocious enemies…. These are the people who continually by their heresies have provoked the anger of God against them and profaned and disgraced the orthodox [Catholic] church. These are the people who continually persecute us Friars and the servants of God…. These are dominated by the Turks and they are dispersed throughout the world like the Jews."
—Ibid., 84–85

"The Georgians are the worst heretics, like to the Greeks, and equal in malice…. They are our great and chief enemies, as the Greeks are…."
—Ibid., 87

"The Armenians are a very beautiful race, rich and generous…. They are deadly enemies of the Greeks and Georgians."
—Ibid., 88

"Baldwin I, king of Jerusalem… never wished to be called king nor to be crowned, saying that it did not behoove a temporal king to carry a crown of gold where the celestial king had carried a crown of thorns."
—Ibid., 105

"[T]hough it be small, yet all the world will congregate [in the Valley of Jehoshaphat] for judgment…."
—Ibid., 112

"In this valley [Silwan] is the…well…where the Jews…hid the fire which ever burned in the Temple. And in this well the Blessed Virgin used to wash the little clothes of Christ."
—Ibid., 119

"The cross…was of four woods… olive, cypress, cedar and palm."
—Ibid., 146

"The country of 'Ein el Karem is pleasing, full of fruit and vines and olive trees."
—Ibid., 147

William Wey
ENGLISH PILGRIM
(1458, 1462)

"There is more pardon in that hill*

Than any Christian man can tell."
—*Itineraries*, 10

*Calvary.

"There is a chapel* that stands right high

From the which Jesus to heaven did fly,

The steps of his feet [be] there in a stone,

Which men may see…."
—Ibid., 13

*On the Mount of Olives.

"Lap strat di trivium flent sudar sincopizavit por pis lap schola domus Her Symonis Pharisey."*
—Ibid., 20

*Wey's mnemonic listing to recall the fourteen Stations of the Cross. The words evoke in specific terms each of the Stations. Wey was the first writer to use the term "stations" – meaning "some place particularly venerated" – in reference to the Via Dolorosa (Storme, *The Way of the Cross*, 98).

#8
Ottoman Period

UP TO NINETEENTH CENTURY

- Ottoman Turks enter Jerusalem in 1516
- Suleiman the Magnificent (builder of the present walls, 1536–40) rules 1520–60

Christianus Adrichomius

1533–85; DUTCH ROMAN CATHOLIC PRIEST, ACCOUNT PUBLISHED 1595

"We have made such exact description…of the way of the cross…to the end that every Christian man, in all places, even in the doors of his house…may by the Imagination of his mind conceive the like way…."*
—*A Briefe Description of Hierusalem*, 59

*Adrichomius was the first to attempt to "arrange in Jerusalem the 14 Stations of the Way of the Cross as they were practiced in Europe" but "as he had not sufficient regard for the places and traditions of Jerusalem, which he knew from books only, his attempt was rejected as unrealistic by the Franciscans living in Jerusalem" (B. Bagatti, Notes, in Horn, *Ichnographiae*, 8).

Anonymous

LATTER PART OF SIXTEENTH CENTURY

"A Song Mad[e] by F.B.P."*

"Hierusalem, my happie home,

When shall I come to thee?

When shall my sorrowes have an end,

Thy joys when shall I see?"
—Julian, *Dictionary of Hymnology*, 580

*The poem, which appears in numerous later versions, is from the late sixteenth or early seventeenth century, and is frequently ascribed to Augustine. F.B.P. was probably a Roman Catholic, possibly a priest (Julian, *Dictionary of Hymnology*, 580, 583).

Pierre Belon

1517–64; FRENCH NATURALIST (IN MIDDLE EAST 1546–49)

"[T]he Franciscans and the Greek [priests] and men of other orders of the Christian faith can enter [the Church of the Sepulcher] and leave without price."
—*Plurimarum Singularium*, 335

"Jerusalem has been surrounded by new and very high, but weak, walls, which could not at all endure bombarding."
—Ibid., 336

William Biddulph

APPOINTED IN 1602 AS
PROTESTANT CHAPLAIN TO
ENGLISH TRADING OUTPOST
IN ALEPPO
(1602)

"We dismounted from our Horses at the West gate of the City, called Joppa [Jaffa] gate; which is a very strong gate of Iron, with thirteen Pieces of Brasse-ordnance planted on the wall about the gate."
—*Purchas His Pilgrimes* 8:300

"[T]here is not one fair street in all Jerusalem as it now is."
—Ibid., 301

"...I admonish those who have a desire to travel to Jerusalem...to take heed...that they make not shipwreck of conscience; for if they come not well commended, or well moneyed, or both, there is no being for them, except they partake with them [the Franciscan guardians of the Christian sites] in their idolatrous services."
—Ibid., 303

"[W]e gave [our Franciscan guide] the hearing of all [his descriptions], but did not believe all, for they seemed to me to be of three sorts, viz. 1. Either apparent Truths. 2. Manifest Untruths. 3. Or thing Doubtful. Those I account apparent Truths, which I could either confirm by reading, or reason."
—*Travels into Africa*, 123

"[I]t seems to a me a manifest truth, that Jerusalem (that now is) stands upon the same place where the old Jerusalem did...."
—*Travels of Four Englishmen*, 822

Napoleon Bonaparte

1769–1821; FRENCH MILITARY
AND POLITICAL LEADER

"Bonaparte a fait publier une proclamation dans laquelle il invite tous les Juifs de l'Asie et l'Afrique à venir se ranger sous ses drapeaux pour établir l'ancienne Jérusalem."*
—French newspaper report on proclamation issued by Napoleon in Acre dated April 19, 1799; quoted in Tuchman, *Bible and Sword*, 166

#8 Ottoman Period

*"Bonaparte has issued a proclamation inviting all the Jews of Asia and Africa to espouse the cause of re-establishing ancient Jerusalem." In his campaign in the Holy Land, Napoleon got as far as Acre but did not reach Jerusalem.

John Bunyan
1628–88; ENGLISH AUTHOR KNOWN FOR HIS SPIRITUAL FERVOR

"This book will make a traveller of thee,

If by its counsel thou wilt ruled be;

It will direct thee to the Holy Land,

If thou wilt its directions understand;

Yea, it will make the slothful active be;

The blind also delightful things to see."
—"The Author's Apology for His Book," *The Pilgrim's Progress*, 36–37

John Calvin
1509–64; FRENCH PROTESTANT THEOLOGIAN

"There is no abbey so poor as to not have a specimen [of the Cross]. In some places there are large fragments, as at the Holy Chapel in Paris, and at Rome, where a good-sized crucifix is said to have been made of it. In brief, if all the pieces that could be found were collected together, they would make a big ship-load. Yet the Gospel testifies that a single man was able to carry it."
—Traité des Reliques; quoted in "True Cross," Wikipedia encyclopedia. http://en.wikipedia.org/wiki/True_Cross

Evliye Chelebi
SEVENTEENTH CENTURY; OTTOMAN NOBLE (1648–50)

"[A]ll the religious scholars went out to meet [the Ottoman conqueror] Selim Shah in 922 [1516 CE]. They handed him the keys to the Mosque al-Aksa and the Dome of the Rock of God. Selim prostrated himself and exclaimed 'Thanks be to God!

I am now the possessor of the Sanctuary of the first *kiblah*.'"
—*Travels in Palestine*; quoted in Peters, Jerusalem, 479

"The corner tower of the right-hand side of the entrance to the Citadel is the tower and noble dwelling built by David himself. For sentimental reasons it is not inhabited but used as an ammunition depot and treasury.... Sultan Isa [al-Mu'azzan] of the Ayyubids had this prayer place of David [in the Citadel] transformed into a mosque and placed a white marble slab in the left wall of it with a dated inscription [1213–1214 CE]."
—Ibid., 481

"There are eight hundred salaried servants employed at this mosque of al-Aksa. That is to say, it has prayer leaders for the four schools [of Islamic law] and as many preachers. On Fridays the preacher ascends the pulpit with the sword in his hand."
—Ibid., 494

Count Eberhard of Wurtemberg

1450–96; GERMAN NOBLEMAN AND PILGRIM

"There are three acts in a man's life which no one ought either to advise another to do or not to do. The first is to contract matrimony, the second is to go to the wars, the third is to visit the Holy Sepulcher."
—Quoted in Fabri, introduction to *Wanderings*, Palestine Pilgrims' Text Society, 7:3–4

Thomas Fuller

1608–61; ENGLISH CLERGYMAN AND AUTHOR

"[W]hen a City in diverse Ages has different names, this speaks her successive subjection to several Lords, new owners imposing on her new appellations...."
—*A Pisgah-Sight*, 313

Jerusalem "was distanced from the sea well-nigh forty miles, having no navigable River near unto it. For God

intended not Jerusalem for a staple of trade, but for a Royal Exchange of Religion, chiefly holding correspondency with Heaven itself, daily receiving blessings thence, duly returning praises thither."
—Ibid., 315

Gedaliah of Siemiatycze

EIGHTEENTH CENTURY;
JEWISH IMMIGRANT
FROM POLAND
(1716)

"There are many Christians in [Jerusalem], almost more than Turks and Arabs. They are also in exile as are the Jews and, like them, must also pay all the onerous taxes."
—Yaari, *Masa'ot Eretz Yisrael*, 341

"Only Ishmaelites are permitted to enter the site of the Temple, but not Jews and other peoples unless, God forbid, they convert to Islam."
—Ibid., 344

"Jerusalem has two Jewish cemeteries, one from ancient times lying at a distance south of the town [Silwan], and a new one…on the slopes of the Mount of Olives. No gravestone can be recognized any more in the old cemetery, and there are many caves to be found there."
—Ibid., 347

"If a Jew makes a Turk angry, then the latter beats him shamefully and dreadfully with his shoe, and nobody delivers the Jews from his hand. Nor is it otherwise with the Christians."
—Ibid., 358

"Ishmael goes to the place of the Temple, but does not permit entry to the Jews, reviling them as 'impure! impure!'"
—Ibid., 366

"And we see that the Arab enters the Temple of the Lord, and says that we are strangers [forbidden] to enter the place of our Temple."
—Ibid., 367

Edward Gibbon

1737–94; ENGLISH HISTORIAN OF THE ROMAN EMPIRE

"After the final destruction of the temple...by Titus and Hadrian, a ploughshare was drawn over the consecrated ground, as a sign of perpetual interdiction."
—*Decline and Fall*, ch. 23

"[I]t was found convenient to suppose that the marvelous wood [of the Cross] possessed a secret power of vegetation; and that its substance, though continually diminished, still remained entire and unimpaired."
—Ibid.

"The holy instruments of the Jewish worship, the gold table, and the gold candlestick with seven branches...placed in the sanctuary of (God's) temple, had been ostentatiously displayed to the Roman people in the triumph of Titus.... At the end of four hundred years [they] were transferred from Rome to Carthage...."*
—Ibid., ch. 36

*Following the sack of Rome by the Vandals in 455.

"The harmony of prayer in so many various tongues, the worship of so many nations in the common temple of their religion [the Church of the Sepulcher], might have afforded a spectacle of edification and peace; but the zeal of the Christian sects was embittered by hatred and revenge; and in the kingdom of a suffering Messiah...they aspired to command and persecute their spiritual brethren."*
—Ibid., ch. 57

*The reference is to the period after the Crusader conquest.

George Herbert

1593–1633; ENGLISH POET, CLERGYMAN

"Lord, with what glory wast thou serv'd of old,

When Solomon's temple stood and flourished!"
—"Sion," in Cattermole, ed., *Sacred Poetry* 1:264

"All Solomon's sea of brass
and world of stone

Is not so dear to thee
as one good groan."
—Ibid.

Thomas Heywood

DIED 1650; ENGLISH DRAMATIST

"Behold the high walls
of Jerusalem

Which Titus and Vespasian
once brake down.

From off these turrets
have the ancient Jews

Seen worlds of people
mustering on these plains.

Oh, princes, which of
all your eyes are dry,

To look upon this temple,
now destroyed?"
—*Four Prentices of London*, quoted
in Tuchman, *Bible and Sword*, 56

Father Elzear Horn

EIGHTEENTH CENTURY;
FRIAR IN JERUSALEM'S
FRANCISCAN COMMUNITY
(1724–44)

"The Golden Gate: formerly in
the days of the Christians and
the Saracens, it was opened only
on Palm Sunday; at present it
is closed by a permanent wall,
for in 1541 the Turks removed
the wooden doors and closed
it with a wall (so that it might
not be accessible)…for they
believed that at some time the
Christians would enter by this
gate and capture the city.…"
—*Ichnographiae*, 28

"The west approach [to the city]
is called the Gate of Bethlehem,
of Ramleh, of Jaffa…also
the Gate of the Citadel.…"
—Ibid., 29

"On the exterior of [Jaffa] gate
the Emperor Hadrian caused
a pig to be sculptured…for
the Jews…indicating that they
were subject to the power of

Rome…but at present that pig is no longer visible…."*

—Ibid.

*Cf. Fabri.

The Citadel of David is "an ancient fort to which this day the name Pisan is attached…."

—Ibid., 33

"The Greeks…impede the [Sepulcher's] restoration… since they unjustly claim in regard to the edifice of the Most Holy Tomb part of the absolute jurisdiction which the Latins [Franciscans] enjoy by right of purchase."

—Ibid., 37

"[T]he Muslims…Greeks and Copts detest every kind of Latins [Franciscans]."

—Ibid., 70

"Godfrey de Bouillon…the first Christian Catholic Latin King of Jerusalem…greatly enlarged this church [of the Sepulcher] and in it united in a wondrous way under one roof Mount Calvary, the Stone of Anointing, the Tomb of the Lord, etc.…"

—Ibid.

The Franciscan "Friars obtained permission to live in the Church of the Holy Tomb shortly after the Latins lost the Holy Land, which took place about the year 1244, at which time Jerusalem [finally] ceased to be Christian and passed to Saracen sovereignty."*

—Ibid., 82–83

*This represented the first European (Latin) Christian return to the churches of Jerusalem after the Muslim reconquest (Peters, Jerusalem, 369).

"Muslims hold the keys of this door [to the Church of the Sepulcher] and they do not open it except to those who pay a certain sum of money."

—Ibid., 84

"[I]n former years many bells were suspended in this tower [of

the Church of the Sepulcher]. Saladin, having captured Jerusalem in 1187, had these... bells broken with hammers...."
—Ibid., 85

"The Muslims do not have bells, nor do they allow their use to Christians."
—Ibid., 86

"It is the opinion of nearly all the ancients that the...skull of Adam was buried at the place where Christ suffered on the Cross."
—Ibid., 112–13

The church [of St. Anne] "which St. Helena, the mother of Constantine, is believed to have built in honor of the grandmother of Christ, St. Anne...at present is shamefully abused by the Turks."
—Ibid., 137

"The Friars...go forth from St. Savior's Convent and with very great devotion, barefooted, make the Way of the Cross, which also the faithful of Jerusalem do frequently, especially on Fridays and during Lent; by saying only an Our Father and Hail Mary at each station [of the Cross], they make a great gain of indulgences for themselves and the souls in Purgatory."
—Ibid., 160

"When Father Boniface of Ragus, then superior of the Holy Land, saw that the convent of Holy Mount Zion, from which the Friars had been expelled shortly before [in 1523], would not be recovered, he used the services of the Venetian ambassador at the Ottoman Porte...to obtain a decree from the...Sultan [Suleiman]...to acquire another covenant in the Holy City...very near to the Christian Catholic quarters and to the Holy Sepulcher.... [In 1559]...they took possession of the little monastery, on condition...that for the land there should be paid annually to the Muslims the sum of 1,700 aspers.... They called this church that of St. Savior...."*
—Ibid., 162–63, 165

*The reference is to the Franciscan monastery in the Christian Quarter.

"During the eight years I lived in Jerusalem there came from Europe [to the Franciscan convent] pilgrims of different states and nations...[including] other Orders [as well as] lay people...Germans, Belgians, Bohemians, Poles, Italians, Hungarians, French, Spanish and English...."
—Ibid., 185

In 1099 when "the Temple [Dome of the Rock] was captured by the Christians under the brave leadership of Godfrey of Bouillon...[and] when the Temple had been cleansed...[he] immediately founded in it the famous College of Canons and...[provided] suitable dwellings around the Temple for those who were to serve God in day and night offices...and who were to celebrate the sacrifice of the Mass on the said rock, after it had been covered with white marble and an altar had been erected on it.... The Temple [was] solemnly dedicated...in...1136...."
—Ibid., 205

The Monastery (and church) of the Cross was "built by St. Helena...because on the spot according to common tradition stood that tree from which the holy cross of Christ was made."
—Ibid., 237

Rabbi Joseph Karo

1488–1575; AUTHOR OF THE AUTHORITATIVE CODIFICATION OF JEWISH LAW, THE *SHULHAN ARUCH*

"A bridegroom puts ashes on his head where *tefillin* are worn in order to remember Jerusalem. There are places where the custom is to break a glass at the time of the wedding ceremony or to place a black cloth or other signs of mourning on the head of the groom."
—*Shulhan Aruch, Orach Haim* 560

Joseph Ha-Kohen

SIXTEENTH CENTURY;
JEWISH PILGRIM

"...God aroused the spirit of Suleiman...and he set out to build the walls of Jerusalem.... And he sent officials who built its walls and set up its gates as in former times and its towers as in bygone days. And his fame spread throughout the land...."
—"Jerusalem under Ottoman Rule," Encyclopedia Judaica, 1972

Rabbi Levi Yitzchok of Berditchev

1740–1810; HASSIDIC LEADER RENOWNED FOR HIS COMMITMENT TO SEEK PRAYERFUL INTERCESSION ON BEHALF OF THE JEWISH PEOPLE

"The marriage will take place on such a date in Jerusalem, except if the Messiah has not yet come; in which case the ceremony will be performed in Berditchev."
—Quoted in Wiesel, Souls on Fire, 103

William Lithgow

SEVENTEENTH CENTURY;
ENGLISH PROTESTANT TRAVELER
(1612)

"The Gates of the City [Jaffa Gate] are of iron outwardly, and above each Gate are brazen Ordonance planted, for their defence."
—Travels and Voyages, 223

Upon Lithgow's arrival at the Franciscan monastery, "the Guardian washed my right foot with water, and his Vicar my left: and done, they kissed my feet.... But when they knew afterward that I was no Popish Catholic, it sore repented them of their Labor."
—Ibid., 224

"Jerusalem stands in the same place where old Jerusalem stood...."
—Ibid., 226

"[A]lthough I rehearse [record] all I saw there [Jerusalem],

yet I will not believe all, only publishing them as things indifferent, some whereof are frivolous, and others somewhat more credible…."
—Ibid., 235

"[W]e saw…the place (as they say) where the Cross grew, whereon Christ suffered: being reserved [retained] by Greeks, who have a Convent builded over it…."
—Ibid., 258

Martin Luther
1483–1546; GERMAN CHURCH REFORMER

"Now…we can go on true pilgrimages in faith, namely, when we diligently read psalms, prophets, gospels, etc. Rather than walk about holy places we can thus pause at our thoughts, examine our heart, and visit the real promised land and paradise of eternal life."
—Table Talk, 1537 [http://www.vision.org/jrnl/0408/jerucenter2.html]

John Mason
DIED 1694; ENGLISH POET

"I bless my God, who is my guide;
I sing in Zion's ways:
When shall I sing on Zion's hill
Thine everlasting praise?"
—"A Song of Praise for a Gospel Ministry," in Cattermole, ed., Sacred Poetry 2:395

Henry Maundrell
BORN 1665; ENGLISH PROTESTANT TRAVELER (1697)

"It is required of all Franks, unless they happen to come in with some public minister, to dismount at the [Jaffa] gate, to deliver [up] their arms, and enter on foot. But we coming in company with the French consul had the privilege to enter mounted and armed."*
—Journey, 89

*Western Christians generally, but not always, entered Jerusalem through Jaffa Gate, which was adjacent to the fortified Citadel. Franciscan Eugene Roger, visiting in the 1630s, reports that Jews and Christians were permitted entry only through Damascus Gate (Naor, *City of Hope*, 190). Horn, in Jerusalem a few decades after Maundrell, writes that Franciscans and the "Religious of other European Orders" entered through Jaffa Gate, while "all secular European pilgrims" were required to go through Damascus Gate (*Ichnographiae*, 30).

"The next day, being Good-Friday in the Latin style…we found the church doors guarded by several Janizaries, and other Turkish officers, who are placed here to watch that none enter in but such as have first paid their appointed caphar [toll]."
—Ibid., 90

"The church [of the Sepulcher] is less than one hundred paces long, and not more than sixty wide; and yet is so contrived that it is supposed to contain under its roof twelve or thirteen sanctuaries, or places consecrated to a more than ordinary veneration, by being reputed to have some particular actions done in them relating to the death and resurrection of Christ."
—Ibid., 92–93

"[T]he great prize contended for by the several sects is the command and appropriation of the Holy Sepulcher, a privilege contested with so much unchristian fury and animosity, especially between the Greeks and Latins, that in disputing which party should go in to celebrate their Mass, they have sometimes proceeded to blows and wounds even at the very door of the sepulcher, mingling their own blood with their sacrifices…. Who can expect ever to see these holy places rescued from the hands of infidels?"
—Ibid., 94–95

"The next morning [in the Church of the Sepulcher]…gave many of the pilgrims leisure to have their arms marked with the usual ensigns of Jerusalem. The artists…have stamps in wood of any figure that you desire, which they first print off upon your arm with powder

of charcoal; then, taking two very fine needles tied close together, and dipping them often, like a pen, in certain ink, compounded, as I was informed, of gunpowder and ox-gall, they make with them small punctures all along the lines of the figure which they have printed, and then, washing the part in wine, conclude the work."
—Ibid., 100

The Monastery of the Cross is so named "because here is the earth, that nourished the root, that bore the tree, that yielded the timber that made the cross. Under the high altar you are shown a hole in the ground, where the stump of the tree stood...."
—Ibid., 126

"The Latins take a great deal of pains to expose this ceremony [the Holy Fire] as a most shameful imposture and a scandal to the Christian religion; perhaps out of envy, that others should be master of so gainful a business; but the Greeks and Armenians pin their faith upon it...."
—Ibid., 131

"In a kind of anti-chapel to this church [of St. James], there are laid up on one side of an altar, three large rough stones, esteemed very precious; as being, one of them, the stone upon which Moses cast the two table[t]s, when he broke them, in indignation, at the idolatry of the Israelites; the other two being brought, one from the place of the Lord's baptism, the other from that of his configuration."
—Ibid., 133

"Here [the Armenian chapel on Mount Zion], under the altar, they tell us is deposited that very stone, which was laid to secure the door of our Savior's sepulcher, Mat. 27.60."
—Ibid., 134

"Near the corner of [the eastern end of the southern wall] there is a short end of a pillar, jetting out of the wall. Upon this

pillar the Turks have a tradition, that Mohammed shall sit in judgment, at the last day...."
—Ibid., 138

"[T]he [Golden] gate of the Temple...is at present walled up, because the Turks here have a prophecy, that their destruction shall enter at that gate...."
—Ibid.

"...I went out in the afternoon...to pace the walls round. We went out at Bethlehem [Jaffa] gate, and proceeding on the right hand, came about to the same gate again. I found the whole city 4630 paces in circumference, which I computed thus:

From Bethlehem gate to the corner on the right hand...400 [paces]

From that corner to Damascus gate...680

From Damascus gate to Herod's...380

From Herod's gate to Jeremiah's prison...150

From Jeremiah's prison to the corner next the valley of Jehosaphat...225

From that corner to St. Stephen's gate...385

From St. Stephen's gate to the Golden gate...240

From the Golden gate to the corner of the wall...380

From that corner to the Dung gate...470

From the Dung gate to Zion gate...605

From Zion gate to the corner of the wall...215

From that corner to Bethlehem gate...500

In all, paces 4630

...by [my] reckoning the 4630 paces amount to 4167 yards, which make just two miles and a half."
—Ibid., 147–48

John Milton

1608–74; ENGLISH AUTHOR

"If Zion hill

Delight thee more, and Siloa's brook, that flowed

Fast by the oracle of God [the Temple], I thence

Invoke thine aid to my adventurous Song…"
—*Paradise Lost*, bk. 1

"…Moloch, horrid king, besmeared with blood

Of human sacrifice, and parents' tears;

Though for the noise of drums and timbrels loud,

Their children's cries unheard, that passed through fire

To his grim Idol."
—Ibid.

"Here* Pilgrims roam, that strayed so far to seek

In Golgotha him dead who lives in Heaven"
—Ibid., bk. 3

*On the periphery of the universe, as Satan makes his way to the world inhabited by newly created Man.

Fynes Moryson
1566–1630; ENGLISH PROTESTANT TRAVELER (1596)

"…I thought no place more worthy to be viewed in the whole world, than this City.…"
—*Itinerary* 2:1

"[T]he City is now seated in the same place, in which it flourished when our Savior lived there in the flesh. Neither let any man object to me the prophecies of the fatal and irreparable ruine thereof, which all Divines understand of the Temple to be utterly demolished…."
—Ibid., 2:2

"From this place [the Monastery of the Cross], they say, the Tree was taken, upon which the Crosse of Christ was made, and Greek Friars keep the Church that was here built."
—Ibid., 2:24

"[I]n the Church [of the Sepulcher] they [the Greek

friars] show a hole in the pavement compassed with Marble, which they say is the very middle point of the world.... I objected that the earth is round, and that in a Globe the center is in the middest, all centers in the outside being but imaginary...."
—Ibid., 2:31

Rabbi Moses of Basola
1480–1560;
ITALIAN JEWISH SCHOLAR
(1521–23)

"Atop the Mount of Olives is the tomb of Huldah (the Prophetess) in a marble tomb."
—Yaari, *Masa'ot Eretz Yisrael*, 145

"On Mount Zion there is a place for Italian priests.... Adjoining it is a place with a locked iron door; they say that David and Solomon are buried there.... And nearby is another place locked with an iron door where they say [are buried] all the kings of the House of David.... The Ishmaelites never allow anyone to enter these two places."
—Ibid., 145

"...I rented a room in a large house called the House of Pilate. I lived in an upper story, and from there I could see the whole Temple enclosure, including the Temple Court. There is no house in Jerusalem from which as much can be seen."
—Ibid., 148

"There is only one synagogue in Jerusalem."
—Ibid., 149

"The congregation (in Jerusalem) is of all kinds. There are fifteen Ashkenazi householders, but the majority are Spanish; and there are Arabized (Jews), who are Moorish, long-ago natives of that country, and 'westerners' who come from Barbary. In all there are about three hundred householders, excluding widows, who number more than six hundred...."
—Ibid., 149

Rabbi Moses ben Elijah the Karaite

SEVENTEENTH CENTURY;
KARAITE CHRONICLER
(1654–55)

"There is an expansive area in the city of Zion [the Armenian Quarter], where a building [the Church of St. James] has been erected in the name of Jesus the Christian to which come all Christian visitors to Jerusalem. Within [that complex] are gardens and orchards and houses…near the Gate of David [Zion Gate]."
—Yaari, *Masa'ot Eretz Yisrael*, 314

John Pascha

DIED 1532; GERMAN CARMELITE,
ACCOUNT PUBLISHED 1568

"Those who cannot go [along the Via Dolorosa in Jerusalem] in person, can still make this voyage by the grace of God, through devout and pious meditations.… You will find here [in meditations] the holy places depicted as if before your very eyes, all shown by the descriptions of the pilgrims, who have themselves been personally to these same holy places."*
—*A Devout Way of Making a Spiritual Pilgrimage to the Holy Land…*; quoted in Storme, *The Way of the Cross*, 116

*"From the fifteenth century onwards…a 'spiritual pilgrimage' was thought to be endowed with the same indulgences as those of the Sorrowful Way in Jerusalem" (Storme, *The Way of the Cross*, 147).

Richard Pococke

1704–65; ENGLISH SCHOLAR
AND CLERGYMAN
(CA. 1743)

"[T]he Christians built a church on this spot [the Temple Mount], which the Saracens, under Omar, converted into a mosque; and when Jerusalem was taken in the holy war,* it was again made a place of Christian worship."
—*Description of the East* 2:14

*By the Crusaders in 1099.

Moses ben Israel Poryat (Praeger) of Prague

CA. 1600–70; AUTHOR OF *DARKEI ZION*, A JUDEO-GERMAN HANDBOOK THAT INFORMED PILGRIMS OF THE ROUTES TO THE HOLY LAND AND THE EXPENSES INVOLVED, AND OF THE RITES AND PRAYERS IN JERUSALEM
(1650)

"Anyone who wears [garments] of green places himself in great danger…because [the wearing of] green is forbidden to Jews in all of Turkey and in Jerusalem."
–Yaari, *Masa'ot Eretz Yisrael*, 277

"Books are not expensive in Jerusalem, so you should not burden yourself with them [on the journey]. Let each person take…only a thick prayer book, a Pentateuch with three commentaries, a Penitential Prayer Book according to the Polish usage, the Mishna with the commentary of Tosfot Yom Tov, Rabbi Mordechai Jaffe's *Lavush* [a compendium of Jewish law and religion], a *Shomrim le-Boker* [dawn prayer service], a Festival Prayer Book according to the Prague usage, Midrash Rabbah, *Ein Yaakov*,…the *Shulhan Aruch*…and the *Yalkut*…. The womenfolk [should] take with them a *Teutsch* [Yiddish] *Humash*,…the Festival Book and *Tehinnah* [a book of vernacular devotions], and other *Teutsch* [Yiddish] books. The prayer books should be small, for there is no lectern in the synagogues and the books must be held in the hand…."
–Ibid., 277–88

"The water is good and healthful…. [It] is rainwater, not from wells…. Every house has a large…cistern under the ground…. In years when there is little water it must be bought from the Turks, who bring it into the house in leather sacks."
–Ibid., 282

"In Jerusalem, and throughout Turkey, there are no clocks; the times are fixed according to the sun. At noon, a Turk [the muezzin] begins to cry out from a very high tower

[minaret]…and similarly three hours before nightfall…."
—Ibid., 283

Francis Quarles
1592–1664; ENGLISH POET

"How hath heaven's absence dark'ned the renown

Of Zion's glory with one angry frown."
—"Sion's Elegies," a paraphrase of *Lamentations of Jeremiah*, in Cattermole, ed., *Sacred Poetry*, 1:213

David de Rossi
SIXTEENTH CENTURY; ITALIAN JEWISH MERCHANT
(1535)

"Here [Jerusalem] we are not in exile as in our own country [Italy]…. Here, those appointed over the customs and the king's tolls are Jews; and there is no wrongdoing anywhere in the kingdom."*
—"A Jewish Merchant from Italy," in Wilhelm, *Roads to Zion*, 35

*The writer is describing the period soon after the Ottoman conquest, when the sultan encouraged the development of a Jewish community in Jerusalem.

John Sanderson
SIXTEENTH–SEVENTEENTH CENTURY; ENGLISH PROTESTANT MERCHANT
(1601)

"Jerusalem has only four gates; at one of which [Jaffa Gate] is the Tower of David, where he fell enamored with Bersaba, as those fondlings [foolish persons] say."
—*Travels*, 102

"I went not at all to the Romish clergy [in Jerusalem] nor visited their father guardian…."
—Ibid., 122–23

George Sandys

1578–1644; ENGLISH PROTESTANT AUTHOR AND POET (1610)

"Although diverse [authors]… have…related the site and state of this City [I provide my own account so] as to deliver the Reader from many erring reports of the too credulous devote, and too too vain-glorious…."
—*Relation of a Journey*, 154

"On the right hand [of Jaffa Gate] and adjoining to the wall, there stands a small ill-fortified Castle; yet the only fort that belongs to the City; weakly guarded, and not over-well stored with munition…."
—Ibid., 158

"O who can without sorrow, without indignation, behold the enemies of Christ to be the Lords of his Sepulcher! who at festival times sit mounted under a Canopy, to gather money of such as do enter…."
—Ibid., 161

"[F]or omitting Pater nosters, and Ave Marias, we lost many years indulgences, which every place does plentifully afford to such as affect them: and contented our selves with an historical relation."
—Ibid., 163

"Thousands of Christians perform their vows, and offer their tears here [at the Holy Sepulcher] yearly, with all the expressions of sorrow, humility, affection, and penitence. It is a frozen zeal that will not be warmed with the sight thereof."
—Ibid., 167

"Within [the Monastery of the Cross is] a handsome chapel; at the upper end an altar; and under that a pit, in which they say that the Palm did grow (but rather, if any, the Olive, whereof that place has store) of which a part of the Cross was made. For it was framed (as they report) of four several woods; the foot of Cedar, the

bole of Cypress, the transome
of Palm, and the title of Olive."
—Ibid., 184

"Ah! See how Zion mourns!

Her gates and ways

Lie unfrequented on
her solemn days,

Her virgins weep, her
priests lament her fall,

And all

Her sweets convert to gall."
—"Judah in Exile Wanders," in
Atwan, ed., *Chapters into Verse* 1:418

"I will to thy house repair;

Worship, and thy power declare;

Offerings on thy altar lay;

All my vows devoutly pay...."
—Paraphrase of Psalm 66, in
Cattermole, ed., *Sacred Poetry* 1:57

"O Solyma! thou that
art now become

A heap of stones, and
to thyself a tomb!"
—Paraphrase of Psalm 137, in
Cattermole, ed., *Sacred Poetry* 1:62

William Shakespeare
1564–1616

"[T]hose holy fields

Over whose acres walk'd
those blessed feet

Which fourteen hundred
years ago were nail'd

For our advantage on
the bitter cross."
—*Henry the Fourth*, pt. 1, 1.1

"So part we sadly in this
troublous world

To meet with joy in
sweet Jerusalem.
—*Henry the Sixth*, pt. 3, 5.5

Suleiman the Magnificent
1494–1566; OTTOMAN
SULTAN, 1520–66

"It is neither just nor appropriate
that this most noble place
[i.e., the Cenacle, above the
traditional tomb of David
on Mount Zion] remain in
the hands of the infidels and
that, in obedience to their

impious customs, their feet foul the places sanctified by the prophets.... We order, then, upon receipt of this August order that you [the governor of Damascus] expel from the church and the convent immediately...the religious [i.e., Franciscans] and all those who reside there."
—Imperial decree by Suleiman, 1523; quoted in Peters, *Jerusalem*, 498

Torquato Tasso
1544–95; NOTED ITALIAN POET OF THE RENAISSANCE

"Jerusalem, behold, appear'd in sight,

Jerusalem they* view, they see, they spy;

Jerusalem with merry noise they greet,

With joyful shouts, and acclamations sweet."
—*Jerusalem Delivered*, 3.3

*The Crusader conquerors.

"But through the way that to the west hill yood [went],

Whereon the old and stately temple stands,

All soil'd with gore and wet with lukewarm blood,

Rinaldo ran and chas'd the pagan bands."
—Ibid., 19.31

Henry Timberlake
DIED 1626; ENGLISH PROTESTANT TRAVELER (1601)

"[S]uch sway do the papists [Franciscans] carry there that no Christian stranger can have admittance there but that he must be protected under them, or not enter the city."
—*Discourse*, 342

"I noted hanging outside the gate [of the Church of the Sepulcher], at least an hundred lines and strings and in the gate a great hole...; whereof...they told me the hole served to give victuals... for them which lie within the church, which are above three

hundred persons.... The strings... have each one a bell fastened at the lodgings [of the various sects], and when the servants, (which are without), bring them any meat, each rings the bell belonging to his household, and so come accordingly (each knowing his own bell) for receipt of their food...."
—Ibid., 347

"In the city of Jerusalem are three Christians for one Turk...but they all live poorly under the Turk."
—Ibid., 349

Thomas Tymme

DIED 1620; ENGLISH TRANSLATOR AND DEVOTIONAL WRITER

"[B]ecause the master workman [Adrichomius] in this new plat [map] of old decayed Jerusalem, has left behind him some rubbish and reliques of the Romish superstition, I have in some measure swept the street and corners of the same, with the broom of truth...."
—Epistle Dedicatory to his English translation of Christianus Adrichomius's *Briefe Description of Hierusalem*

William Tyndale

1494–1536; ENGLISH RELIGIOUS REFORMER AND BIBLE TRANSLATOR

"Neither need a Christian man to run hither or thither, to Rom[e], to Jerusalem, or St. James, or any other pilgrimage far or near, to be saved...."
—*Doctrinal Treatises and Introduction to Different Portions of the Holy Scriptures*, 281

Count Constantin Volney

1757–1820; FRENCH ARISTOCRAT, HISTORIAN AND PHILOSOPHER (1784)

Jerusalem "presents a striking example of the vicissitude of human affairs: when we behold its walls leveled, its ditches

#8 Ottoman Period

filled up, and all its buildings embarrassed with ruins, we can scarcely believe we view that celebrated metropolis, which formerly withstood the efforts of the most powerful empires.... By a whimsical change of fortune, its ruins now receive her homage and reverence; in a word, we with difficulty recognize Jerusalem."
—*Travels through Egypt and Syria* 2.303

"To judge from the respect the inhabitants profess for the sacred places it contains, we should be ready to imagine there is not in the world a more devout people; but this has not prevented them from acquiring, as well deserving, the reputation of the vilest people in Syria...."
—Ibid., 2.304

"[T]he different communions of schismatic, and Catholic Greeks, Armenians, Copts, Abyssinians and Franks, mutually envying each other the possession of the holy places, are continually endeavoring to outbid one another in the price they offer for them to the Turkish governors. They are constantly aiming to obtain some privilege for themselves, or to take it from their rivals, and each sect is perpetually informing against the other for irregularities."
—Ibid., 2.305

"[T]he number of pilgrims has diminished, and they are now reduced to a few Italian, Spanish and German monks, but the case is different with the Orientals [Eastern Christians].... The Greeks, especially, declare that the pilgrimage ensures plenary indulgence not only for the past, but even for the future...."
—Ibid., 2.308

"The Orientals [Eastern Christians] still believe in this miracle [of the Holy Fire], though the Franks acknowledge that the priests retire into the scarcity and effect what is done by very natural means."
—Ibid., 2.311

"The convent of these Franks, called St. Savior's, is the principal religious house [headquarters] of all the missions of the Holy Land which are in the Turkish empire."
—Ibid., 2.313

John Winthrop
1588–1649; A LEADER OF THE PURITAN SETTLERS IN NEW ENGLAND

"[W]e shall find that the God of Israel is among us...when he shall make us a praise and a glory, that men shall say of succeeding plantations: the lord make it like that of New England: for we must Consider that we shall be as a City upon a Hill, the eyes of all people are upon us...."*
—"A Modell of Christian Charity," lecture delivered aboard the ship *Arrabella* in 1630 on the voyage to New England; in Miller, ed., *The Puritans* 1:198–99

*Cf. Jeremiah 30:18–19: "[A]nd the City [Jerusalem] will be built upon its hill.... The sound of thanksgiving and the sound of merrymakers will emanate from them...."Winthrop's image has often served as a metaphor for the vision of America. For example, Ronald Reagan in his farewell address from the White House: "I've spoken of the shining city all my political life.... In my mind it was a tall, proud city built on rocks stronger than oceans, windswept, God-blessed, and teeming with people of all kinds living in harmony and peace...."

Moses Yerushalmi
EIGHTEENTH CENTURY; KARAITE PILGRIM
(1769)

"The [Hebrew] word [*kotel* = Western Wall] is to be divided into two words: *ko* which has the same numerical value as God's name [26] and *tel* which means 'the hill' towards which all turn and direct their prayers...."*
—Yaari, *Masa'ot Eretz Yisrael*, 449

*Naor, *Western Wall*, 69, attributes this quotation to Moses the Karaite in 1658.

"There [on the Mount of Olives] is the tomb of Huldah [the prophetess]."
—Ibid., 450

#9
Ottoman Period
UP TO 1917

Karl Baedeker

1801–59; PUBLISHER AND GUIDEBOOK AUTHOR

"[Caliph] Abd el-Malik was moved by political considerations to erect a sanctuary on this spot [the Rock on the Temple Mount], as admission to the Kaaba in Mecca was at that time refused to the Umayyads."
—*Palestine and Syria* [1912], 53

"As David and his descendants were buried in 'the city of David' (1 Kings 2:10, etc.), the expression was once thought to mean Bethlehem.... The earliest Christians, however... appear to place it in Jerusalem (Acts 2:29), where by that time Hyrcanus and Herod had robbed the tombs of all their precious contents."
—Ibid., 72

"The foundation of the monastery [Monastery of the Cross] is attributed to the Empress Helena; according to another tradition it was founded by Mirian (265–342), the first Christian ruler of Georgia.... It is at any rate certain that it was founded before the introduction of Islam."
—Ibid., 92

J. T. Barclay

1807–74; AMERICAN PHYSICIAN AND MISSIONARY, AMONG THE FIRST RELIGIOUS COLONISTS WHO WENT TO THE HOLY LAND WITH THE INTENTION OF CONVERTING JEWS TO CHRISTIANITY (1851–54)

Jerusalem, "the theater of the most memorable and stupendous events that have ever occurred in the annals of the world."
—*City of the Great King*, xii

The Sepulcher was "perhaps quite down in the gloomy vale of the Kedron."
—Ibid., 79

"[T]he traditionalist that has credulity enough to believe

in the 'invention' of the cross, as its discovery is called...."
—Ibid., 222

"And though you may give no credit whatever to the tradition [of the site of the Sepulcher], and may be heartily disgusted with the mummery all around, yet little is hazarded in saying that when you place your hands on that cold marble [of the tomb]...you will feel an indescribable emotion felt never or since."
—Ibid., 235–36

"The identification and aggregation of so many sites of important events within so small a compass is an absurdity at which credibility itself must stagger, and the most ardent devotee of tradition stands abashed."
—Ibid., 238

"[A]l-Aksa is not an original Saracenic structure, but is unquestionably the Church of Mary [the Nea Church] built by Justinian...."
—Ibid., 336

"This [Jewish] quarter of the city, though assigned to one-half of the entire population, is by far the smallest, being about one-third the size of the Christian, and one-fifth that of the Mohammedan."
—Ibid., 444

"[The residents of Silwan] are, with few exceptions, real troglodytes – dwelling not only in natural caves, but in the tenements of the dead, with which that cliff abounds...."
—Ibid., 455

"There is no place on earth concerning which there has excited a curiosity half so intense and prurient as that in relation to the sacred enclosure of the Temple, the Haram-a-Sherif, which can only perish with the faith it typifies."
—Ibid., 470

W. H. Bartlett
1809–54; ENGLISH PAINTER, AUTHOR, AND TRAVELER
(1834, 1842, 1854)

"We had to wait some time outside the Jaffa Gate before the Turkish sentinel unbarred it."
–*Walks*, 14

"There is not the slightest ground for supposing that the modern Zion, Moriah, or Acra are not the same as the ancient."
–Ibid., 29

"It is a great enjoyment to sit here [atop Mount Zion] as the evening declines, and the long shadows are projected from the city walls over the valley below, and up the breasts of the hills, gradually gaining upon the outstretched view, till the last roseate glow, beautiful beyond description, lingers for a brief moment on the distant mountains. Nowhere is the arch of heaven more pure, intense, and cloudless than above the proud heights of Zion; and no one who has sat there, at the hour when the evening wind springs up, sweeping freely over it, and rustling the few trees upon the ancient mount, will fail to record it among the choicest recollections of his life."
–Ibid., 71

"The church of St. James…is considered by travelers as one of the most sumptuous in the East, enriched by the liberality of wealthy Armenian pilgrims."
–Ibid., 79

"From the extreme summit [of the Mount of Olives] the view is perhaps the most interesting in the world. Jerusalem is spread out like a map below the eye on one hand, and on the other is a wide and dreary horizon of desert country – the Moab Mountains, the Valley of the Jordan and the Dead Sea…."
–Ibid., 100

"[W]here the bodies of the nobles of Judah were borne to their last home [on the Mount of Olives], with 'burnings' [sacrifices] and all the pomp

of funeral ceremony, the flocks of sheep and goats, which wander over the valley, are driven for nightly shelter."
—Ibid., 110

"[T]his small but gallant band,* the flower of Christendom...."
—Ibid., 125

*The Crusaders.

"If the traveler can forget that he is treading on the grave of a people from whom his religion has sprung, on the dust of her kings, prophets, and holy men, there is certainly no city in the world that he will sooner wish to leave than Jerusalem."
—Ibid., 133

"Humanly speaking, Jerusalem is the last place where we may expect to meet with converts, where every object tends to keep alive among the Jews the spirit of their religion – the sacred hills, the cemeteries of their fathers, the walls of their once proud temple."
—Ibid., 190

"[I]t is sad to think that the spot whence the divine doctrines of mutual love and good-will went forth to mankind, has ever been the chosen seat of strife and contention, and that the real influence of Christianity is less felt in Jerusalem, than in regimes unheard of at the time of its promulgation from her holy soil."
—Ibid., 199

"The climate of Jerusalem is on the whole good. It would be one of the finest in the world, were common attention paid to the cleanliness of the streets and houses."
—*Jerusalem Revisited*, 53

"A ramble through the Jewish quarter will convince the traveler that whatever improvement may have taken place [in the city], little, if any, has been effected among the squalid habitations of the Jews upon Mount Zion...."
—Ibid., 78

"Were we to judge of the moral condition of Jerusalem from

the number of its convents and hospitals, we might esteem it to be the most pious and charitable city in the world, where self-renunciation and active benevolence were the only principles that actuated its citizens."
—Ibid., 91

"These legendary localities [multiple sites identified with the crucifixion] were gradually accumulated around that of the Sepulcher, as medieval darkness became more dense, and the credulity of pilgrims more craving, and the fraud of the priests more barefaced."
—Ibid., 100

"I cannot describe the mingled emotions by which I was agitated during our perambulation of this most singular edifice [Church of the Sepulcher]. Its venerable antiquity and gorgeous gloom… could not but produce a solemn and affecting influence, and call to mind the long series of pilgrims, monks, and warriors, who during so many centuries had worshiped around the Sacred Tomb. On the other hand…everything connected with the place seem[ed] to bear the dark stamp of a superstition little, if at all, better than that of the old Pagans."
—Ibid., 101

"Of all the traditions of Jerusalem…the one which seems most palpably to contradict the plain letter of the New Testament, is that which places the scene of the Ascension on the summit of Mount Olivet."
—Ibid., 117

"…Justinian's Church of St. Mary [the Nea], [is] either identical with the Aksa [Mosque], or standing over this very site."
—Ibid., 158

"[I]t would have been strange…if an age which witnessed the discovery, or, as it is otherwise called, the *invention* of the Holy Cross, should have failed to discover also the

precise spot where grew the tree of which it is made...."*
—Ibid., 191

*The reference is to the Monastery of the Cross.

"Of all cities in the world [Jerusalem] has the distinction of being the battle-ground for religious creeds – the field where the fanaticism of the Jew, the Christian, and the Turk has met, and alternately triumphed."
—Ibid., 192

Philippe Berger

NINETEENTH CENTURY; FRENCH ARCHEOLOGIST

(1894)

"You expect to see [a] huge [Western] wall reminiscent of Herod and Solomon, with the sky and countryside as a horizon. Instead you are in a narrow passage so crowded with people that you must use your elbows to get through."
—C. Adler, "Memorandum on the Western Wall" –1930; quoted in Ben-Arieh, *Jerusalem in the Nineteenth Century: The Old City*, 372

William Blake

1757–1827; ENGLISH POET AND ARTIST

"And did the Countenance Divine

Shine forth upon our clouded hills?

And was Jerusalem builded here

Among these dark Satanic mills?"

...

"I will not cease from Mental Fight

nor shall my sword sleep in my hand

Till we have built Jerusalem

in England's green and pleasant land.
—"Milton," *The Portable Blake*, ed. Alfred Kazin, 412

"England! awake! awake! awake!
Jerusalem thy Sister calls!"
—"Jerusalem," ibid., 457

"Jerusalem the Emanation of the Giant Albion! Can it be? Is it a Truth that the Learned have explored? Was Britain the Primitive Seat of the Patriarchal Religion? …It is True and cannot be controverted."
—"To the Jews,'Jerusalem,'" ibid., 447

Edward Wilmot Blyden
1832–1912;
AFRICAN-AMERICAN AUTHOR
(1866)

"No site in Jerusalem affected me more" than the Western Wall.
—*From West Africa to Palestine;**
quoted in Obenzinger,
American Palestine, 245

*This 1873 account is "the most significant African American contribution to Holy Land literature" in the nineteenth century (Obenzinger, *American Palestine*, 227).

"…Jews, Christians and Muslims [all agree] as to the final destiny of Jerusalem; that it is to be the scene of latter-day glories; that the Jews are to be restored to the land of their fathers, and the Messiah is to be enthroned in personal reign in the 'City of the Great King.'"
—Ibid.

John Ross Browne
1821–75; AMERICAN JOURNALIST,
AUTHOR AND TRAVELER
(1851)

"Perhaps upon the whole face of the globe there could not be found a spot less holy than modern Jerusalem."
—*Yusef…, A Crusade in the East*; quoted in Walker, *Irreverent Pilgrims*, 223

James Silk Buckingham

1786–1855; ENGLISH TRAVELER AND MERCHANT
(1816)

"The appearance of this celebrated city, independently of the feelings and recollections which the approach cannot fail to awaken, was greatly inferior to my expectations, and had certainly nothing of grandeur or beauty, of stateliness or magnificence about it. It appeared like a walled town of the third or fourth class...."
—*Travels in Palestine*, in Osband, *Famous Travellers*, 27

"Not even in a solitary instance did I hear a word of resignation,* or of the joy of suffering for Christ's sake, or the love of persecution, or of the paradise found in a life of mortification, so often attributed to these men."
—Ibid.

*Among the Franciscan friars in the Convent of Terra Sancta.

Samuel Butler

1835–1902; ENGLISH AUTHOR

"The new Jerusalem, when it comes, will probably be found so far to resemble the old as to stone its prophets freely."
—Quoted in Eckardt, ed., *Jerusalem: City of the Ages*, 231

George Gordon Byron

1788–1824; ENGLISH POET

"And where shall Israel lave her bleeding feet?

And when shall Zion's songs again seem sweet?"
—"Oh! Weep for Those," *Byron's Hebrew Melodies*, 138

"How long by tyrants shall thy land be trod?

How long thy temples worshipless, Oh God?"
—"On Jordan's Banks," ibid., 143

"Our Temple hath not left a stone,

And Mockery sits on Salem's throne."
—"The Wild Gazelle," ibid., 154

François-René de Chateaubriand

1768–1848; FRENCH WRITER, POLITICIAN, AND DIPLOMAT
(1806)

"I am certain that whoever has had the patience, as I did, to read nearly two hundred modern accounts of the Holy Land [and Jerusalem], the rabbinic collections, and the passages of the ancients on Judea, would still understand nothing."
–*Itinéraire de Paris à Jérusalem* 2:42*

*Except as noted, translations are mine.

"Christian readers will perhaps wish to know what I did feel on entering that awesome place [the Church of the Sepulcher]. Actually, I cannot say. So many impressions came upon me that I could not pause on any one of them. I remained for about a half hour on my knees in the small chamber of the Holy Sepulcher, my gaze so firmly attached to that stone that I could not tear it away.... All I am certain of is that at the sight of this triumphant tomb I was aware only of my own weakness, and when my guide cried out with St. Paul, 'Death, where is thy victory? Death, where is thy sting?' I listened attentively, as if death were about to respond that it was conquered and chained in that monument."
–Ibid., 2:102; translation in Peters, *Jerusalem*, 579

"I did not leave the sacred structure [the Church of the Sepulcher] without stopping at the monuments of Godfrey and Baldwin. They face the entrance of the church....* I saluted the ashes of these royal chevaliers, who were worthy of reposing near the tomb which they had rescued. These ashes are those of Frenchmen.... What an honorable distinction for my country!"
–Ibid., 2:103; translation in Osband, *Famous Travellers*, 35

*The monuments were removed by the Greeks during their repairs to the church in the early nineteenth century.

"St. Helena [mother of Constantine] built a church where one finds today the octagonal mosque [the Dome of the Rock]."
—Ibid., 2:119

"To see in the Crusades only armed pilgrims who went out to deliver a tomb in Palestine, is to take a very narrow view of history. It was not merely a question of liberating this Holy Sepulcher but even more of knowing who should have the upper hand in this world, a cult which is the enemy of civilization, systematically supporting ignorance, despotism and slavery or a cult which revived in modern times the genius of a learned antiquity and abolished slavery.... If the cries of so many suffering victims in the East, if the forward march of the Barbarians even to the gates of Constantinople, reawakened Christianity and made it rush to its own defense, who would dare to say that the cause of the Holy Wars was unjust?"
—Ibid., 130; translation in Peters, *Jerusalem*, 580

"Saladin's soldiers cast down [the] cross of gold above the Temple* [and] dragged it through the streets to the summit of Mount Zion, where they destroyed it."
—Ibid., 133

*Erected by the Crusaders atop the Dome of the Rock.

"Over the past century the Fathers of St. Savior's [Franciscan convent] have seen perhaps [only] two hundred Catholic travelers, made up of religious of their own orders and missionaries to the East."
—Ibid., 171

"The greatest expense of the pilgrims are the dues which they are expected to pay to the Turks and Arabs, whether as entry fees to the holy places or as caphars, or tolls, upon the roads."
—Ibid.

"The [Franciscan] Fathers permitted me to examine the library and archives of their convent. Unfortunately the

contents...were scattered a century ago when the pasha put the Fathers in irons and carried them captive to Damascus. A few documents escaped the destruction.... One sees [from them] that these unfortunate Fathers, guardians of the Tomb of Jesus Christ, were solely occupied over several centuries in defending themselves, day by day, against all types of insults and tyranny."
—Ibid., 177; translation in Peters, *Jerusalem*, 560

"Crushed by the Cross that condemns them, skulking near the Temple, of which not one stone is left upon another, they continue their deplorable infatuation. The Persians, the Greeks, the Romans are swept from the earth; and a petty tribe, whose origins preceded that of those great nations, still exists unmixed among the ruins of its native land."
—Ibid., 203; translation in Eckardt, ed., *Jerusalem: City of the Ages*, 231

"Civita Cattolica"

1897 STATEMENT ISSUED BY THE VATICAN, IN RESPONSE TO CONVENING OF FIRST ZIONIST CONGRESS

"One thousand eight hundred and twenty seven years have passed since the prediction of Jesus of Nazareth was fulfilled, namely that Jerusalem would be destroyed.... A rebuilt Jerusalem, which would become the center of a reconstituted state of Israel...is contrary to the prediction of Christ Himself."*
—quoted by Paula Fredriksen, "The Holy City in Christian Thought," in Rosovsky, ed., *City of the Great King*, 80

*In December 1993 the Holy See and Israel formally established diplomatic relations.

Daniel Edward Clarke

BORN 1769; ENGLISH GEOGRAPHER
(1801)

The church [of the Sepulcher] has the appearance of "any common Roman Catholic church."
—Quoted in Silberman, *Digging for God and Country*, 19

Claude Reignier Conder

1848–1910; JERUSALEM EXCAVATOR AND MEMBER OF PALESTINE EXPLORATION FUND (1872)

"It [Church of the Sepulcher] is a grim and wicked old building.... Perhaps no other edifice has been directly the cause of more human misery, or defiled with more blood.... I should be loathe to think that the Sacred Tomb had been a witness for so many years of so much human ignorance, folly, and crime."
– *Tent Work in Palestine*, 170

The Church of the Sepulcher has an "open court in which according to the legend the Wandering Jew stays for a moment once in every century to beg admission, and hears a voice which bids him resume his endless journey."
–Ibid., 172

"The most impressive portion of the church [of the Sepulcher] is…the nave east of the rotunda belonging to the Greeks, with its great screen in front of the three apses."
–Ibid., 173

"The next [chant in the Holy Fire ceremony] was rarely heard: 'O Jews, O Jews! your feast is a feast of apes.'"
–Ibid., 177

"The Latins have long discountenanced the imposture [of the Holy Fire], though it was once recognized by them, and dates back to the miraculous lighting of lamps in the time of the Christian kings of Jerusalem…. Every educated Greek knows it to be a shameful imposition; but the ignorant Syrians and the fanatical Russian peasants still believe the fire to descend from Heaven."
–Ibid., 181

"[W]e have no sound reason for supposing that the early Christians paid any attention to the site of the Sepulcher."
–Ibid., 191

"[T]he present site of the Holy Sepulcher will probably be discarded by any unprejudiced inquirer...."
—Ibid., 193

"The Jewish quarter…in the middle ages was…that now occupied by Muslims."
—Ibid., 351

George W. Curtis
1824–92; AMERICAN ESSAYIST AND TRAVELER, ACCOUNT PUBLISHED 1852

"[G]oing up to Jerusalem as to the holiest city of the purest faith, you are disappointed by what you see of that faith there, as you would be upon approaching a banquet of wit and beauty, to find it a festival of idiots and the insane."
—*The Howadji in Syria*; quoted in Obenzinger, *American Palestine*, 50

Robert Curzon
1810–73; ENGLISH TRAVELER, DIPLOMAT
(1834)

"There is a round hole in one part of the chapel of the sepulcher, out of which the holy fire is given, and up to this the man who had agreed to pay the highest sum for this honor was conducted by a strong guard of soldiers. There was silence for a minute; and then a light appeared out of the tomb, and the happy pilgrim received the holy fire from the Patriarch within.… This was the whole ceremony; there was no sermon or prayers, except a little chanting during the processions, and nothing that could tend to remind you of the awful event which this feast was meant to commemorate."*
—*Visits to the Monasteries in the Levant*, in Osband, *Famous Travellers*, 38

*In the course of the ceremony Curzon witnessed, five hundred pilgrims died by asphyxiation.

Benjamin Disraeli

1804–81; ONLY PRIME MINISTER OF ENGLAND OF JEWISH DESCENT

(1831)

"Yes, I am a Jew, and when the ancestors of the Right Honorable gentleman [Irish MP O'Connell] were living as savages in an unknown island, mine were priests in the Temple of Solomon."*
—1848 House of Commons speech; quoted in Tal, *Whose Jerusalem*, 286

*In response to disparaging remarks by O'Connell about Disraeli's Jewish ancestry.

Charles W. Elliott

NINETEENTH CENTURY; AMERICAN TRAVELER, ACCOUNT PUBLISHED 1867

"On the same ridge of Zion…lies the Jewish Quarter, which a man may smell afar off…once covered with palaces of priests and kings, but now the danger and opprobrium of the Holy Land."
—*Remarkable Characters and Places of the Holy Land*; quoted in Vogel, *To See a Promised Land*, 83

"[T]he Kingdom of Christ is a spiritual kingdom…and not the old, dirty Jewish city which once was (but not now) the type of a heavenly city."
—Ibid.; quoted in Obenzinger, *American Palestine*, 187

Jacob Freese

NINETEENTH CENTURY; AMERICAN TRAVELER, ACCOUNT PUBLISHED 1869

(1867)

"To see the representatives of a people once so glorious, and once the possessors and rulers of this land, now so abject and downtrodden that only by permission dare they lift their eyes toward the outer walls of their once glorious temple…."
—*The Old World*; quoted in Vogel, *To See a Promised Land*, 84

James Finn

1806–72; BRITISH CONSUL IN JERUSALEM, ACCOUNT PUBLISHED 1872
(1845–63)

"The water-supply of Jerusalem is not from springs, but each house has its own cistern, into which the rain is collected as it falls upon the flat roofs and terraces."
–*Stirring Times*, in Osband, *Famous Travellers*, 45

"The state of poverty among the Jews at this time exceeded anything we had before known. Parents were said to be selling their children to Muslims, as the only way of preserving their lives."
–Ibid., 46

Asher Hirsch Ginsberg (Ahad HaAm)

1856–1927; ZIONIST WRITER UNDER PSEUDONYM AHAD HAAM
(1891)

"Obviously my first stop [in Jerusalem] was the [Western] Wall. There I found crowds of our brothers, dwellers of Jerusalem, standing and praying in loud voices. Their thin faces, their strange motions and their odd dress seemed to fit the terrible state of the Wall. As I stood and contemplated them and the Wall one thought filled my mind: these stones are witnesses to the destruction of our land; these men – to the destruction of our people. Which is the greater destruction?"
–Yaari, *Masa'ot Eretz Yisrael*, 732

Heinrich Heine

1797–1856; GERMAN JEWISH POET

On the ninth day of the month of Av – myself, with streaming eyes,

I have seen the heavy teardrops

From the mighty stones that trickled,

Hear the broken temple pillars

Utter cries and lamentations....
–"Hebrew Melodies"; quoted in Tal, *Whose Jerusalem*, 293

Theodor Herzl

1860–1904;
ZIONIST VISIONARY
(1898)

"Even now, in its destruction, it is a beautiful city, and when [the Jews] come it will become one of the world's most beautiful cities."
—Diary, Oct. 29, 1898, in Yaari, *Masa'ot Eretz Yisrael*, 743*

*Except as noted, translations are mine.

"When I remember you in days to come, O Jerusalem, it will not be with delight. The musty deposits of two thousand years of inhumanity, intolerance, and foulness, lie in your reeking alleys. The one man who has been present here all this while, the lovable dreamer of Nazareth, has done nothing but help increase the hate.

"If Jerusalem is ever ours, and if I were still able to do anything about it, I would begin by cleaning it up."
—Diary, Oct. 31, 1898, in Yaari, *Masa'ot Eretz Yisrael*, 743–44; translation from Holtz, *The Holy City*, 146

"We visited the Western Wall. I experienced no deep [religious] emotion as a result of the hideous, miserable, scrambling beggary that prevails there."
—Diary, Oct. 31, 1898, in Yaari, *Masa'ot Eretz Yisrael*, 744

"My friends restrained me from entering the Church [of the Sepulcher].... It is also forbidden to set foot in the Mosque of Omar and the site of the Temple, under pain of excommunication by the rabbis.... What superstition and fanaticism on every side."
—Ibid., 745

"The Kaiser is consecrating the Church of the Redeemer today."
—Ibid.

"What couldn't be made of this prospect [from the Mount of Olives]. A city like Rome – and the Mount of Olives furnishing a panorama like the Giancolo."
—Diary, Nov. 1, 1898, in Yaari, *Masa'ot Eretz Yisrael*, 750

"I would enclose the Old City and its sacred shrines as in a box, and would remove all business and commercial activities."
—Ibid.

My "brief reception [by Kaiser Wilhelm II in Jerusalem] will be eternally remembered in Jewish history. It is not unlikely that it will have historical consequences."
—Diary, Nov. 2, 1898, in Yaari, *Masa'ot Eretz Yisrael*, 751

A.S. Hirschberg

JEWISH AUTHOR; ACCOUNT WRITTEN 1901

"[W]e came to a small, narrow alley. One side of this was the Western Wall and the other side was a solid wall of one of the hovels of the Magreb Quarter."
—*Eretz Hemdah*; quoted in Ben-Dov, *The Western Wall*, 77

"All kinds of Jews are there [at the Western Wall]. Thin, scrawny, sharp-nosed Yemenites dressed in poor, worn Arab robes…; rich, fat, elegantly clad Sephardim…their black coats and tarbooshes on their well-groomed heads…Perushim, dressed in a weird mixture of east and west with medieval Polish fur hats on their heads…[;] groups of Hasidim, in their kaftans of red, gold or sky-blue silk and velvet…."
—Ibid., 78

Naftali Herz Imber

1856–1909; GALICIAN-BORN POET AND ZIONIST

"To live in freedom in the land of Zion and Jerusalem."
—"Hatikvah"*

*Adopted as the national anthem upon the establishment of the State of Israel in 1948.

William Jowett

1787–1855; ENGLISH MISSIONARY, ACCOUNT PUBLISHED 1826 (1823)

"Like many other cities of the East, the distant view

of Jerusalem is inexpressibly beautiful, but the distant view is all. On entering at the Damascus Gate, meanness, filth and misery, not exceeded if equaled by anything which I had before seen, soon told the tale of deprivation."
–*Christian Researches in Syria and the Holy Land*, in Schur, *Twenty Centuries of Christian Pilgrimage*, 111

Mousa J. Kaleel

BORN 1892; CHRISTIAN ARAB FROM RAMALLAH, ACCOUNT PUBLISHED 1914

"Pilgrims from all parts of the world are in Jerusalem; most of these are Russians in long boots and heavy fur clothing. Greek priests with their chimney-pot hats are seen all over the city, selling candles and souvenirs and extorting coins…[and] these contemptible priests…[strip] them of all their money and even the choice pieces of fur…."
–"When I Was a Boy in Palestine," in Shadur, *Young Travelers to Jerusalem*, 152

Alexander William Kinglake

1809–91; ENGLISH HISTORIAN AND DIPLOMAT
(1835)

"The Church of the Holy Sepulcher comprises very compendiously almost all the spots associated with the closing career of our Lord. Just there, on your right, he stood and wept; by the pillar on your left he was scourged; on the spot just before you he was crowned with the crown of thorns; up there he was crucified, and down here he was buried. A locality is assigned to every, the minutest, event connected with the recorded history of our Savior; even the spot where the cock crew, when Peter denied his Master…. Many Protestants are wont to treat these traditions contemptuously…."
–*Eothen*; quoted in Walker, *Irreverent Pilgrims*, 29

Alphonse-Marie-Louis de Lamartine

1790–1869; FRENCH POET, NOVELIST, AND STATESMAN (1832)

"I reached the summit [of the Mount of Olives], crowned by a ruined mosque, covering the spot where our Lord ascended to Heaven after his resurrection."
—entry for Oct. 28, 1837, *Souvenirs d'Orient*, in Osband, *Famous Travellers*, 70

"This magnificent platform… was the sublime pedestal upon which arose the Temple of Solomon; it now supports two Turkish mosques…."
—Ibid.

Jerusalem "is a city shining in light and color! … The view is the most splendid that can be presented to the eye of a city that is no more…."
—Ibid., 70–71

"I, the feeble poet of an age of silence and decay, had I domesticated at Jerusalem, I should have selected, for my residence and abiding place, precisely the spot which David chose for his at Zion."
—Ibid., 72

Edward Lear

1812–88; ENGLISH POET AND ILLUSTRATOR

"[I]f I wished to prevent a Turk, Hebrew, or Heathen from turning Christian, I would send him to Jerusalem."
—Quoted in Rosovsky, ed., *City of the Great King*, 231

Guy Le Strange

1854–1933; FRENCH HISTORIAN OF ISLAM

"Politically, Jerusalem was never the Muslim capital of the province…of Palestine, this being at Ar Ramlah."
—*History of Jerusalem under the Moslems*, 4

"In the matter of the Rock which the Dome is intended to cover, it must be remembered that this was held sacred, in the eyes of Muslim true believers, both as representing the ancient *Kiblah* of Moses – for on the Rock they say the Ark of the Covenant was placed – and as the first *Kiblah* in Islam…."
—Ibid., 34

Abraham Lincoln

1809–65; SIXTEENTH PRESIDENT OF THE UNITED STATES

"How I should like to visit Jerusalem sometime."
—April 14, 1865, to Mrs. Lincoln; in Kunhardt and Kunhardt, *Twenty Days*; quoted in Obenzinger, *American Palestine*, 161

Norman Macleod

1812–72; SCOTTISH MISSIONARY, CHAPLAIN TO QUEEN VICTORIA
(1864)

"It is not…the vast multitude who sleep here [on the Mount of Olives], but the faith which they held in regard to their Messiah, that makes this spectacle so impressive."
—*Eastward*; quoted in Millgram, *Jerusalem Curiosities*, 129

"Standing here [in the Dome of the Rock] one loves to linger on earlier days and to recall the holy men and women, the kings, high priests and prophets who came to this spot to pray – whose faith is our own, whose sayings are our guide, whose life is our example, and whose songs are our hymns of worship."
—*Eastward*; quoted in Kernohan, *The Road to Zion*, 56

Reverend Samuel Manning

1822–81; ENGLISH BAPTIST MINISTER AND INITIATOR OF THE RELIGIOUS TRACT SOCIETY SERIES ON WORKS OF TRAVEL
(1873)

"Several fortified and castellated convents – Greek, Latin, Copt and Armenian – remind us that Christianity is but

encamped as a foreigner in the land which gave it birth...."
—*Those Holy Fields*, 29

"[I]n seeking the place 'where the Lord lay,' we have nothing to guide us but vague conjecture and dubious tradition."
—Ibid., 38

"Here [in the Church of the Sepulcher] are shown not only the sites of the crucifixion and the resurrection, but the tombs of Adam, Melchizedek, Joseph of Arimathea, and of Nicodemus; the place where our Lord was crowned with thorns, and where He appeared to Mary Magdalene; the pillar to which he was bound during the scourging; the slab upon which His body was laid for anointing; the spot where He first appeared to his mother after the resurrection; the center of the world; the place whence the earth was taken from which Adam was made, and many other marvels."
—Ibid., 98

"The superstitious zeal of the Empress Helena prompted her to visit the sacred places...."
—Ibid., 101

"I came to the conclusion that the place of the crucifixion and entombment must be sought elsewhere, and not on the spot which tradition points out."
—Ibid., 104

"We have but to transfer the scene of the crucifixion from the northern to the eastern side of the city, in the valley of the Kedron, to find all the requirements of the [New Testament] narrative satisfied."
—Ibid., 106

"[T]he Jewish quarter [is] the foulest, most squalid and wretched part of the city."
—Ibid., 112

"[T]he scene [at the Western Wall] is strangely affecting, leading back our thoughts to the

self-invoked curse of eighteen hundred years ago – 'His blood be on us, and on our children.'"
—Ibid., 115

David Samuel Margoliouth

1858–1940; ENGLISH ORIENTALIST, ACCOUNT PUBLISHED 1907

"The enthusiasm which characterized the descriptions of those who arrived [in Jerusalem] at the cost of vast sacrifices is wanting in the memoirs of the traveler who is conveyed thither comfortably by steam…."
—*Cairo, Jerusalem and Damascus*, 364

Harriet Martineau

1802–76; ONE OF MOST WIDELY READ NINETEENTH-CENTURY ENGLISH AUTHORS
(1847)

"I much doubt whether there will ever be Jewish converts enough to fill [Christ Church].*"
—*Eastern Life*, 376

*The first Protestant church in Jerusalem, it was established at the initiative of the London Society for Promoting Christianity among the Jews. Its cornerstone was laid in 1842.

"After all these years, the converts are very few; they are not all Jews."
—Ibid.

"While we have millions of savages in our own island…I cannot see why we should spend on a handful of strangers, who have already a noble faith of their own."
—Ibid.

"The massive stone walls [of Jerusalem] and substantial character of the buildings remove every appearance of sordidness, when the place is seen from a height."
—Ibid., 377

"It was always a treat to walk through the Jew quarter, and especially on the Sabbath.... They are a very handsome race, with eyes which seem to distinguish them from the rest of mankind – large, soft, and of the deepest expression."
—Ibid., 378

"No Jew or Christian can pass the threshold of the outermost courts [of the Haram-a-Sharif] without certain and immediate death by stoning or beating."
—Ibid.

"What a contrast did these humbled people [Jews, at the Western Wall] present to the proud Mohammedans within!"
—Ibid., 380

"This Jerusalem is the most sacred place in the world, except Mecca, to the Mohammedan; and to the Christian and Jew it is the most sacred place in the world."
—Ibid.

Karl Marx
1818–83; FOUNDER OF COMMUNISM

"Nothing equals the misery and the suffering of the Jews at Jerusalem, inhabiting the most filthy quarter of the town...between Mount Zion and Mount Moriah, where their synagogues are situated – the constant objects of Mussulman oppression and intolerance, insulted by the Greeks, persecuted by the Latins and living upon the scanty alms transmitted by their European brethren."*
—"Declaration of War – on the History of the Eastern Question," dispatch to the *New York Daily Tribune*, April 15, 1854, Marx/Engels, *Collected Works* 13:107–8

*In this article on the background of the Crimean War (1853–56), Marx describes the parlous state of the various non-Muslim religious communities in Ottoman Jerusalem.

Herman Melville

1819–91; AMERICAN NOVELIST, ESSAYIST AND POET

(1857)

"[H]ard by Ophel's winding base...

A spot they found, not lacking grace,

Named Garden of King Solomon,

Though now a cauliflower bed

To serve the kitchens of the town."
—*Clarel*, "Jerusalem," canto 10

"A rotting charnel-house forlorn*

Midway unearthed, caved in and torn."
—Ibid.

*Aceldama.

"The port* walled up by Muslim hands

In dread of that predicted day

When pealing hymns, armed Christian bands –

So Islam seers despondent vouch –

Shall storm it, wreathed in Mary's May."**
—Ibid.

*The Golden Gate.

**Branches or flowers of the English hawthorn.

"The Turk permits the tribes* to creep

Abject in rear of those dumb stones,

To lean or kneel, lament and weep"
—Ibid., canto 16

*The Jews (at the Western Wall).

"Pronounce its name, this natural street's:

The *Via Crucis** – even the way

Tradition claims to be the one

Trod on that Friday far away

By Him our pure exemplar shown."
—*Clarel*, "Bethlehem," canto 34

*Way of the Cross, the Via Dolorosa.

#9 Ottoman Period

The facade of the Church of the Sepulcher looked "like so much spoiled pastry at which the mice have been at work...."
—*Journal*; quoted in Walker, *Irreverent Pilgrims*, 123

Jerusalem "looks at you like a cold grey eye in a cold grey man."
—Ibid., 124

In the "wretched settlement of Siloam...living persons dwelt in tombs in the hillside."
—Ibid., 125

I saw "Jerusalem from [the] distance – unless [I] knew it, could not have recognized it – looked exactly like arid rocks...."
—*Journal*; quoted in Silk, *Retrievements*, 86

"[T]he wall of Omar [Dome of the Rock] rises upon the foundation stones of Solomon['s Temple], triumphing over that which sustains it, an emblem of the relationship of the two faiths."
—Ibid., 87

"*Talk of the guides* 'Here is the stone where Christ leaned against, & here is the English Hotel. Yonder is the arch where Christ was shown to the people, & just by that open window is sold the best coffee in Jerusalem.'"
—Ibid., 89

"No country will more quickly dissipate romantic expectation than Palestine – particularly Jerusalem."
—*Journal*; quoted in Obenzinger, *American Palestine*, 79

"One of the missionaries...confessed...that out of all the Jew converts, but one he believes to be a true Christian."
—*Journal*; quoted in Millgram, *Jerusalem Curiosities*, 238

Rabbi Menahem Mendel of Kamieniec

1800–37; FOLLOWER OF GAON OF VILNA
(1833)

"All those approaching the [Western] Wall remove their shoes."
—Yaari, *Masa'ot Eretz Yisrael*, 542

Sir Moses and Lady Judith Montefiore

1784–1885; ENGLISH FINANCIER AND PHILANTHROPIST
(1827; FIRST OF EIGHT VISITS)

"We prayed the evening service on the Mount of Olives, lifting our eyes to the site of our Temple, venerated since ancient times even by idol worshipers."
—*Journal of Lady Judith Montefiore*, 1839 visit, in Yaari, *Masa'ot Eretz Yisrael*, 566

"Its walls are in ruins and the Temple plundered, but the sacred hills of Zion stand."
—Ibid., 567

"[W]e entered the Jewish quarter of the town and which appeared the cleanest of any we had traversed."
—Ibid., 570

The Western Wall, with its "massive interlocking stones is a guardian of Israel. And I thought, is this not a sign to Israel that hope has not yet been lost?"
—Ibid., 572–73

"[O]ur eyes felt that they could never grow weary of contemplating the Holy City.…"
—*Journal of Lady Judith Montefiore*, 1839 visit, in Osband, *Famous Travellers*

"The walls of the temple may have yielded to the devastating arm of the conqueror; but Mount Zion itself stands for ever."
—Ibid.

"Great was my delight when I considered that but a few years had passed since the time when not one Jewish family was living

outside the gate of Jerusalem...
and now I beheld almost a
new Jerusalem springing up,
with buildings, some of them
as fine as any in Europe."
—*A Narrative of a Forty Days'
Sojourn in the Holy Land*;
quoted in Hammer, ed.,
Jerusalem Anthology, 198

"Friday...I proceeded to the Western Wall to offer up the customary prayers. The road leading to that hallowed spot, and the houses in its vicinity, are still in a state of ruin, causing man and horse to stumble over detached fragments of ancient structures.... When I visited Jerusalem in...1866, I exerted myself very much to have an awning made in front of the Western Wall...but unexpectedly some obstacles occurred, which could not be surmounted.... A gentleman recently tried to place there some seats...and not succeeding...he asked permission to have at least a number of large square marble stones placed there, and was allowed to do so. But they did not remain [there] long...."
—Ibid., 200

"...I was the first who introduced a printing-press in Jerusalem...."*
—Quoted in Silk, *Retrievements*, 104

*Cf. Ben-Dov, below.

Robert Morris

BORN 1818; AMERICAN TRAVELER
AND HOLY LAND POPULARIZER
(1867)

"Earth from the Garden of Gethsemane" – "This...is an honest portion of Gethsemane; a portion upon which the Divine *feet* may have trodden, the Divine knees pressed, the Divine *tears* and *sweat* moistened."
—Quoted in Davis,
The Landscape of Belief, 50–51

Mordecai Emanuel Noah

1785–1851; AMERICAN
JEWISH JOURNALIST AND
PROMOTER OF JEWISH
RESTORATION TO PALESTINE

"...Christian and Jew will together, on Mount Zion, raise their voices in praise of Him whose covenant with Abraham

was to endure forever, and in whose seed all the nations of the earth are to be blessed."
—"Discourse on the Restoration of the Jews," in Schappes, *A Documentary History of the Jews*, 250

Laurence Oliphant

1829–88; ENGLISH AUTHOR AND TRAVELER
(1879, 1882)

"[T]he Jerusalem of the present day, the Holy City of the world par excellence…contain[s] within its walls more sacred shams and impostures than any other city in the world."
—*Haifa*, 377

"With considerate ingenuity, and possibly with a view to lightening the labors of the pilgrims as much as possible, the early Church crowded as many sacred stones together under the roof of the holy edifice [the Church of the Sepulcher] as it could with decency."
—Ibid., 378

"Golgotha, or Calvary, was a knoll outside the Damascus Gate, exactly in the opposite direction to that affixed by Christian tradition, and which would do away with the Via Dolorosa…."
—Ibid., 381

"[T]he mere fact that so many nations and races of diverse religions…center their political and religious aspirations upon this spot [Jerusalem] makes it the most interesting city upon the earth's surface…."
—Ibid., 401

Ermete Pierotti

MID-NINETEENTH CENTURY; ITALIAN ARCHITECT AND ENGINEER TO TURKISH AUTHORITIES IN JERUSALEM

"On Good Friday the Jews cannot quit their own quarters, as the Latins, Greeks, and Armenians would insult and otherwise ill-treat them…. No Jew, who lives at Jerusalem, dares to pass in front of the Church of the Holy Sepulcher…. If, on an occasion like this, he were

murdered, the malefactors would not be severely punished; for all the native population unfortunately hold the opinion that to injure a Jew is a work well pleasing in the sight of God."
—Quoted in Silk, *Retrievements*, 139

Edward Robinson
1794–1863; AMERICAN GEOGRAPHER-HISTORIAN, ACCOUNT PUBLISHED 1841 (1838, 1852)

"In every view which I have been able to take of the question, both topographical and historical, whether on the spot or in the closet, and in spite of all my previous prepossessions, I am led irresistibly to the conclusion that the Golgotha and the tomb now shown in the Church of the Holy Sepulcher, are not upon the real places of the crucifixion and resurrection of our Lord. The alleged discovery of them by the aged and credulous Helena, like her discovery of the cross, may not improbably have been the work of pious fraud...."
—*Biblical Research in Palestine*; quoted in Millgram, *Jerusalem Curiosities*, 152

"The whole scene [of Holy Week services in the Church of the Sepulcher] was to a Protestant painful and revolting. It might perhaps have been less so had there been manifested the slightest degree of faith in the genuineness of the surrounding objects. But even the monks themselves do not pretend that the present sepulcher is anything more than an imitation of the original. But to be in the ancient city of the Most High and to see these venerated places and the very name of our holy religion profaned by idle lying and mummeries, while the proud Mussulman looks on with haughty scorn, all this excited in my mind a feeling too painful to be borne...."
—*Biblical Research in Palestine*; quoted in Peters, *Jerusalem*, 585

"The simplicity and spirituality of the Protestant worship [at a service in the home of a Jerusalem Protestant] was to me affecting and doubly pleasing, in contrast with the pageant [Holy Week services in the church] of which we had just been spectators."
—Ibid.

"The glory of Jerusalem has indeed departed. From her ancient estate as the splendid metropolis of the Jewish commonwealth and of the whole Christian world, the beloved of nations and the 'joy of the whole earth,' she has sunk into the neglected capital of a petty Turkish province...."
—*Biblical Research in Palestine*; quoted in Ben-Arieh, *Jerusalem in the Nineteenth Century*, 53

"This arch* could only have belonged to the bridge which...led from this part of the temple to Xystus** on Zion; and it proves incontestably the antiquity of that portion of the wall from which it springs...."
—*Biblical Research in Palestine*; in Osband, *Famous Travellers*, 100

*Now known as Robinson's Arch.

**Xystus refers to a building with a covered colonnade, mentioned by Josephus, which stood opposite Wilson's Arch.

Theodore Roosevelt

1858–1919; TWENTY-SIXTH PRESIDENT OF THE UNITED STATES
(1873)*

"Under the rock [in the Dome of the Rock] we saw the places where Abraham, Jacob, David and Solomon prayed, all conveniently near each other. In one place where the room was small Mohammed had enlarged it by putting up his head."
—*Diaries of Boyhood and Youth*, 315

*When T.R. was fourteen years old.

"It seems to me that it is entirely proper to start a Zionist State around Jerusalem."*
—Quoted in Oren, *Power, Faith and Fantasy*, 359

*Written by the former president during the administration of Woodrow Wilson as part of the effort to spur American support for Jewish statehood.

Joseph Schwarz

1804–65; BAVARIAN JEWISH GEOGRAPHER (SETTLER IN JERUSALEM FROM 1833)

"There is, thank God, an abundance of food, and in recent times we live in peace and quiet. The one, increasingly onerous, burden on the community is the cost (of living)…the main reason being the upkeep of the army brought…to Jerusalem by Ibrahim Pasha after the recent revolution to assure security."*
—Yaari, *Igrot Eretz Yisrael*, 377

*Palestine was under Egyptian rule 1831–39.

"As German [citizens], and all those from Europe who are not subjects of the Turkish sultan – known in the local language as Franks – [we] are exempt from the above-mentioned taxes and from other oppressive measures imposed by the pasha on [Turkish] subjects.… We enjoy the special protection of our respective European consuls."
—Ibid.

Ulrich Seetzen

1767–1811; GERMAN EXPLORER (1806)

"Beside the Church of the Holy Sepulcher there is a large factory for leather manufacture.… The factory is the source of the most terrible smells.… The Christians are convinced that the Muslims built this factory [at this site] out of contempt.… In the Jewish quarter there is a slaughterhouse which produces the same ugly odors, and the Jews too are convinced that their fellow inhabitants have chosen this place…out of hatred for them."
—Quoted in Peters, *Jerusalem*, 551–52

"This convent [of St. James in the Armenian Quarter] lies near the Citadel [of David] and is favorably situated in a more spacious area than the churches and convents of the other religious groups. It is of considerable size...."
—Ibid., 556

"Jerusalem has no suburbs, that is, all the houses and buildings are located inside the city walls.... There are no significant public squares.... The open places in front of the Citadel and the entrance to the Holy Sepulcher are insignificant because they are so small, and the beautiful wide platform of the Haram, which is one of the most beautiful places in the Ottoman Empire, does not merit being called a public place since Jews and Christians may not enter it without risking their lives.... There are at most only a half a dozen date palms in Jerusalem."
—Ibid., 565

"[D]uring the flourishing time of their nation [the Jews] owned one of the most important temples in the world, whose holy site they can still look upon every day, though they dare not even look through the gates which lead to it. This luckless people, which here as elsewhere is among the most despised, is much like Tantalus, who is always so close to what he so deeply yearns for and yet will never be able to attain it...."
—Ibid., 569

Sherif Pasha

1818–87; GOVERNOR GENERAL OF SYRIA 1831–40

"[T]he place the Jews asked for permission to pave adjoins the [western] wall of the Haram-a-Sharif and also the spot where al-Burak was tethered.... It has also been established that paving it by the Jews would be inadmissible under the Islamic Law. Therefore the Jews must not be enabled to pave the place. They must be warned against raising their voices and forbidden to proclaim their doctrines."

—Communication from the governor of Syria to his deputy in Jerusalem, 1840, ratifying a recommendation of the Muslim Consultative Council of Jerusalem; quoted by A.L. Tibawi, *The Islamic Pious Foundations in Jerusalem*, in Peters, *Jerusalem*, 541–42

George Adam Smith
1856–1942; SCOTTISH BIBLICAL RESEARCHER
(1880, 1890, 1901, 1904)

"Nowhere else has the universal struggle (between the spirit of God and the spirit of man) been waged so consciously, so articulately, as in Jerusalem."

—*Jerusalem* 1:5

"Though other great cities of Christendom, Antioch, Alexandria, Carthage and Rome, were by far her superiors in philosophy and spiritual empire, Jerusalem remained the religious center of the earth…the original of the heavenly city which would one day descend from God among men."

—Ibid., 1:7

"He who would raise the Essential City must wait for night, when Jerusalem hides her decay.…"

—Ibid., 1:25

"Even before the great Sanctuary perished at the hand of Rome…Jesus in the experience of His followers had taken the place of the Temple and of everything for which it stood."

—Ibid., 2:522

Arthur P. Stanley
1815–81; DEAN OF WESTMINSTER
(1852–53, 1862)

"It is useless to seek for traces of His [Jesus'] presence in the streets of the since ten times captured city. It is impossible not to find them in the free open space of the Mount of Olives."

—*Sinai and Palestine*, 189

"The desolation and degradation, which have so often left on those who visit Jerusalem the impression of an accursed city, read in this sense a true lesson: 'He is not here: He is risen.'"

—Ibid., 195

"It is startling to hear that this [the "Mosque of the Tomb of David" on Mount Zion] is the scene of the Last Supper, of the meeting after the Resurrection, of the miracle of Pentecost, of the residence and death of the Virgin, of the burial of Stephen."
—Ibid., 456

"There [in the Church of the Sepulcher] is the place in which to study all the diverse rites and forms of the older churches of the world. There alone are gathered together all the altars of all the sects which existed before the Reformation. On one side is the barbaric splendor of the Greek Church, exulting in its possession of Constantine's basilica and of the rock of Calvary. In another corner is the deep poverty of the Coptic and Syrian Churches, each now confined to one paltry chapel, forcibly contrasted again with the large portions won by the rich revenues of the merchant Church of Armenia. And intermingled with each of these is the more chastened and familiar worship of the Latin Church, here reduced from the gigantic proportions which it bears in its native seat to a humble settlement in a foreign land…. High on the platform of Calvary…it has claimed a separate altar for the Exaltation of the Cross. Deep in the Armenian chapel of St. Helena it has seated itself in the corner where the throne of Helena was placed during the 'Invention.' In the Chapel of the Holy Sepulcher itself…the Latin Church…has adopted for its altar the Holy Tomb itself. For good or for evil – for union or for disunion – the older forms of Christendom are gathered together, as nowhere else in Europe or in Asia, within those sacred walls."
—Ibid., 461–62

"[C]onsidering the the place, the time, and the intention of the professed miracle [of the Holy Fire, it is] probably the most offensive delusion to be found in the world."
—Ibid., 469

John Lloyd Stephens

1805–52; FIRST AMERICAN TRAVELER TO WRITE ABOUT PALESTINE
(1836)

"The road between these oldest of cities [Bethlehem and Jerusalem] was simply a mule-path over rocky mountains, descending occasionally into rich valleys."
—*Incidents of Travel*, 327

"[A]s I walked along the bank, or stood on the margin, or descended the steps to the water's edge [of the "Pools of Solomon"], it seemed almost the wild suggestion of a dream to imagine that the wisest of men had looked into the same pool, had strolled along the same bank, and stood on the very same steps. It was like annihilating all the intervals of time and space. Solomon and all his glory are departed, and little could even his wisdom have foreseen that, long after he should be laid in the dust…a traveler from a land he never dreamed of would be looking upon his works, and murmuring to himself the words of the preacher [Solomon], 'Vanity of vanities, all is vanity.'"
—Ibid., 327–28

"What authority she [Helena] had for fixing here the site of the Redeemer's burial-place I will not stop to inquire. Doubtless she had her reasons; and there is more pleasure in believing than in raising doubts which cannot be confirmed."
—Ibid., 346

"The holy sepulcher…is still in the hands of the infidels; and it would have made the sword of an old crusader leap from its scabbard to behold a haughty Turk, with the air of a lord and master, standing sentinel at the door and with his long mace beating and driving back the crowd of struggling Christians."
—Ibid.

"I could not help thinking of it as a strangely interesting fact that here, in the holy city of Jerusalem, where Christ preached and died, though thousands were calling upon his name, the only persons who were praising him in simplicity and truth were a [Protestant] missionary and

his wife, and a passing traveler, all from a far-distant land."*
—Ibid., 347

*Stephens is drawing a contrast with the contention of the Christian sects in the Church of the Sepulcher which he has witnessed.

"If I can form any judgment from my own feelings, every man other than a blind and determined enthusiast, when he stands by the side of that marble sarcophagus, must be ready to exclaim, 'This is not the place where the Lord lay'; and yet I must be wrong, for sensible men have thought otherwise…."
—Ibid., 353

"Here I was indeed among the hallowed places of the Bible. Here all was as nature had left it, and spared by the desecrating hand of man; and as I gazed upon the vast sepulchral monuments, the tombs of Absalom, of Zachariah, and Jehoshaphat, and the thousands and tens of thousands of Hebrew tombstones covering the declivity of the mountain [the Mount of Olives], I had no doubt I was looking upon the great gathering place, where, three thousand years ago, the Jew buried his dead under the shadow of the Temple of Solomon; and where, even at this day, in every country where his race is known, it is the dearest wish of his heart that his bones may be laid to rest among those of his long-buried ancestors."
—Ibid., 355

"[T]he tomb of Absalom is a single stone, as large as an ordinary two-story house…. [N]o pilgrim, whether Jew or Christian, ever passes through the Valley of Jehoshaphat without casting a stone at the sepulcher of the rebellious son."
—Ibid., 358

"I came to the Aceldama, or field of blood, the field bought with 'thirty pieces of silver,' which to this day remains a public burying place or potter's field. A large chamber excavated in the rock is still the charnel-house of the poor and unhonored dead of Jerusalem."
—Ibid., 360

"[A]nd now, as in the days of David, old men may be seen at the foot of Mount Zion, teaching their children to read from that mysterious book [the Bible] on which they have ever fondly built their hopes of a temporal and eternal kingdom."
—Ibid., 367

"The tradition which leads them to pray *through* this wall is that during the building of the temple a cloud rested over it so as to prevent any entrance; and Solomon stood at the door and prayed that the cloud might be removed and promised that the temple should be always open to men of every nation desiring to offer up prayers, whereupon the Lord removed the cloud and promised that the prayers of all people offered up in that place should find acceptance in his sight; and now, as the Mussulman lords it over the place where the temple stood and the Jews are not permitted to enter, they endeavor to insinuate their prayers through the crevices in the wall, that thus they may rise from the interior to the Throne of Grace. The tradition is characteristic and serves to illustrate the devoted constancy with which the Israelites adhere to the externals of their faith."
—Ibid., 368–69

"[T]here are few things connected with my journeying in the Holy Land which I look back upon with a more quiet satisfaction than my often repeated and almost daily walk around the walls of Jerusalem. It was a walk of between three and four miles; and I always contrived, about half an hour before the gates were closed, to be sitting on a favorite tombstone near St. Stephen's Gate."
—Ibid., 378–79

"I had regretted that I could not stay for the great Greek jugglery, the drawing down fire from heaven, where every pilgrim considers himself bound to light his taper at the sacred flame; and those who light first are considered the most fortunate and the most favored in the

sight of God. I could imagine the wild and frantic struggling among more than ten thousand bigots and fanatics for the first rays of the heavenly light...."
—Ibid., 406

"Refused by the Latins, the friends of Dr. Dodge [a Protestant] had asked permission of the Greeks to lay his body for a while in their burying-ground; and negotiating with the dragoman of the [Catholic] convent, they thought that permission had been granted; but, while they were in the act of performing the funeral service, a messenger came in to tell them that the grave had been filled up. They protracted the service till the delay excited the attention of his unhappy widow, and they were obliged to tell her that they had no place where they could lay the head of her young husband. A reluctant permission was at length granted...."
—Ibid., 409–10

"Galloping back to [St. Stephen's] gate, I turned to look at them...a living, moving mass of thousands, thousands of miles from their homes, bound for the sacred Jordan, and strong in the faith that, bathing in its hallowed waters, they should wash away their sins."
—Ibid., 412

"[T]he reader will see that, whatever may be his fate hereafter, a pilgrimage to the holy city gives a man temporal honors, and has transformed a republican citizen of America into an 'illustrissimus dominus [illustrious lord].'"
—Ibid., 414

"...I mounted my horse for the last time at the door of the convent. I lost my way in going to the Damascus Gate, but a friendly Jew conducted me to it; a Jew was the first to welcome me to the Holy Land, and a Jew was the last to speed me on my way from the holy city of Jerusalem."
—Ibid.

Bayard Taylor
1825–78; AMERICAN TRAVELER, ACCOUNT PUBLISHED 1859
(1846)

"It is estimated that each member of the community [of Jewish converts] has cost the Mission about 4,500 (English pounds): a sum which would have Christianized tenfold the number of English heathen. The Mission, however, is kept up by its patrons as a sort of religious luxury."
—*Land of the Saracens*; quoted in Millgram, *Jerusalem Curiosities*, 238

W.M. Thackeray
1811–63; ENGLISH AUTHOR
(1844)

"The Latin fathers have long given up and disowned the disgusting mummery of the Eastern [Holy] Fire – which lie the Greeks continue annually to tell."
—*Notes of a Journey*, in *Sketch Books*, 688

"...the stinking ruins of the Jewish quarter."
—Ibid., 689

"As elsewhere in the towns I have seen, the Ghetto of Jerusalem is preeminent in filth."
—Ibid., 690

"I think the Valley of Jehoshaphat is the most ghastly sight I have seen in the world."*
—Ibid.

*apparently a reference to the Jewish cemetery on the Mount of Olives

"I don't believe the Episcopal apparatus – the chaplains, and the colleges, and the beadles – have succeeded in converting a dozen of them [Jews]...."
—Ibid.

"What they call the tomb [of David] is now a crumbling old mosque; from which Jew and Christian are excluded alike."
—Ibid., 692

"Then, after three days of butchery,* they purified the desecrated mosque [al-Aksa] and went to prayer."
—Ibid.

*describing the Crusader conquest in 1099

"The Church of the Holy Sepulcher…seems to an Englishman the least sacred spot about Jerusalem."
—Ibid., 695

"It is the lies, and the legends, and the priests, and their quarrels, and their ceremonies, which keep the Holy Place out of sight."
—Ibid.

"The situation of the Tomb [of Jesus] (into which, be it authentic or not, no man can enter without a shock of breathless fear, and deep and awful self-humiliation) must have struck all travelers."
—Ibid., 696

"A colony of ruffians inhabit the dismal place [Silwan], who have guns as well as sticks at need."
—Ibid., 701

William McClure Thomson

1806–94; AMERICAN MISSIONARY
(1857)

"Jerusalem is the common property of the whole Christian world…."
—*The Land and the Book*, 626*

*The book sold 200,000 copies, surpassed in the nineteenth century only by *Uncle Tom's Cabin* and *Innocents Abroad* (Rosovksy, *Jerusalem*, 220).

"The temporal Zion is now in the dust, but the true Zion is rising and shaking herself from it, and putting on her beautiful garments to welcome her King when he comes to reign over the whole earth."
—Ibid., 631

"[T]he so-called Garden of Gethsemane.... The authenticity of this sacred garden...I do not even choose to believe.... The Greeks have invented another site...and, of course, contend that they have the true Gethsemane. My impression is that both are wrong."
—Ibid., 634

"The various altars [chapels and tombs in the church] bear witness to the divisions of Christendom...."
—Ibid., 635

The "sepulchers...in the Valley of the Kidron...are frequented exclusively by the Jews, and mostly on their festival days. I once entered them on the thirty-third day after the Passover [Lag B'Omer].... Many Jews were there with their children. Like all other sects in the East, they make vows [sic] in reference to shaving off the hair from their own and their children's heads in honor of some saint or shrine."
—Ibid., 639

"The greatest sin of Israel and of the world *was*, and *is*, apostasy from the true God and his worship by idolatry; and the most prevalent mode of this apostasy is sacrilegious reverence for dead men's tombs and bones."
—Ibid., 640

"[O]ne of [the monks] showed us the place [the Monastery of the Cross] where the tree grew from which the cross was made! Whether true or not, let others discuss; but one thing is certain, – this great convent, with all its revenues, has grown up out of that hole in the ground in which the tree is said to have stood."
—Ibid., 663

"Our padre [friar, guide] labors hard to explain how it could possibly come to pass that [John] the Baptist should be born *in two places* [in Ein Kerem] – beneath the rich altar within the convent, and in the grotto at least a quarter of a mile from it, where a convent was also erected, over

the house of Elizabeth. It is not very important how we dispose of this difficulty [the padre explains]. Elizabeth may possibly have divided the time of that important occasion between the two, in order to multiply the number of sacred places, and thereby increase the piety of future generations."
—Ibid., 663–34

"I have come to regard [the site of the Church of Sepulcher] as the most interesting half acre on the face of the earth."
—Ibid., 674

"…[I] looked at the three holes in which the crosses are said to have stood; but this seems to me the most bungling arrangement in the whole 'invention' [of the sacred sites]. The three holes are too close together, and there is an air of desperate improbability about the entire contrivance that cannot be overcome."
—Ibid., 677–78

"Now I am devoutly thankful that no amount of learning or research can establish the remotest connection between any act of our Savior and any one of these so-called holy places. And I seem to find, in this uncertainty which hangs over every sacred locality, the indications of a watchful Providence in beautiful accordance with many similar interpositions to save God's people from idolatry."
—Ibid., 679

"[S]ince God has concealed the *realities* [the precise location of the sacred places], we have no need of these fictitious sites to confirm our faith. We are surrounded by witnesses, and these mountains, and valleys, and ruins, that cannot be effaced or corrupted…. The great atoning sacrifice of the Lamb of God…was offered up here, on this unquestioned platform of the Holy City. This is all I care for, all that mere topography can offer."
—Ibid., 679–80

Samuel Langhorne Clemens (Mark Twain)

1835–1910; AMERICAN AUTHOR
(1867)

We were shown (in the Cathedral of Notre Dame) "some nails of the true cross, a fragment of the cross itself, a part of the crown of thorns. We had already seen a large part of the true cross in a church in the Azores, but no nails."
—*Innocents Abroad* 1:126

"Among the most precious of relics [in the Cathedral of Milan] were, a stone from the Holy Sepulcher, part of the crown of thorns…a fragment of the purple robe worn by the Savior [and] a nail from the Cross…."
—Ibid., 1:178

"They have [in St. Peter's Church]…a piece of the true cross, and some nails, and a part of the crown of thorns."
—Ibid., 1:284

"Heaven protect the Sepulcher when this tribe* invades Jerusalem."
—Ibid., 2:196

*Twain's fellow travelers who chipped relics from the holy sites.

"The appearance of the city is peculiar. It is as knobby with countless little domes as a prison door is with bolt-heads."
—Ibid., 2:197

"Rags, wretchedness, poverty and dirt, those signs and symbols that indicate the presence of Muslim rule more surely than the crescent flag itself, abound…. Jerusalem is mournful and dreary and lifeless. I would not desire to live there."
—Ibid., 2:298–99

"The greatest [proof of the site of Adam's creation] lies in the fact that from under this very column [in the Church of the Sepulcher] was taken the *dust from which Adam was made*. This

can surely be regarded in the light of a settler [convincing proof]. It is not likely that the original first man would have been made from an inferior quality of earth when it was entirely convenient to get first quality from the world's center.... That Adam was formed of dirt procured in this very spot is amply proven by the fact that in six thousand years no man has ever been able to prove that the dirt was *not* procured here whereof he was made."
—Ibid., 2:306

"There is no question that [Adam] is actually buried in the grave [in the Church of the Sepulcher] which is pointed out as his…because it has never been proven that that grave is not the grave in which he is buried."
—Ibid., 2:307

"The monks call this apartment the 'Chapel of the Invention of the Cross' – a name which is unfortunate, because it leads the ignorant to imagine that a tacit acknowledgment is thus made that the tradition that Helena found the true cross here is a fiction – an invention."
—Ibid., 2:310

The visitor to the Church of the Sepulcher "looks at all these places [the designated shrines] with interest, but with the same conviction he felt in the case of the Sepulcher, that there is nothing genuine about them, and that they are imaginary holy places created by the monks. But the place of the Crucifixion affects him differently. He fully believes that he is looking upon the very spot where the Savior gave up his life."
—Ibid., 2:312

"It is not possible that there can be any mistake about the locality of the Crucifixion…. [It] was too notable an event in Jerusalem, and the Hill of Calvary made too celebrated by it, to be forgotten in the short space of three hundred years."*
—Ibid., 2:313

*Helena, the mother of Emperor Constantine, is said to have

identified the site in the fourth century.

"When one stands where the Savior was crucified, he finds it all he can do to keep it strictly before his mind that Christ was not crucified in a Catholic Church."
—Ibid., 2:314

"With all its claptrap sideshows and unseemly postures of every kind, [the Church of the Sepulcher] is still grand, reverend, venerable – for a god died there…."
—Ibid., 2:315

"History is full of this old Church of the Holy Sepulcher – full of blood that was shed because of the respect and the veneration in which men held the last meeting-place of the meek and lowly, the mild and gentle, Prince of Peace!"
—Ibid., 2:316

"[T]he guide began to give name and history to every bank and boulder we came to: 'This was the Field of Blood; these cuttings in the rocks were shrines and temples of Moloch; here they sacrificed children; yonder is the Zion Gate; the Tyropean Valley; the Hill of Ophel; here is the junction of the Valley of Jehoshaphat – on your right is the Well of Job. We turned up Jehoshaphat. The recital went on."
—Ibid., 2:328

"I cannot say anything about the stone column that projects over [the Valley of] Jehoshaphat from the Temple wall like a cannon, except that the Muslims believe Mohammed will sit astride of it when he comes to judge the world. It is a pity he could not judge it from some roost of his own in Mecca, without trespassing on *our* holy ground."
—Ibid., 2:329–30

"[T]he thirst, the tiresome volubility of the guide, the persecutions of the beggars – and then, all that

will be left will be pleasant memories of Jerusalem...."
—Ibid., 2:330

"Renowned Jerusalem...the stateliest name in history, has lost all its ancient grandeur, and is become a pauper village; the riches of Solomon are no longer there to compel the admiration of visiting Oriental queens; the wonderful temple which was the pride and glory of Israel, is gone, and the Ottoman crescent is lifted above the spot where, on that most memorable day in the annals of the world, they reared the Holy Cross."
—Ibid., 2:358–59

"It was suggested that we might hire parties to visit these [tiring sites] for us and thus see them by proxy, but after some deliberation it was decided that such a course would be discreditable. Still, we had got altogether enough, for the present."
—Twain report to the Alta newspaper, 1868; quoted in Walker, Irreverent Pilgrims, 187

Eliot Warburton
1810–52;
ENGLISH NOVELIST AND TRAVELER WHOSE BOOK WAS ONE OF THE MOST POPULAR NINETEENTH-CENTURY GUIDEBOOKS
(1844)

"Apart from all associations, the first view of Jerusalem is a most striking one. A brilliant and uncheckered sunshine has something mournful in it, when all that it shines upon is utterly desolate and drear."
—Crescent and Cross, 232

"The chief place of interest in Jerusalem is the Holy Sepulcher, whose site I believe to be as real, as the panorama that the priests have gathered round it must needs be false."
—Ibid., 239

"At the Savior's Tomb, the infidel* watches with drawn saber to prevent his followers from destroying one another."

*The Muslim guards.

Charles Dudley Warner

1829–1900; AMERICAN AUTHOR AND TRAVELER
(1875)

"Indeed, the greatest wonder to me in the whole East is that there has not been a good road built from Jaffa to Jerusalem…."
—*In the Levant* 1:33

"Within the door of the church [of the Sepulcher], upon a raised divan at one side, as if this were a bazaar and he were the merchant, sat a fat Turk, in official dress, the sneering warden of this Christian edifice, and the perhaps necessary guardian of peace within."
—Ibid., 1:42

"I do not know how many times the houses along [the Via Dolorosa] have been destroyed and rebuilt since their conflagration by Titus, but this destruction is no obstacle to the existence intact of all that are necessary to illustrate the Passion-pilgrimage of our Lord."
—Ibid., 1:49

"[I]t is the tradition that it was from this tower [of David] that the king first saw Bathsheba, the wife of Uriah…."
—Ibid., 1:52

"I wish [the Armenian Quarter] were the Christian quarter, for it is the only part of the town that makes any pretension to cleanliness, and it has more than any other the aspect of an abode of peace and charity."
—Ibid., 1:53

"The men stand together at one part of the [Western] wall, and the women at another."
—Ibid., 1:67

"This platform [the Haram-a-Sharif (Temple Mount)] is beyond all comparison the most beautiful place in Jerusalem, and its fairy-like buildings, when seen from the hill opposite [Mount of Olives], give to the city its chief claim to Oriental picturesqueness."
—Ibid., 1:83

"The dome of the mosque Kubbet es-Sukhrah [Dome of the Rock] is perhaps the most beautiful in the world; it seems to float in the air like a blown bubble...."
—Ibid.

"[W]e passed the village of Siloam, which is inhabited by about a thousand Muslims – a nest of stone huts and caves clinging to the side-hill.... The occupation of the inhabitants appears to be begging, and hunting for old copper coins, mites [coins of small value], and other pieces of Jewish money.... There is a great choice of disagreeable places in the East, but I cannot now think of any that I should not prefer as a residence to Siloam."
—Ibid., 1:99

"The Jerusalem donkey is a good enough donkey, but he won't go.... No persuasions of mine, such as kicks and whacks of a heavy stick, could move him on; he would turn out of the road, put his head against the wall, and pretend to go to sleep. You would not suppose it possible for a beast to exhibit so much contempt for a man."
—Ibid., 1:109

"Bethany is a squalid hamlet clinging to the rocky hillside, with only one redeeming feature about it – the prospect. A few wretched one-story huts of stone, and a miserable handful of Muslims, occupy this favorite home and resting-place of our Lord."
—Ibid., 1:114

"The visitor expects too much; he is unreasonably impatient of the contrast between the mean appearance of the theater and the great events that have been enacted on it; perhaps he is not prepared for the ignorance, the cupidity, the audacious impostures under Christian names, on the spot where Christianity was born."
—Ibid., 1:116

"Nor do I know whether the true cross has still the power of growing, which it had in

the fourth century, to renew itself under the constant demand for pieces of it."
—Ibid., 1:117

Charles Warren
1840–1927; ENGLISH ARCHEOLOGIST IN THE SERVICE OF THE PALESTINE EXPLORATION FUND
(1867)

"A city of contradictions, Jerusalem excels in the anomaly of her customs, which can scarce be called civilized, though she is the center of religious attraction to the civilized world."
—*Underground Jerusalem*, 82

"The ancient Holy of Holies has become the shrine of Islam; the stronghold of Zion, the holy place of David, is the Kiblah of the Christians; there, fire is worshiped after the example of the Magi...."
—Ibid., 83

"[C]auliflowers...grow to an enormous size and in great profusion on the slopes of Ophel, the finest I have ever seen."
—Ibid., 89

The "military Pacha" (governor) "expressed much astonishment at my mission [to explore under the Temple Mount]: what could it be for? there was nothing to learn about the Noble Sanctuary! He could tell me what was under every stone."
—Ibid., 96

"Now we have ascertained that this arch was not one of a series, reaching across the valley to the Upper City, and so far Dr. Robinson was mistaken...."
—Ibid., 319

Chaim Weizmann
1874–1952; FIRST PRESIDENT OF ISRAEL

"'Mr. Balfour,* supposing I were to offer you Paris instead of London, would you take it?'

"He sat up...and answered:

"'But Dr. Weizmann, we have London.'

"'That is true,' I said. 'But we had Jerusalem when London was a marsh.'"
—*Trial and Error*, 110–11

*Arthur James Balfour, the future prime minister, at Weizmann's first meeting with him in 1906, when the British government had proposed Uganda as an alternative to Palestine.

"There were innumerable churches, of every sect and nationality. We had not a decent building of our own. All the world had a foothold in Jerusalem – except the Jews."
—1907 visit, ibid., 131

John Greenleaf Whittier

1807–92; AMERICAN QUAKER POET AND REFORMER

"Our wasted shrines – who weeps for them?

Who mourneth for Jerusalem?"
—"Ezekiel," in Atwan, ed., *Chapters into Verse* 1:429–30

William Robert Wilde

1815–76; SURGEON AND WRITER, FATHER OF OSCAR WILDE, ACCOUNT PUBLISHED 1840 (1838)

"Much as [Jews] venerate the very stones that now form the walls of this enclosure [the Haram-a-Sharif (Temple Mount)], they dare not set foot within its precincts; for the crescent of the Muslim is glittering from the minaret, and the blood-red banner of Mohammed is waving over their heads."
—*Narrative of a Voyage to Madeira, Teneriffe, and along the Shores of the Mediterranean*, in Osband, *Famous Travellers*, 155

"Were I asked what was the object of the greatest interest that I had seen, and the scene that made the deepest impression upon me…I would say that it was a Jew mourning over the stones of Jerusalem."
—Ibid., 155

Charles W. Wilson

1836–1905; ENGLISH EXPLORER AND RESEARCHER; LED ORDNANCE SURVEY OF JERUSALEM (1864)

"The view from the Mount of Olives is one which, from its strange beauty and its extraordinary interest, lingers long and lovingly in the memory of those who have seen it."
—*Jerusalem: The Holy City*, 4

"Within the Citadel there is ruin and rubbish everywhere; without, in the moat, soldiers' gardens, beds of cactus…and filth of every possible description…."
—Ibid., 11

"The view from the top of David's Tower is extensive, embracing the whole town, the Mount of Olives, the Dead Sea, and the Mountains of Moab – a pleasant sight to feast the eyes upon for half an hour before the sun goes down."
—Ibid.

"A bright flame as of burning wood appears…the light, as every educated Greek knows and acknowledges, kindled by the bishop within – the light, as every pilgrim believes, of the descent of God himself upon the Holy Tomb."
—Ibid., 28

"The houses and the streets of Siloam [Silwan]…are filthy in the extreme, and the villagers are notorious thieves, sometimes not over-courteous to visitors."
—Ibid., 94

"The Sephardim have a curious tradition that their ancestors were settled in Spain before the days of the Crucifixion, and they thus claim to be exempt from the consequences of the outcry of the Jews, 'His blood be upon us and our children.'"
—Ibid., 118

"The Armenians…form a thriving community, and occupy one of the pleasantest quarters of Jerusalem."
—Ibid., 119

#10 BRITISH MANDATE PERIOD
UP TO 1948

General Edmund Allenby

1861–1936; COMMANDER OF BRITISH FORCES THAT CONQUERED JERUSALEM IN 1917 (1917)

"…I make it known to you that every sacred building, monument, holy spot, shrine, traditional site, endowment, pious bequest of customary place of prayer of whatsoever form of the three religions will be maintained according to the existing customs and beliefs of those to whose faiths they are sacred…."
—Proclamation after entry into Jerusalem, 1917; quoted in Hammer, ed., *Jerusalem Anthology*, 231

Arthur James Balfour

1848–1930; BRITISH FOREIGN SECRETARY IN WORLD WAR I

"His Majesty's Government views with favor the establishment in Palestine of a national home for the Jewish people, and will use their best endeavors to facilitate the achievement of this object, it being clearly understood that nothing shall be done to prejudice the civil and religious rights of existing non-Jewish communities in Palestine…."
—"Balfour Declaration," issued November 2, 1917

"[I]t would be interesting to be present at the reconstitution of the [ancient] kingdom of Jerusalem."*
—Quoted in David Pryce-Jones, "Jews, Arabs, and French Diplomacy," *Commentary Magazine*, May 2005

*Response to French ambassador in London, January 1919, in reaction to French initiative to thwart growing Jewish nationalism.

David Ben-Gurion

1886–1973; FIRST PRIME MINISTER OF ISRAEL

"Jerusalem does not cease being to the Jewish people what it was during King David's time and still is today: the heart of the Jewish people and its joy. It has not been designated [by the United Nations Special Commission on Palestine, 1947] the capital of the Jewish

state, but it was and will always remain the capital of the Jewish people, the very core of the entire Jewish people...."*
—Quoted in Naor, *City of Hope*, 246

*Response to 1947 UN partition plan calling for internationalization of Jerusalem.

British Secretary of State for the Colonies

BRITISH CABINET OFFICE 1768–82

"The importation of the screen* [at the Western Wall] and its attachment to the pavement constituted an infraction of the status quo, which the Government were unable to permit."
—Memo to Parliament, 1928; quoted in Silk, *Retrievements*, 160–61

*To separate male worshippers from female, as required by Jewish law.

G.K. Chesterton

1874–1936; ENGLISH CATHOLIC WRITER

"...Jerusalem might be called a city of staircases. Many streets are steep and most actually cut into steps."
—*New Jerusalem*, 60

"For there is a strange Muslim legend that through this [Golden] gate, so solemnly sealed up, shall ride the Christian King who shall again rule in Jerusalem."
—Ibid., 64

"Strange scenes have already been enacted round that fane [temple] where the Holy Fire bursts forth to declare that Christ is risen; and whether or no we think the thing holy there is no doubt about it being fiery."
—Ibid., 89

"Jerusalem is a small town of big things; and the average modern city is a big town full of small things. All the most important and interesting powers in history

are here gathered within the area of a quiet village; and if they are not always friends, at least they are necessarily neighbors."
—Ibid., 122

"In the First Crusade it was the ordinary man who was right or wrong. He came out in a fury at the insult to his own little images or private prayers.... [T]he typical leader...was... Peter the Hermit.... And it was his army, or rather his enormous rabble, that first marched across the world to die for the deliverance of Jerusalem."
—Ibid., 233–34

Winston Churchill

1874–1965; ENGLISH STATESMAN

"You [the Jews] have prayed for Jerusalem for 2,000 years, and you shall have it."
—*The London Times*, May 5, 1938; quoted in Tal, *Whose Jerusalem*, 285

Rudyard Kipling

1865–1936; INDIAN-BORN ENGLISH AUTHOR

"And burthened Gentiles o'er the main

Must bear the weight of Israel's hate

Because he [Israel] is not brought again

In triumph to Jerusalem."
—"The Burden of Jerusalem," unpublished poem, sent by Winston Churchill to President Roosevelt in 1943, with the notation that Mrs. Kipling withheld publication "in case [it] should lead to controversy" [David Noone, http://www.exterminationist.com/kiplingunpublishedpoems.htm]

Rabbi Abraham Isaac Kook

1865–1935; CHIEF RABBI OF PALESTINE FROM 1921

"There are men with hearts of stone, and there are stones with human hearts."*
—Quoted in Ben-Dov, *Western Wall*, 36

*The reference is to supplications at the Western Wall.

David Lloyd George

1863–1945; PRIME MINISTER OF BRITAIN, 1916–22

"I want Jerusalem as a Christmas present for the British people."*
—Quoted in Naor, *City of Hope*, 222

*Said to General Edmund Allenby, 1917.

Vincent Sheehan

AMERICAN AUTHOR AND JOURNALIST, ACCOUNT PUBLISHED 1935
(1929)

"There were…mosques everywhere, and Islam's call to prayer haunted the still air of the evening, so that I could scarcely see a photograph of the roofs of Jerusalem afterwards without hearing the long cry of the Muezzin as a part of it."
—*Personal History*; quoted in Khalidi, *From Haven to Conquest*, 275

"The Muslims made no objections to such visits [to the Haram-a-Sharif]. In this and in other respects the Muslims of Palestine were less jealous of their holy places than Muslims elsewhere.…

"[I]t was possible, at first, to assume that the Muslims of Palestine did not regard their holiest shrine with the extreme religious passion characteristic of Muslims elsewhere. [However] it seemed to me that [the more permissive Muslim attitude regarding the] Haram-a-Sharif was due to the Westernized character of life in Jerusalem…[;] its Muslim leaders were constrained by Western taste and manners to open their great sanctuary to the visits of the infidel."
—Ibid., 282–83

Sir Ronald Storrs

1881–1955; BRITISH MILITARY GOVERNOR OF JERUSALEM, 1918–26

"There is no promotion after Jerusalem."
—*Orientations*, 1937; quoted in Kernohan, *The Road to Zion*, 117

Arnold Toynbee

1889–1975; ENGLISH HISTORIAN

"If any Jerusalem survives, this will be the Jerusalem of the Wailing Wall and the Holy Sepulcher and the Dome of the Rock, not the Jerusalem that has been David's and Godfrey's and Ben-Gurion's secular capital city."
–Introduction, *Cities of Destiny*; quoted in Millgram, *Jerusalem Curiosities*, xiv

H.A. Zuta and L. Sukenik

HEBREW EDUCATORS AND AUTHORS; ZUTA, 1868–1939, WAS A FOUNDER OF THE MODERN HEBREW SCHOOL SYSTEM IN ISRAEL

"To this very day, it is almost impossible for Jews to walk freely in the alley near the Church of the Holy Sepulcher."
–*Our Country: Guide to Eretz-Israel and the Neighboring Countries*, 1930 [Hebrew]; quoted in Ben-Arieh, *Jerusalem in the Nineteenth Century: The Old City*, 238

#11
*I*srael *P*eriod
UP TO PRESENT

- In June 1967, as a result of the Six-Day War, Jerusalem became again a united city

S.Y. Agnon

1888–1970; ISRAELI AUTHOR

"I found a place for myself at the Wall, standing at times amongst the worshipers, at times amongst the bewildered bystanders. I was amazed at the peoples of the world; as if it were not enough that they oppressed us in all the lands, yet they must also oppress us in our home."
—*Tehilla*; quoted in Holtz, *The Holy City*, 155–56

"Through a historical catastrophe – the destruction of Jerusalem by the emperor of Rome – I was born in one of the cities of the diaspora. But I always deemed myself a child of Jerusalem, one who is really a native of Jerusalem."
—Nobel Prize acceptance speech, 1966; quoted in Gilbert, *Jerusalem*, 270

Avigad, Nahman

1905–92; ISRAELI ARCHEOLOGIST INVOLVED IN OLD CITY EXCAVATIONS AFTER 1967

"[T]wo thousand years later, when the descendants of the slaughtered returned to the site,* they uncovered the physical traces of the [Roman] destruction and rebuilt their homes over the ruins. Now they too…can look out through their windows and see the Temple Enclosure.…"
—*Discovering Jerusalem*, 137–38

*the "Burnt House," excavated in the Jewish Quarter

Menachem Begin

1913–92; SIXTH PRIME MINISTER OF ISRAEL, 1977–83

"Our capital was not determined by a Basic Law [of the Knesset]… nor by our liberation of new Jerusalem in [1948] or when we were privileged to liberate the Old City. When was this capital determined? When it was written eternally in the Book of Books about the young king who ruled forty years. There* it says of David…: 'The length of David's reign over Israel was forty years: he reigned seven years in Hebron, and…thirty-three years in Jerusalem.'"
—Address to the Knesset, July 21, 1976

*1 Kings 1:51.

Saul Bellow

1915–2005; AMERICAN
JEWISH NOVELIST

"As we go into the Via Dolorosa, we hear an exciting jingle. Arab boys are racing their donkeys down the hill. You look for sleighs and frost when you hear this jingle-belling. Instead, there are boys stern and joyous, galloping hell-bent on their donkeys toward the Lions' Gate."
—*To Jerusalem and Back*, 16

"…Jerusalem is the only ancient city I've ever seen whose antiquities are not on display as relics but are in daily use."
—Ibid., 25

"…I, too, feel that the light of Jerusalem has purifying powers and filters the blood and the thoughts; I don't forbid myself the reflection that light may be the outer garment of God."
—Ibid., 93

Meir Ben-Dov

ISRAELI ARCHEOLOGIST, LED
EXCAVATIONS IN THE OLD CITY
AFTER THE 1967 SIX-DAY WAR

"The longest of the [Temple Mount's] buttress walls was the western wall; it measured 485 feet from the southern extremity to the Antonia citadel…at its northern end."
—*Western Wall*, 41

"It is in the Middle Ages that the term Western Wall begins to appear in Jewish sources. In *Sefer Ha-Yuhasin* (*Megilat Ahimaatz*, an 11th-century chronicle) we learn of one, Samuel, the son of Paltiel (980–1015) who gave '…oil for the sanctuary at the Western Wall….'"
—Ibid., 66

"In the first years of the common era, it seems that the western wall of the Temple building itself still existed."
—Quoted in Hammer, ed., *Jerusalem Anthology*, 407

The wakf's "resistance was anchored in two fears. One

was that the excavations might turn up finds that contradicted the tenets of Islam. But far more decisive was the fact that the trustees knew the Temple Mount had been built over the foundations of an infrastructure from the Second Temple period and that excavations might well reveal who had preceded the Muslims in the area."
–*In the Shadow of the Temple*, 16

"[T]he chief importance of the Temple Mount for Christianity during the early Byzantine era was the fact that it lay in ruins – vindication of Jesus' prophecy that the Temple would be destroyed…."
–Ibid., 25

"[B]y the end of the First Temple period organized settlement extended to the western hill."
–Ibid., 34

"From the eighth century onward, the cemeteries of Jerusalem's upper classes were located southeast of the city, among the houses of what is now the Arab village of Silwan."
–Ibid., 41

"The hand of fate must have been behind the fact that the building from the Second Temple period began to show through the earth on the 17th of Tammuz, the date of a fast commemorating the breach of the city walls by the Romans, and the pottery vessels in the First Temple structure were found on the 10th of Av, a day after the date on which the Temple was destroyed."
–Ibid., 46

"The dimensions of the Temple Mount…the largest site of is kind in the ancient world, were as follows: the southern wall, the shortest of the retaining walls…280 meters…; the eastern wall…460 meters; the western…485 meters; …the northern…314 meters. The Temple Mount is…a trapezoid covering 144,000 square meters."
–Ibid., 77

"Imagine actually standing on a stone pavement from the Second Temple period, wedged in between the stones that had smashed down on the 9th of Av [in 70 CE] – and on the eve of Jerusalem Day, at that."
–Ibid., 106

Examination of the site of the Nea Church "makes it difficult to avoid the conclusion that Justinian's builders dismantled the porticoes of the ruined Temple Mount and hauled off their columns to build the church."
—Ibid., 239

"[A] Byzantine emperor [Justinian] used the remains of the Temple Mount to build an enormous church [the Nea] and did his best to cover the fact; the Jews of the country [in 614, as part of the conquering Persian forces] destroyed the church at the first opportunity [in an act of revenge for the Temple Mount's despoilation]; the Muslims built in the area of the Temple Mount using the remains of that same destroyed church; and after hundreds of years of silence, Israeli scholars [after the Six-Day War] redeemed this intricate tale from the depths of oblivion."*
—Ibid., 241

*Cf. Le Strange, *History of Jerusalem under the Moslems*, 11: "Perhaps…the remarkable silence of all the Arab writers in regard to the date of 'Abd al Malik's rebuilding of the Aksa may be taken as an indirect proof that that Caliph did not erect that edifice from its foundations, but that he made use of the remains of the St. Mary [Nea] Church… incorporating these into the new Aksa, which thus rose on the ruins of the Christian edifice."

"…'Jerusalem' proper is the Old City and its environs. If King David were to visit Jerusalem today and were invited to visit the Knesset, he would surely ask in surprise whether he was in Jerusalem."
—*Historical Atlas*, 365

David Ben-Gurion
1886–1973; FIRST PRIME MINISTER OF ISRAEL

"[I]f a land can have a soul, Jerusalem is the soul of the land of Israel."*
—Quoted in Naor, *City of Hope*, 256

*Recounting his concerns during Israel's 1948 War of Independence.

"We will not countenance a UN effort to tear Jerusalem from the State of Israel – it is the eternal capital of the Jewish people...."*
—Ibid., 259

*Response in Knesset to UN plan to internationalize Jerusalem, 1949.

"For the State of Israel there has always been and always will be one capital only – Jerusalem the Eternal. Thus it was 3,000 years ago – and thus it will be, we believe, until the end of time."
—Speech to Knesset, Dec. 13, 1949; quoted in Slonim, *Jerusalem in America's Foreign Policy*, 144

Winston Churchill
1874–1965; ENGLISH STATESMAN

"You ought to let the Jews have Jerusalem; it was they who made it famous."*
—Quoted in Gilbert, *Jerusalem*, 262

*1955, to diplomat Evelyn Shuckburgh, whose father had helped draft the clauses of the British Mandate.

Bill Clinton
1946–; FORTY-SECOND PRESIDENT OF THE UNITED STATES

"I do recognize Jerusalem as Israel's capital, and Jerusalem ought to remain an undivided city. But I think that timing is the real issue."
—Interview, 1992; quoted in Slonim, *Jerusalem in America's Foreign Policy*, 303

Moshe Dayan
1915–81; ISRAELI MILITARY LEADER AND POLITICIAN

"We have united Jerusalem, the divided capital of Israel. We have returned to our holiest of holy places, never to part from it again."*
—Quoted in Gilbert, *Jerusalem*, 287

*Spoken standing before the the Western Wall, June 7, 1967.

"We have not come to Jerusalem to conquer the holy sites of others...but to guarantee the

wholeness of this city, and to live side by side in brotherhood."*
—Quoted in Naor, *City of Hope*, 278

*Statement on Israel's return to the Old City in 1967.

Abba Eban
1915–2002; ISRAELI DIPLOMAT AND POLITICIAN

"Perhaps in this as in other critical periods of history a free Jerusalem may proclaim redemption to mankind."
—Voice of Israel broadcast, 1967; quoted in Holtz, *The Holy City*, 162

Rabbi Shlomo Goren
1917–94; CHIEF RABBI OF ISRAEL DEFENSE FORCES UNTIL 1968, ASHKENAZI CHIEF RABBI OF ISRAEL, 1973–83

"The dream of all the generations has been fulfilled before our eyes. The City of God, the Temple site, the Temple Mount, and the Western Wall – symbol of the Jewish People's Messianic Redemption – has been delivered this day by you, heroes of the Israel Defense Forces."
—Address to troops who liberated Western Wall, June 7, 1967; quoted in Hammer, ed., *Jerusalem Anthology*, 295

Mordecai Gur
1930–95; COMMANDER OF PARATROOP BRIGADE THAT TOOK OLD CITY IN 1967, LATER CHIEF OF STAFF OF ISRAEL DEFENSE FORCES, 1974–78

"*HaKotel b'yadeinu* – the Temple Mount is ours! …I repeat, the Temple Mount is ours."
—Radio message to General Uzi Narkiss, June 7, 1967

Shulamith Hareven
1930–2003; ISRAELI AUTHOR

"Jerusalem is a veiled lady on a still, torrid day, feminine, forlorn, softly dreaming, self-absorbed, sucking time sweetly like an old sugar candy, her sons gathered under the many folds of her robe, picking rockrose and herbs. Other days she is a man, fierce, dry, and ancient, smelling of

thyme and wild goat, his head covered with a sack against the wind, bare feet viny-veined, brusque-voiced and ornery, sniffing the slippery scent of sin in abandoned alleys, the odor of prophecy in public squares."
—*City of Many Days*, 1993; quoted in Hammer, ed., *Jerusalem Anthology*, 327

"Some neighborhoods…have names like prayers for succor and strength that never seem to come. As the present is always bad, the Jews have learned to live in a future that is always sure to be better. Romema, 'Uplifted.' Ruhama, 'The Pitied one.' Ezrat Yisra'el, 'The Aid of Israel.' Ge'ula, 'Redemption.' Talpiot, 'Great Heights.' Yemin Moshe, 'The Right Hand of Moses' – perhaps …[in reference] to Sir Moses Montefiore…[its builder], perhaps to Moses…. Some live in Mekor Hayyim, 'Life's Source,' while others dream of Sha'arei Hesed, 'Mercy's Gates'; still others who never planted a seed in their lives named their quarter Me'ah She'arim, 'The Hundredfold Crop.'"
—Ibid., 329

Samuel Heilman
CONTEMPORARY AMERICAN JEWISH SOCIOLOGIST AND AUTHOR

"And so in the end, Jerusalem must be understood as a tapestry in time. Woven into its present is an unforgettable past, and intertwined with both is an idealized future."
—*A Walker in Jerusalem*, 22

Abraham Joshua Heschel
1907–72; NOTED JEWISH THEOLOGIAN AND PHILOSOPHER

"Once you have lived a moment at the Wall, you never go away."
—*Israel: An Echo of Eternity*, 1967; quoted in Hammer, ed. *Jerusalem Anthology*, 316

"Joseph"
TREASURER OF NARKIS STREET BAPTIST CONGREGATION, JERUSALEM

"We [of the Narkis Street Baptist Congregation in Jerusalem] are not trying to substitute

circumcision for baptism or anything like that. The Jews are welcome to remain as Jews and to accept the Lord Jesus as the Savior. That fits the Scriptures exactly."*
—Milton, *The Riddle and the Knight*, 163

*Comment made in early 1990s to G. Milton in Jerusalem.

Kathleen Kenyon
1906–78; ENGLISH ARCHEOLOGIST
(1961–67)

"If one had to depend only on the evidence of excavations in Jerusalem, one would have no idea at all of Solomon's building operations. The site of the Temple is not in doubt."
—*Digging up Jerusalem*, 110

"One can…take it as certain that Zerubbabel's work was based on Solomon's foundations. Ruined as it was, the Temple had remained in existence."
—Ibid., 177

"[T]he interest of tourists is aroused by a story vividly told which does not conflict too seriously with known facts."
—Ibid., 226

"The ruthlessness and efficiency of Rome succeeded in obliterating Jerusalem and indeed Palestine as a Jewish state. Today one must, of course, recognize that Rome could not obliterate the concept of Jerusalem and Palestine as the Jewish homeland."
—Ibid., 249

"Titus decided to rely for the final capture on the cumulative effect of famine and the really horrible internecine struggles of the sects and parties in Jerusalem. Josephus shows us all too clearly that Titus was fully justified in waiting for the Jews to destroy each other."
—Ibid., 251

"Hadrian…abolished Jewish Jerusalem with his construction of Aelia Capitolina. Within

his city he buried it to level up the site for his regular lay-out. Outside it he threw it away in order to use the very rock on which it was built for his own city."
—Ibid., 264

"The site of the Temple lies beneath the Muslim sanctuary, the Haram-a-Sharif, in the center of which is the Dome of the Rock."
—*Archaeology in the Holy Land*, 239

R.D. Kernohan

CONTEMPORARY SCOTTISH JOURNALIST, AUTHOR, AND AUTHORITY ON THE CHURCH OF SCOTLAND

"[T]he first bishop, the Jewish-born Michael Solomon Alexander, laid the foundation stone [of Christ Church, the first Protestant church in Jerusalem] in 1842...."
—*The Road to Zion*, 42

"Save for the Haram built on the foundations of the Temple, with the great Dome of the Rock and some lesser buildings of grace and beauty, it has surprisingly few Islamic monuments of importance. The last centuries of Muslim Government left a memory of insufficiency, cruelty, extortion, and tyranny.... For though Jerusalem was a place of Arab holiness and Muslim pilgrimage it was not a place of activity and achievements like Damascus and Baghdad. The future dialogues of Christianity and Islam will probably be based and inspired elsewhere."
—Ibid., 165

"In the words of the Scots metrical form of Psalm 122,

'Pray that Jerusalem may have

Peace and felicity;

Let them that love thee and thy peace

Have still prosperity.'"
—Ibid., 167

Teddy Kollek
1911–2007; MAYOR OF JERUSALEM, 1965–94

"Everybody has two cities, his own and Jerusalem...."
—Quoting participant at town-planners' meeting in Jerusalem; quoted in Eckardt, ed., *Jerusalem*, 218

"The thing I dread most is that this city, so beautiful, so meaningful, so holy to millions of people, should ever be divided again...."
—"Jerusalem," *Foreign Affairs*, July 1977

Jerusalem "has been coveted and conquered by a host of peoples: Canaanites, Jebusites, Jews, Babylonians, Assyrians, Persians, Romans, Byzantines, Arabs, Crusaders, Mamlukes, Ottomans, British, Jordanians, Jews. But throughout those thousands of years, Jerusalem has been divided for less than two decades, from 1948 to 1967. It must never again be divided."
—Ibid.

"Jews care intensely about Jerusalem. The Christians have Rome and Canterbury and even Salt Lake City; Muslims have Mecca and Medina. Jerusalem has great meaning for them also. But the Jews have only Jerusalem, and only the Jews have made it their capital."
—Ibid.

"This beautiful golden city is the heart and soul of the Jewish people. You cannot live without a heart and soul. If you want one simple word to symbolize all of Jewish history, that word would be Jerusalem."
—Ibid.

"Since June 1967...freedom of [worship] is absolute.... There is no Saracen guard to control Christian entry into the Church of the Holy Sepulcher; no Crusader to bar the Muslim from the Haram-a-Sharif; and neither Christian nor Muslim to prevent the Jewish pilgrim from visiting the Temple Mount, sounding the Shofar at the

Western Wall, or entering the Cave of Machpelah in Hebron."
—*Pilgrims to the Holy Land*, 204

Bernard Lewis
1916–; AMERICAN
SCHOLAR OF ISLAM

"It is surely significant that the Koranic and other inscriptions on the Dome of the Rock [when built in 691]…included a number of directly anti-Christian polemics: 'Praise be to God, who begets no son, and has no partner,' and 'He is God, one, eternal. He does not beget, nor is he begotten, and he has no peer.'"
—"The Revolt of Islam,"
New Yorker, Nov. 19, 2001

James Michener
1907–93; AMERICAN AUTHOR

"I tried to visit the Wailing Wall…. First, it was almost impossible to find, for the narrow streets leading to it were winding and unmarked. Second, when I did get there, I found myself in a miserable little alley about as wide as a very small room. Third, when I got that far, armed soldiers prevented me from going too near the great old Wall, lest I turned out to be a Jew who wanted to pray, which was, of course, forbidden."*
—Quoted in Eckardt, ed.,
Jerusalem, 277

*Recalling a visit to the Western Wall before 1967.

Abraham E. Millgram
BORN 1901; AMERICAN
RABBI AND AUTHOR

"The most intriguing of…[the legends] is…that it was from this tower [the present Tower of David] that King David gazed at the beautiful Bathsheba as she was taking her bath…. Pilgrims were shown the exact spot where the King stood, the 'window' through which he gazed, and the spot where Bathsheba was taking her bath."
—Hammer, *Jerusalem Curiosities*, 63–64

General Uzi Narkiss

1925–97; LED BATTLE THAT LIBERATED THE OLD CITY IN 1967

"Silently I bowed my head. In the narrow space were paratroopers, begrimed, fatigued, overburdened with weapons. And they wept.... These were tears of joy, of love, of passion, of an undreamed first reunion with the ancient monument to devotion and to prayer. They clung to the stones, kissed them, these rough, battle-weary paratroopers, their lips framing the *Shema*."
—Hammer, *Jerusalem Curiosities*, 292

Benjamin Netanyahu

1949– ; NINTH PRIME MINISTER OF ISRAEL

"Israel could not under any circumstances negotiate over any aspect of Jerusalem, any more than Americans would negotiate over Washington, Englishmen over London, or Frenchmen over Paris. Israel is prepared to offer the Arabs full and equal rights *in* Jerusalem – but no rights *over* Jerusalem."
—*A Place among the Nations*, 346

Wajeen Yacob Nuseibeh

CUSTODIAN (1990S) OF CHURCH OF SEPULCHER, DESCENDANT OF TRADITIONAL MUSLIM CUSTODIANS

"To have a Muslim unlocking the doors [of the Church of the Sepulcher] is symbolic of the friendship between Christianity and Islam.... But most importantly, it cuts down the wrangles between the different Christian groups."
—Milton, *The Riddle and the Knight*, 144

Msgr. John M. Oesterreicher

1904–93; ROMAN CATHOLIC THEOLOGIAN

"Many thousand tombstones were taken from the ancient cemetery on the Mount of Olives to serve as building

material or paving stones. A few were even used to surface the footpath leading to a latrine in a Jordanian army camp."
—"Jerusalem the Free," in Oesterreicher and Sinai, eds., *Jerusalem*, 251

Amos Oz

1939–;
ISRAELI AUTHOR

"City of my birth. City of my dreams. City of my ancestors' and my people's yearnings. And I was condemned to walk through its streets armed with a sub-machine gun…. To be a stranger in a very strange city."
—*The Seventh Day*, 241–42

Yitzhak Rabin

1922–95; PRIME MINISTER OF
ISRAEL 1974–77 AND 1992–95

"There are not two Jerusalems. There is only one Jerusalem. For us, Jerusalem is not subject to compromise and there is no peace without Jerusalem."
—Remarks in Rotunda of US Capitol, Washington, 1995; quoted in Naor, *City of Hope*, 301

Edward Said

1935–2003;
ARAB INTELLECTUAL

"The [Church] of the Holy Sepulcher…was exactly as I recalled it, an alien, run-down, unattractive place full of frumpy middle-aged tourists milling about in the decrepit and ill-lit area where Copts, Greeks, Armenians and other Christian sects nurtured their unattractive ecclesiastical gardens in sometimes open combat with each other."*
—Quoted in Gilbert, *Jerusalem*, 346–47

*Reflections on 1992 visit.

Naomi Shemer

1931–2004; ISRAELI
SONGWRITER AND POET

"To reach a wall where men stand weeping."
—"Jerusalem of Gold"

David K. Shipler

1942– ; AMERICAN
JOURNALIST AND AUTHOR

"In Jerusalem, the moment of harmony comes at dawn. The first light sings a pastel tune on ancient stone. As the sun rises from behind the desert mountains across the Jordan and the Dead Sea, the rays touch the curve of the Mount of Olives, then illuminate the creations of man. The sunlight kindles the brilliant gold of the Dome of the Rock.... Then the adjacent al-Aksa mosque is lit, followed by the newest blocks of towering stone yeshivas in the Jewish Quarter of the Old City.... The light catches the dome and eclectic superstructure of the Church of the Holy Sepulcher...."
– *Arab and Jew: Wounded Spirits in a Promised Land*, 3–4

"[I]n Jerusalem it is the pious who greet the dawn – the Muslims, Jews, and Christians who sacrifice sleep for prayer."
–Ibid., 4

Albert Storme

1917–97; FRANCISCAN AUTHOR

"Today it is no longer necessary to remind the faithful that the main purpose of the Stations of the Cross is not to gain indulgences, but to participate in the Passion of Christ."
–*The Way of the Cross*, 163

Elie Wiesel

1928–; HOLOCAUST
SURVIVOR AND AUTHOR

"Jerusalem: the city which miraculously transforms man into pilgrim: no one can enter it and go away unchanged."
–*A Beggar in Jerusalem*

Rev. John Wilkinson

CONTEMPORARY ENGLISH
SCHOLAR, AUTHORITY ON
EARLY CHRISTIAN TRAVEL
TO THE HOLY LAND

"The authenticity of the Holy Places for the early Christians was to be measured by a standard of faith and prayer

rather than of logical proof. Thus Eusebius tells us that at its discovery the Tomb of Christ in Jerusalem 'by its very existence bore clearer testimony of the Savior's resurrection than any words.'"
—*Jerusalem Pilgrims*, 37

A.B. Yehoshua
1936–; ISRAELI AUTHOR

"The city must remain united from the human point of view, but diversified from the point of view of sovereignty; it must be a single city for all its inhabitants, yet at the same time two capitals for two peoples…."
—"Jerusalem," *The Jewish Quarterly*, spring 1981; quoted in Hammer, *Jerusalem Anthology*, 453

Topical Index

A

Aceldama, pointed out until today in Aelia, 31; a rotting charnel-house forlorn, 160; to this day, public burying place, 172

Abd al-Malik (Umayyad Caliph), erected above the Rock the Dome, 47; noting the greatness of Dome of Holy Sepulcher, 47

Adam
    buried: (tomb of) in Golgotha (Calvary), 19, 56, 65, 157, 180; in Hebron, 65, 68
    created: (at Golgotha), 28; cast out from paradise 100; descent from paradise, 90; earth from which made, 157; no man proved dirt *not* procured there, 180; raised to life, 68
    died: (in Golgotha) 82
    head of: blood of Jesus washed away sins, 56, 65; at place of Crucifixion, 55, 88, 91, 117; within wood of Cross, 55
    in Judaism: created from soil of Moriah, 18; offered sacrifice at site of Temple, 66

Aelia Capitolina (see Hadrian; Aceldama)

al-Aksa Mosque, about 10,000 beheaded within, 57; clappers silenced, 64; corruption and shame ceased, 64; eight hundred salaried servants, 112; on Fridays preacher ascends, sword in hand, 112; Koran raised and Testaments cast down, 64; no Christian or Jew suffered to enter, 78; prayer in worth 10,000, 89
    appearance: more beautiful than that of Damascus, 48
    built: beside which small oratory made into church, 71; commencement of before Shem, 89; erected on very spot of *sakhrah* (the Rock), 43; 40 years after Sacred Mosque of Mecca, 89; had as rival great church (of Sepulcher), 48; identical with Nea Church, 138; not

the Temple Solomon built, 58; Solomon built the Holy House, 47, 54; Solomon's Temple, 57; Templars had built living quarters, 54, 63, 64; unquestionably the Church of Mary (Nea), 138
and al-Burak: where Prophet tied al-Burak, 42
and Mohammed: night of ascension, 44
and Saladin: ordered *mihrab* to be uncovered, 64

Antiochus IV (Epiphanes), ordered pollution of Temple, 11

Antiochus VII (Sidetes), advised to take city by storm, 15

Armenian Chapel (Mount Zion), stone laid to secure Savior's Sepulcher, 122

Armenian Quarter, an abode of peace and charity, 183; gardens and orchards and houses, 126; one of pleasantest of Jerusalem, 187; only part of town that makes pretension to cleanliness, 183; to which come all Christian visitors, 126

Armenians (see Christians; Church of St. James)

Ascension (site of) (see also Church of), ruined mosque covering spot where Lord ascended, 155; site most palpably contradicted by New Testament, 141; spot where Jesus wrote Lord's prayer in Hebrew, 69; very beautiful church destroyed by Pagans, 69

B

Baldwin I (Crusader king of Jerusalem), did not behoove temporal king to carry crown of gold, 104; never wished to be called king, 104

Bethany, wretched huts and miserable handful of Muslims occupy resting place of Lord, 184

Bethseda, name of Sheep Pool in language of Jews, 19

al-Burak, brought to Dome of Gabriel for Prophet to mount, 44; footprint of Prophet when he mounted, 97; spot under corner of al-Aksa Mosque, 42; tied up at south side of the Rock, 97; Western Wall, where tethered, 168

C

Caligula (Emperor), ordered Jews to set up his statue in Temple, 21

Calvary (See also Church of Sepulcher; Sepulcher of Jesus)
  location: alleged discovery by Helena a pious fraud, 165; Golgotha and tomb not the real places, 165; knoll outside Damascus Gate, 164; more pardon there than Christian man can tell, 105; where they crucified him, 19
  rock of: Abraham blessed by Melchizedek, 82; brazen serpent set up, 82; Isaac brought hither, 82; Jesus crucified here, 82; there Abraham offered his son, 28, 36, 82; where Abraham offered sacrifice, 57
  and Adam (see Adam)

Castle of David (see Tower of)

Castle of the Pisans (see Jaffa Gate; Tower of David)

Charlemagne, came to Most Holy Tomb of Our Lord, 41

Christ Church, Jewish-born (Bishop) Alexander laid foundation stone in 1842, 207

Christians
  meaning of Jerusalem to: all profit from my enterprise for recovery of Jerusalem, 81; Christianity encamped as foreigner in land which gave it birth, 157; the City upon a Hill, 134; city where Jesus suffered had to be destroyed, 19; if Divine grace more abundant in Jerusalem, sin would not be so much the fashion, 32; Holy City has to be given back to Christian Church, 80; Jerusalem, common property of whole Christian world, 176; Kingdom of Christ is spiritual...not old dirty Jewish city, 150; pilgrimage to Jerusalem not among good deeds, 32; real influence of Christianity less felt in Jerusalem, 140
  presence in Jerusalem: many, almost more than Turks and Arabs, 113; only 200 Catholic visitors in a century, 146; 300 survivors of Sultan, 98
  Protestants: contempt for traditions of sites linked to Jesus, 154; to deliver Reader from erring reports, 129; Franciscans knew I was no Popish Catholicke, 119; a frozen zeal that will not be warmed, 129; Holy Week

service painful and revolting to, 165; I have swept the streets with broom of truth, 132; I went not at all to the Romish clergy, 128; I will not believe all, 120; no need of fictitious sites to confirm our faith, 178; only persons praising Jesus in simplicity and truth, 171; refused access to burial ground, 174; simplicity and spirituality of worship, 166; we did not believe all, 160

relations between denominations: Armenians deadly enemies of Greeks and Georgians, 104; Armenians very beautiful race, 104; Georgians are worst heretics, 104; Greeks and Armenians pin faith on Holy Fire, 122; Greeks and Copts detest Latins, 116; Greeks cry out "Hasten to religion of Cross," 96; Greeks impede restoration of Church of Sepulcher, 116; Greeks our worst enemies, 104; Greeks unjustly claim in Holy Tomb part of absolute jurisdiction, 104; Latins expose Holy Fire as shameful imposture, 122; profaned by lying and mummeries, 122; seat of strife, 140; unchristian fury over Sepulcher, 121; various communions endlessly fighting over holy places, 133; zeal of sects embittered by hatred and revenge, 114

and Jews: also in exile as are the Jews, 113; Jerusalem last place to meet Jewish converts, 140; must bear the weight of Israel's hate, 193; welcome to remain as Jews and accept Lord Jesus as Savior, 206; will not turn Christian in Jerusalem, 155

and Muslims: Christians make public manifestation of infidel faith, 96; neither would Saracens mind if Christians were lords, 86; since Christians and Saracens cannot agree, 86; would care little about Saracens' rule, provided allowed freedom, 86

Church of Ascension (on Mount of Olives), footprints of Jesus, 84; where Jesus ascended to heaven, 84, 88

Church of Assumption, where Virgin ascended into heaven, 84

Church on Mount Zion (Church of Last Supper), cornerstone rejected by builders, 27; crown of thorns Jesus received, 29; pillar at which

Lord scourged, 34; monuments of King David and Solomon under, 91

Church of Redeemer, Kaiser consecrating, 152

Church of St. Anne, explained to Christians by old Saracen woman, 93; heathen turned into mosque, 77; Helena believed to have built, 117; Saracens made church of their own, 93; shamefully abused by Turks, 117; spot where Mary was born, 93, 100

Church of St. James, large, inhabited by Armenian monks, 65; more spacious than churches and convents of other groups, 168; one of most sumptuous in East, 139; stone from Jesus' configuration, 122; stone from place of Lord's baptism, 122; stone upon which Moses cast tablets, 122

Church of Sepulcher (See also Calvary; Sepulcher of Jesus)
appearance: alien, run down, unattractive, 211; like common Roman Catholic church, 147; lines and strings hanging outside, 136; eight doors, 39; Greek nave most impressive portion, 148; most beautiful yet rendered hideous by abominable errors, 83; never covered, 57; one of most wonderful buildings, 53; quite round and open from above, 55; shabby, facade looked like spoiled pastry, 161; supposed to contain twelve or thirteen sanctuaries, 121; two main domes, 103; very large and round, 39;
authenticity: bungling arrangements in "invention," 178; Chapel of Invention of Cross unfortunate name for, 180; for Englishman, least sacred place in Jerusalem, 176; lies and legends keep Holy Place out of sight, 176; on monument of salvation was new Jerusalem built, 31; never able to prove dirt used in Adam's formation *not* procured here, 180; not possible any mistake about locality of Crucifixion, 180; nothing genuine about shrines but place of Crucifixion affects one differently, 180; place of crucifixion must be sought elsewhere, 157; scene of crucifixion in valley of Kidron, 157; seemed to bear dark mark of superstition, 141;

site as real as panorama of priests must needs be false, 182; stood anciently without the town, 73; with all its claptrap, still grand for a god died here, 181;
built: Constantine built church of wondrous beauty, 28; St. Helena caused this wonderful temple to be built, 79
center of the earth: 56; Compas is middle of the world, 69; hole they say is middle of world, 125; I objected that earth is round, 125
history: Charlemagne said to have visited, 41; contended for with so much unchristian fury, 121; everyone proceeds to the greater church, built by Constantine, 29; Franciscan Friars obtained permission to live in, 116; Helena called church St. Constantine, 46; history is full of this old Church, 181; monuments of Godfrey and Baldwin a distinction for the French, 145; locality assigned to minutest event connected with Savior, 154; older forms of Christendom gathered together as nowhere else, 170; perhaps no other edifice cause of more human misery, 148; place in which to study diverse forms of older churches, 170; so many sites within so small a compass, 138; zeal of Christian sects embittered by hatred and revenge, 114
pilgrims: all he can do to keep in mind Christ not crucified in Catholic Church, 181; cannot describe mingled emotions, 141; carved on pillars and marble slabs, 85; a frozen zeal that will not be warmed, 129; Heaven protect the Sepulcher when this tribe invades, 179; painted coats of arms, 85; third act to visit Holy Sepulcher, 112
relics: *Adam*: buried where Christ suffered, 117; head of came forth when blood flowed, 55; head of near hole where cross fixed, 88; no question Adam buried there – never proven not the grave, 180; redeemed by blood of Christ, 65; skull of beneath this rock, 55; *Cross*: chapel where St. Helena found, 55; large piece of in Chapel of our Lady, 79; *other*: cup of our Lord, 39; comprises almost all spots in closing career of Lord, 154; early Church crowded as many sacred stones as it could, 164; horn with which David and Solomon anointed, 28;

lamp which goes out by itself, 53 lance with which soldier pierced Lord's side, 40; not only sites of crucifixion and resurrection but many other marvels, 157; pillar to which Jesus bound during scourging, 157; sponge held up to our Lord's mouth, 39
and Jews: almost impossible for Jews to walk freely near, 195
and Muslims: *attitude towards*: Christians convinced nearby leather factory built out of contempt, 167; demolishing would serve no purpose, 64; al-Hakim ordered destruction of, 45, 61; to have Muslim unlocking symbolic of friendship between Christianity and Islam, 210; infidel watches to prevent followers destroying one another, 182; profaned altars, 86; proud mussulman looks on with haughty scorn, 165; Saladin had bells broken, 117; Saracens respect as Christians do Jewish synagogue, 94; site was place of refuse, 60; still in hands of the infidels, 171; sword of old crusader would leap to behold haughty Turk, 171; torn down, 97; *called*: Beytu-l-makamah, 45; Kanisah al Kumanah, 47; Kumanah, not Kayamah, 73; *in control of*: all Christians pay stipulated tax, 88; Christ's worshippers let into by Christ's blasphemers, 82; Christians go in and out at pleasure of the dog, 79; doors guarded by Turkish soldiers, 121; enemies of Christ Lords of his Sepulcher, 129; fat Turk sneering warden of, 183; Franciscans and Greek priests enter without price, 109; key held by Saracens, 99,103; Moor who auctions tolls, 79; no Saracen guard to control entry, 208; none enter but such as paid, 121; Saracens present with their sticks, 91; who can expect to see rescued from, 121

Churches, have no bells, 81

Citadel of David (see Tower of)

City of David, Ark of God brought there by David, 7

Constantine (Emperor), built Church of Sepulcher, 28; church built by, behind the Cross, 29; gave orders to purify Tomb, 31

Convent of Armenians, in honor of St. Sabas, **65**

Cross (Holy) (see also Church of Sepulcher), people kiss the sacred wood, 30; star appears when brought out, 27; upright beam found near Temple, 55; which for you is simply a piece of wood, 68

authenticity and fragments: all pieces would make shipload, 111; alleged discovery by Helena a pious fraud, 165; already seen large part of in the Azores, 179; Chosroes carried to Persia, 72; convenient to suppose wood possessed power of vegetation, 114; Helena brought Constantine part of, 93; "invention" as discovery is called, 138; invention of, 141; nail from in Cathedral of Milan, 179; nails and fragments of in Cathedral of Notre Dame, 179; part of sent to Constantinople, 64; piece of the true cross in St. Peter's Church, 179; portion of stolen, 30; power to renew itself under constant demand for pieces, 185; saw nails of in Belvieu, 87; taken by the Persians, 29; wood and nails of in chapel of kings of France, 87

wood of: framed of four woods, 93, 100, 105, 129; was of nut, 27

Crusaders (and Crusades)
carnage: about 10,000 were beheaded, 57; after three days of butchery, purified the desecrated mosque, 176; cut off heads of Saracens, 56; everywhere was frightful carnage, 72; Franks burn synagogue over Jews' heads, 61; Franks slaughtered more than 70,000, 72; Franks stripped Dome of Rock, 161; men rode in blood up to their knees, 67; our squires split bellies of dead Saracens, 58; ran and chased the pagan bands, 131

rectitude of: clerics and laity singing new songs unto Lord, 58; creation, and salvation of man, 73n; the flower of Christendom, 140; the heathen came into your inheritance, 59; Jerusalem, with merry noise they greet, 131; a just and splendid judgment of God, 67; ought not choose king where Lord has suffered, 67; our bishops and priests preached to us, 56; who dare say cause of Holy Wars unjust, 146; who should have upper hand in this world, 146

Crucifixion (see Calvary; Church of Sepulcher)

Cyrus, The Lord has charged me with building Him a House, 10

D

David, brought Ark to the City of, 7; captured stronghold of Zion, 7

Dome of the Chain (on Dome of Rock), here Solomon administered justice, 53; where judgment given to children of Israel, 42

Dome of Gabriel (on Dome of Rock), al-Burak brought to this spot, 44

Dome of the Rock
appearance: city has one beautiful building, 78; dome seems to float in air like blown bubble, 184; greater part covered with gold, 88; a round dome like a hat, 100
built: Abd al-Malik moved by political considerations to erect, 137; cannot believe built by Solomon, 78
and Christianity: altar where priest performs rituals, 57; better to tear up than dedicate to name of Christ, 86; birthplace of Jesus, 44; covered with figure of Holy Cross, 65; Franks groaning in consternation and grief, 63; Franks stripped of candelabra, 61; Godfrey founded College of Canons, 118; had it not been built Christians would never have lost Jerusalem, 86; Holy Cross placed by Christians, 65; Lord's Temple, 73; neither Christian nor Jew can enter, 78; the very cradle in which Jesus lay, 43
and Islam: emblem of relationship of the two faiths, 161; I saw priests and monks in charge of the Sacred Rock, 62; I am now possessor of Sanctuary of first *kiblah*, 112; inscriptions included anti-Christian polemics, 209; *kiblah* changed from Jerusalem to Mecca, 43 Muslims dance as Israelites used to, 92; Muslims take down the cross, 63; rises upon foundation stones of Temple, 161; Saladin's soldiers destroyed cross of gold, 146
and Judaism: Abraham and Isaac, marks of their feet, 44; altar whereon Children of Israel offered sacrifices, 63; Ark of Tabernacle said deposited there, 44; neither Christian nor Jew can enter, 78; no Jew may enter, 101; one loves to

linger on earlier days, 156; on site of Holy of Holies, 92

E

Ein Karem, full of fruit vines, olive trees, 105; John the Baptist born in two places, 177

Eudocia, restored walls of Jerusalem, 29

Execration Texts, first historical mention of Jerusalem, 3

F

Fish Gate (see Jaffa Gate)

Foundation Stone (on Dome of Rock), before the Holy Ark, 17; Ishmaelite kings built house of prayer around, 92

Franciscan Convent (see St. Savior Church)

Franciscans (see also Mount Zion)
church (convent) on Mount Zion: 94, 95, 102; expelled, 82, 131
St. Savior Church (convent): called St. Savior, 117. 134; near Holy Sepulcher, 117; obtained permission to live in Church of Holy Tomb, 116
ministry: Christian stranger must be protected under them, 131; did not hear joy of suffering for Christ's sake, 144; friars make Way of Cross, 117; Guardian washed my right foot, 119; solely occupied over centuries defending against insults and tyranny, 147

G

Garden of Eden, gate near Mount Moriah (Temple Mount), 18

Gate of David (see Jaffa Gate)

Gate of Mercy (Golden Gate), on both sides Muslim graves, 94; consists of two gates, 100; guard closely against Christians and Jews, 77; opened on Palm Sunday, at present closed, 115; no Jew permitted, still less Gentile, 67;
beliefs about: Muslim legend says Christian King will ride through, 192; prophecy that destruction shall enter, 123; tradition among Jews Divine glory appeared, 67; Turks believed Christians would enter, 115; walled up by Muslim hands in dread of that predicted day, 160

Georgians (see Christians)

Gethsemane, earth upon which Divine feet may have trodden, 163; Greeks have invented another site, 177; the so-called Garden of, 177; where Christ was arrested, and prayed, 100

Gihon (Spring of), runs for six days and nights, 28

Godfrey de Buillon, founded College of Canons (at Dome of Rock), 118; I will not wear a crown of gold, 58

Golden Gate (see Gate of Mercy)

Golgotha (see Calvary)

Greeks (see Christians; Holy Fire; Monastery of Holy Cross)

H

Hadrian (Emperor), abolished Jewish Jerusalem with construction of Aelia Capitolina, 206; Jerusalem called Aelia in honor of Hadrian, 30; Jewish race forbidden to set foot in Jerusalem, 30; named Jerusalem after himself, 33; raised new Temple to Jupiter, 15; set up depiction of pig, 85, 115

Haram-a-Sharif (see also Temple Mount), can only perish with faith it typifies, 138; close to mosque, stone that was Solomon's throne, 44; could tell me what was under every stone, 185; nothing to learn about Noble Sanctuary, 185; one of most beautiful places in Ottoman Empire, 168; Solomon sat there, 45

access restricted: Muslim leaders constrained by Western taste to open to infidel, 194; Muslims made no objections to visits, 194; no Jew or Christian can pass threshold without death, 159; not a public place since Jews and Christians may not enter, 168

Helena (mother of Constantine), brought Constantine part of Cross and four nails, 93; doubtless had her reasons for burial-site, 171; found cross, nails, hammer and crown, 55; sent part of cross to Constantine, 35, 46; superstitious zeal prompted visits to sacred places, 157;

churches built by: believed to have built Church of St. Anne, 117; built church where octagonal mosque now stands, 146; caused Church of Sepulcher to be built, 79; enclosed the life-giving Tomb, 49; founded also other churches, 46; founded church where wood of cross found, 46; Monastery of Cross built by, 118

Helene (of Adiabene), tomb opens only on same day every year, 20

Herod, palace exceeds all ability to describe, 16; towers for largeness, beauty and strength beyond all, 16

Herzl, Theodor, beautiful city even in destruction, 152; if Jerusalem ever ours, would begin by cleaning it up, 152; reception by Kaiser Wilhelm will be eternally remembered, 153; restrained from entering Church, Mosque, Temple, 152; no deep emotion at Western Wall, 152; will not remember Jerusalem with delight, 152; would enclose Old City and sacred shrines in box, 153

Holy Fire, all nations save Friars feign to be true, 104; angel kindles light, 41; called "Saturday of the Light," 96; Divine grace lights the lamps, 56; Eastern Christians still believe, 133; educated Greek knows kindled by bishop within, 187; educated Greek knows to be shameful imposture, 148; every pilgrim believes descent of God, 187; fire worshiped after example of Magi, 185; Franks recognized priests bring it about, 133; goes out by itself on Good Friday, 53; the great Greek jugglery, 173; Greeks and Armenians pin faith upon it, 122; Greeks shut priest into Lord's monument, 83; Latins reject divine origins of, 122; not lighted by a miracle, 83; nothing to remind of awful event designed to commemorate, 149; O Jews! Your feast...of apes, 148; probably most offensive delusion, 170; shameful imposture, 122, 148; Syrians and Russian peasants still believe from Heaven, 148; by a trick cause fire to appear, 62; whether we think holy, no doubt fiery, 192

Holy Sites (authenticity of), Garden of Gethsemane, I do not choose to believe site of, 177; identification of so many sites an absurdity, 138; imaginary holy places in Church of Sepulcher, 180; measured by standard of faith rather than proof, 212; no amount of learning can establish connection between Savior and so-called holy places, 178; no need of these fictitious sites, 178; not possible any mistake about locality of Crucifixion, 180; present site of Holy Sepulcher will probably be discarded, 149; site of Temple not in doubt, 206; sites not determined with any degree of certainty, 86

Hospitallers (Knights), four hundred knights, 54; like the Maccabees, 103; take care of sick and needy, 53

I

Indulgences, granted by Pope Sylvester, 102; main purpose of Stations of Cross not indulgences but Passion of Christ, 212; for omitting Paternosters, lost many years, 129; plenary, 81, 82, 117, 126n, 133

J

Jaffa Gate, also called Gate of Bethlehem, Ramleh, Citadel, 115; Franks required to dismount, 120 had to wait before sentinel unbarred, 139; Hadrian set up pig carved in marble, 85; of iron, 119; name Pisan attached, 116

Jerusalem
appearance and condition: from afar, filled with brilliance and beauty, 96; all around many caves (wherein) buried pious and saintly, 95; all houses...inside city walls, 168; beautiful, however filthily maintained, 103; a city of staircases, 192; climate on the whole good, 140; contrast between mean appearance and the great events, 184; customs can scarce be called civilized, 175; distant view beautiful, but distant view is all, 153; entrance under citadel of King David, 68; even in destruction a beautiful city, 152; every sacred shrine will be maintained, 191; by far most famous city of East, 20; first view striking, when all is desolation and drear, 182; 4630 paces in circumference, 123; glory of has indeed departed, 166; greatly inferior to my expectations, 144; has no walls except one side, 94; has two Jewish cemeteries, 113; he who would raise

Essential City must wait for night, 169; it is the pious who greet the dawn, 212; "Jerusalem" proper is Old City, 202; knobby with countless little domes, 179; light of Jerusalem may be outer garment of God, 200; looked exactly like arid rocks, 161; looks at you like a cold grey eye, 161; massive stone walls and character of buildings remove appearance of sordidness, 158; meanness, filth and misery, 154; more ravaged than rest of country, 98; moment of harmony comes at dawn, 212; for most part desolate, 101; mournful and dreary and lifeless, 179; the musty deposits of 2,000 years, 152; never able to see beautiful woman in, 79; no clocks in, 127; no country more greatly dissipates romantic expectation, 161; no longer in place it stood when Jesus was crucified, 55; no place more worthy to be viewed, 124; not a good road built from Jaffa to, 183; not one fair street, 110; only ancient city whose antiquities are in daily use, 200; pleasant memories all that will be left, 182; pleasantest in way of climate, 47; at present not enclosed, 103; the principal quarters, 96; quiet satisfaction of daily walk around, 173; remains of old vaulted roofs under houses, 87; road from Bethlehem simply a mule-path, 171; said to be visible from Jaffa, 20; shining in light and color, 155; stateliest name in history, has lost ancient grandeur, 182; surrounded by new but weak walls, 109; a veiled lady and other days a man, 204; water is good and healthful, 127; water supply not from springs, but cisterns, 151; would scarcely recognize famous metropolis, 133

events: Antiochus advised to take by storm, 15; called Aelia, 15, 30, 35; Charlemagne brought about admirable treaty, 72; colonized by an alien race, 30; destroyed by Nebuchadnezzar, 7; destroyed on the very day of Saturn, 15; by end of First Temple period settlement extended to western hill, 201; first who introduced printing press, 163; for the freedom of, 15; Hadrian names it Aelia Capitolina, 15; the heathen came into your inheritance, 32; I may rebuild the sacred city, 33;

Jews banned from entering, 33; no wrongdoing in kingdom, 128; seventeenth of Tammuz, city breached, 21; Suleiman sent officials who built walls, 119; taken in second year of Vespasian, 16; throughout thousands of years divided for less than two decades, 208; Vespasian gave orders to demolish city and temple, 17

homage and supplication: Ariel, where David camped, 8; to Christian and Jew, most sacred place in world, 159; a city knit together, 9; city which miraculously transforms man into pilgrim, 212; in diverse Ages has different names, 112; has seventy names, 18; heart will rejoice, 27; free Jerusalem may proclaim redemption to mankind, 204; the Holy City par excellence, 164; if I forget thee let my right hand wither, 10; I will protect and save for My sake, 7; for its sake I will not be silent, 8; let us go up to the Mount of the Lord, 8; like praying before throne of Glory, 18; in the midst of the nations, 9; most interesting city on earth's surface, 164; most sacred place in world, except Mecca, to Mohammedan, 159; neighborhoods have names like prayers for succor, 205; new Jerusalem so far resembles old as to stone prophets, 144; nine measures of beauty bestowed, 22; nine measures of wisdom bestowed, 23; no man ever said too confined, 22; our feet stood within your gates, 9; pray for the well-being of, 9; proper to start state around Jerusalem, 167; ransomed of the Lord shall return with joy, 8; rejoice with and be glad for her, 8; squares of the city shall be crowded, 9; there is no promotion after Jerusalem, 194; we shall be as a City upon a Hill, 134; will be called City of righteousness, 8; word of the Lord from, 8, 9

impressions: all most important powers gathered; if not always friends, at least neighbors, 193; if any Jerusalem survives, will be that of Wailing Wall and Holy Sepulcher and Dome of Rock, not secular, 195; battleground for religious creeds, 142; everybody has two cities, his own and Jerusalem, 208; a festival of idiots and the insane, 149; how I should like to visit, 156; I want as Christmas present for British, 194; I would not desire to live there, 179; Jerusalem donkey exhibits contempt for man, 184; must be single city yet two capitals, 213; no city traveler will sooner wish to leave, 140; nowhere else has universal struggle been waged so consciously, 169; ought to remain an undivided city, 203; a tapestry in time, 205; whoever had patience to read accounts would still understand nothing, 145

mourning: bitterly she weeps in the night, 10; lonely sits the city,(10; mourners enter on left, 23; mourners for will behold joy, 22; Rabbi Akiva, why are you smiling? 22; whitewash house but leave area unfinished, 22

and Christians: to allow anyone not belonging to Christian faith a sacrilege, 73; city where Jesus suffered had to be destroyed, 19; clogged with cadavers, 71; common property of whole Christian world, 176; City of God shall descend from heaven, 19, 169; despite professed respect for holy places, vilest people, 133; England! Jerusalem thy Sister calls, 143; exalted above all Judea, 32; God intended for Royal Exchange of Religion, 113; a heart of stones, and to thyself a tomb, 130; heathen have come into your inheritance, 59; here we have no continuing city, 19; I will not cease till we have built Jerusalem in England's green and pleasant land, 142; Jesus took the place of the Temple and everything for which it stood, 169; to judge from convents might esteem to be most pious city, 141; the malevolent one came to destroy the city of God, 35; manifest truth standeth upon same place, 110; with merry noise they greet, 131; on monument of salvation new Jerusalem built, 31; more sacred shams and impostures than any other city, 164; most noble and magnificent above all cities, 99; Mount Zion the heavenly Jerusalem, 19; my country...my mother, 28; new Jerusalem, coming out of heaven, 19; at noon, Turk begins to cry out, 127; now in bondage; Jerusalem above is free, 19; an object of worship we could not give up, 67; Ottoman crescent lifted above spot where they reared Holy Cross, 182; our pure and holy country, 28; over whose acres walk'd those blessed feet, 130; part in troubled world to meet in sweet Jerusalem, 130; perhaps not a spot less holy, 143; the points at issue are Jerusalem, the Cross, and the land, 67; pray that Jerusalem may have Peace and felicity, 207; a rebuilt Jerusalem is contrary to prediction of Christ Himself, 147; religious center of the earth...original of heavenly city, 169; in same place where old stood, 86, 110; so beloved by God, 103; so many places of prayer, 32; subjected to domination of unbelieving enemies, 72; suffer me not to behold Thy Holy City, 68; taken in year of Incarnation of Lord 1099, 72; that eternal Jerusalem which Pilgrim sigheth after, 27; theater of most memorable events, 137; three Christians for one Turk, 132; unhappy Jerusalem has suffered, 86; was Jerusalem builded here among Satanic mills? 142; who mourneth for Jerusalem? 186

and Jews: building from Second Temple period began to show on seventeenth of Tammuz, 201; capital determined by the Book of Books, 199; to caress thy stones, fondle your dust, 98; condemned to walk through streets with sub-machine gun, 217; could never grow weary of contemplating, 162; if ever ours, would begin by cleaning up, 152; every wind comes to prostrate before the Lord, 102; in God's holy court idols resort, 60; he who merits to see ruins merits to see rebuilt, 98; I beheld almost new Jerusalem springing up, 163; I dread it should be divided again, 208; I shall enter Heavenly only after, 21; imagine standing on Second Temple pavement on Jerusalem Day, 201; Israel could not negotiate any more than Americans over Washington, 210; if King David invited to visit Knesset, would ask in surprise, 202; to live in freedom in, 153; lovable dreamer of Nazareth has helped increase the hate, 152; marriage in Jerusalem; if not, in Berditchev, 119; my heart is in the East, 59; no peace without Jerusalem, 211; pottery vessels of First Temple period found on tenth of Av, 201; in recent times, live in peace and quiet, 167; Salem is Jerusalem, 61; sanctity has never lapsed, 66; since June 1967 freedom of worship absolute, 208; the soul of land of Israel, 202; Spain my country, Jerusalem my destiny, 59; sweet would it be to walk naked and barefoot, 59; tore my garments, but felt solace, 98; we had Jerusalem when London a marsh, 186; we have united Jerusalem, 203; what superstition and fanaticism, 152; when the Jews come will become one of most beautiful cities, 152; who shall grant me eagle's wings, 59; whoever mourns for will witness its rejoicing, 22; will not remember with delight, 152; would enclose Old City and shrines in box, 153; you are from the land of the Canaanites, 3; *capital of Jewish people*: eternal, 203; for State of Israel only one, 203; will always remain, 192 *and Muslims*: Allah forgave sins of Israel in, 48; called Kuds, 43; the first land Allah blessed, 48; God allowed to retake on anniversary of Prophet's night journey, 62, 63; has surprisingly few Islamic monuments of importance, 207; heart of every man of intelligence yearns, 47; is ours as much as yours, 70; Jesus born in, 48; Mecca and Medina will come to, 48; mosques everywhere and Islam's call to prayer haunted the still air, 194; neglected capital of a petty Turkish province, 166; never the Muslim capital of Palestine, 155; no Jewish person allowed to dwell in, 49; no mosque existed further away, 74; one prayer in Jerusalem as 25,000 elsewhere, 44; place of Arab (Muslim) holiness but not of activity, 207; Rock in is center of world, 48; symbols of Muslim rule rags, wretchedness, poverty, 179; third in excellence after Mecca and Medina, 88; those unable to go to Mecca tarry at, 43; whoever prays there all guilt forgiven, 89

Jesus (see also Church of Sepulcher; Sepulcher of), blood on Adam's skull washed away sins of man, 55; comes to Gethsemane, 18; crucified at place called Calvary, 19; and disciples, come to Bethpage at Mount of Olives, 18; entered Jerusalem, 18; had a well-shaped foot and handsome face, 34; lines from Sepulcher indicate height and breadth, 57; meek and lowly, mild and gentle, Prince of Peace, 181; place to where he will return on day of judgment, 103; not remotest connection between any acts of Savior and so-called holy places, 178; in rock, footsteps of our Lord, 69; so many events hallowed by Passion, one day cannot suffice, 78; went up to Jerusalem for Jewish festival, 19

Jewish Quarter, always a treat to walk through, especially on the Sabbath, 159; cleanest of any we traversed, 162; Ghetto of Jerusalem preeminent in filth, 175; half of entire population but smallest area, 138; a man may smell it afar off, 150; in middle ages that now occupied by Muslims, 144; most filthy quarter of town, 157; most squalid and wretched part of city, 157; once palaces of priests and kings, now the opprobrium, 150; site of slaughterhouse chosen out of hatred, 167; squalid habitation of the Jews, 140; stinking ruins, 175

Jews

homage and supplication: all world had foothold in Jerusalem except the Jews, 186; born in diaspora but always deemed myself child of Jerusalem, 199; bridegroom puts ashes on head, 118; Christians have Rome and Canterbury, Muslims Mecca and Medina, but Jews only Jerusalem, 208; custom is to break glass, 118; have not come to Jerusalem to conquer holy sites of others, 203; have returned to our holiest of holy places, 203; a Jew mourning over stones of Jerusalem, 186; many visitors come to mourn Sanctuary, 98; on Mount of Olives we worship on holy days, 40; now they too can see Temple Enclosure, 199; rebuilt homes over ruins, 199; rents in garments (mourning for Temple and Jerusalem), 22, 70, 92, 94, 101; take only prayer book, Pentateuch, 127; when descendants of the slaughtered returned to the site, 199; when your ancestors living as savages, mine were

233

priests in Temple, 150; why do you not come? 45; word to symbolize Jewish history: Jerusalem, 208; working day and night at study of Holy Law, 80; if you do not come, send five men, 45; you have prayed for Jerusalem for 2,000 years, and shall have it, 193

and the Christian world: to be restored to land of their fathers, 143; dearest wish that bones be laid to rest among ancestors, 172; first to welcome me last to speed me on way, 174; on Good Friday Jews cannot quit their quarters, 164; His Majesty's Government views with favor national home for Jewish people, 191; let the Jews have Jerusalem; they made it famous, 203; no Jew dares to pass in front of Church of Sepulcher, 164; a people once so glorious, now so abject and downtrodden, 150; petty tribe, still unmixed among the ruins, 147; Sephardim claim to be exempt from outcry "His blood be upon us," 187; skulking near Temple, continue deplorable infatuation, 147; they are a very handsome race, 159; this luckless people much like Tantalus, 168; those miserable people groan, 33; welcome to remain as Jews and accept Lord Jesus as Savior, 206; wretched congregate while Church flows, 33; *converts (to Christianity):* after all these years very few, 158; but one true Christian, 161; cost of would have Christianized tenfold English heathens, 175; don't believe Episcopal apparatus converted dozen, 175; doubt whether enough to fill Christ Church, 158; each cost Mission 4,500 English pounds, 175; last place we may expect to meet, 140; why spend on strangers who already have noble faith, 158; *converts (from Christianity):* fell away to Jewish sect, 77

and Crusader period: about 200 Jews, 54; dwell under Tower of David, 54; Franks burn synagogue over their heads, 61; only Jew is Rabbi Abraham the dyer, 66; pay rent for dyeing house, 53

and Muslim periods: about 300 householders excluding widows, 125; appointed over king's tolls, 128; Arab says we are strangers to enter place of Temple, 113; beaten if makes Turk angry,

113; community quite numerous, 80; dare not look through gates to Temple, 168; green forbidden to, 127; habitations in caves as wild beasts, 92; to injure a Jew is work well pleasing, 165; live in happiness and tranquility, 80; majority are Spanish, 125; many forsaken widows, 101; may not rebuild house without permission, 101; no Jews except two dyers, 98; not in exile as in own country, 128; not permitted to enter Temple Mount, insinuate prayers through crevices, 173; nothing equals the misery and suffering of, 159; ply trades side by side with Ishmaelites, 81; poverty exceeded anything we had known, 151; in recent times live in peace and quiet, 167; seventy families of poorest, 101; 250 Jewish householders, 94; we enjoy special protection of European consuls, 167; when did Jews return here, 60

and Roman period: banned from entering Jerusalem, 33; differed from neighbors, 21; Hadrian abolished Jewish Jerusalem with construction of Aelia Capitolina, 206; offer their prayers for my imperial office, 33; Rome could not obliterate concept of Jerusalem as Jewish homeland, 206; sacred rites at variance with glory of Rome, 15; Titus justified in waiting for Jews to destroy each other, 206

Joseph of Arimathea, shown tomb of (in Church of Sepulcher), 157

Julian (Emperor), I may rebuild sacred city, (33); Jews offer prayers for my imperial office, 33

Justinian (Emperor), dedicated church to Mother of God, 34; sent Temple treasures to sanctuaries of Christians in Jerusalem, 35

Kiblah (see Dome of Rock; Rock)

Koran, raised to the throne and Testaments cast down, 64; sent down in three places including Jerusalem, 90

verses: does not behoove God to have son, 39; God has not begotten a son, 33; Jesus only an apostle, 33; so turn towards the Holy Mosque (Mecca), 43

M

Mary (Virgin), Church where born, 93, 100; departed this life at Mount Zion, 49; pious belief not only her soul but also body raised, 65; place in valley of Gethsemane (Jehoshaphat) at which taken from this life, 33; snatched up to heaven from Valley of Jehoshaphat, 71; the spot on Mount Zion where she died, 40; taken into heaven from Mount of Olives, 27; from this place (in Church of Assumption) ascended into heaven, 84; where Jesus first appeared to (in Church of Sepulcher), 157

Mary Magdalene, shown where Jesus appeared to in Church of Sepulcher, 157

Matathias (Maccabee), why was I born to behold destruction, 11

Melchizedek, blessed Abraham on Rock of Calvary, 82; king of Salem, 3; shown tomb of, 157

Mohammed, apostle of Allah transported to Jerusalem, 42; companions of did not regard Rock as *kiblah*, 90; conquest on anniversary of ascension to heaven, 63; on day of judgment will take his seat, 85; footprint of, when he mounted Burak, 97; go to Prayer Niche of David, 96; good work in Jerusalem equal to thousand, 96; Jerusalem site of Prophet's nocturnal journey, 70; Muslims believe will sit astride stone column to judge, 181; Night Journey originated in Jerusalem, 74; pity he could not judge world from roost of his own in Mecca, 181; sin in Jerusalem equivalent of thousand, 96; successors employed sword and violence, 72; this firstborn son of Satan, 72; visitor to Jerusalem should bathe himself in fountain of Siloam, 96

Monastery (Church) of Holy Cross, built by St. Helena, 137; great convent grown out of hole in the ground, 177; laid waste by Pagans, 69; Solomon had a garden, 84; tradition it was founded by ruler of Georgia, 137; wall on which painted St. Abraham, 100; in which abide schismatic monks, 97
in the keeping of the Greeks: Friars, 124; Greeks, 120; Monks, 69

source of wood of Cross: the earth that nourished the root, 122; pit in which they say Palm did grow, 129; spot where arm of cross grew, 102; where grew the tree, 84, 118, 142; where holy cross was cut out, 69; where stump of tree stood, 122; from which one part of cross made, 100

Monastery of Mary, in the Valley of Jehoshaphat, 71; from which Mary's body snatched to heaven, 71

Monastery of St. Elias, halfway on road from Jerusalem to Bethlehem, 100

Monument (Pillar) of Absalom, even Muslims throw a stone, 95; every year heap is removed, 95; no pilgrim passes without casting stone, 172; stones thrown at it, 91

Mount of Olives, atop is tomb of Huldah, 125, 134; furnishing a panorama like the Giancolo, 152; most attractive view of Jerusalem, 96; scarcely olive tree to be found, 102; view from lingers long and lovingly, 187

and Christianity: below, basilica of Blessed Mary, 27; Christians have constructed 24 churches, 36; crowned by ruined mosque covering site of Ascension, 155; desolation and degradation provide true lesson: He is not here, 169; impossible not to find traces of Jesus in the free open space, 169; not multitude who sleep here, but faith held in the Messiah, 156; last print of our Lord's feet, 40; site of Ascension most palpably contradicted by New Testament, 141; steps of Jesus' feet in a stone, 105; where our Lord ascended into heaven, 40, 155

and Judaism: gather in month of Tishri to weep, 41; mourn destruction on ninth of Av, 95; there is a synagogue, 40; tombstones from ancient cemetery serve as paving stones, 211; we prayed the evening service, 162; where bodies of nobles of Judah, flocks of sheep and goats, 140; where the red heifer was burnt, 70; worship facing Temple, especially on Hoshana Rabba, 41

Mount Scopus, we see Jerusalem and make one rent, 92

Mount Zion, Christian and Jew will together raise voices in praise, 163; I should have selected for my residence, 155; last roseate glow, beautiful beyond description, 139; on ninth of Av mourners weep, 95; nowhere is arch of heaven more pure, 139; stands for ever, 162

and Christianity: in basilica, stone rejected by builders, 27; Helena founded immense church, 46; Jesus had holy Supper with Apostles, 99; marble column to which our Lord bound, 40, 157; no buildings except place of Christians, 54; once was built Convent of St. Mary, 93; site of martyrdom of St. Stephen, 40; site of our Lord's Supper, 40; spot where Christ appeared to Apostles, 99; spot where Virgin Mary died, 40; startling to hear that this mosque is scene of Last Supper, 170; stone table of altar from exit of Holy Sepulcher, 99; where Holy Ghost descended on apostles, 40

and Franciscans (see Franciscans)

and King David: the chapel in which David wrote Psalter, 42; David and Solomon buried there, 125; as in days of David, old men at foot of, teaching children from Bible, 173; formerly fortress of King David, 80; is the City of David, 7. 87, 93, 95; monuments of David and Solomon under the church, 91; sepulchers of House of David, 54; Tomb of David now crumbling old mosque, 175; Tomb of David once thought to mean Bethlehem, 137

and Muslims: Ishmaelites never allow to enter, 125; neither Christians nor Jews shall have, 82; seizure of tomb of David from Christians, 96; we will take it for ourselves, 82

Muslims (see other headings, especially Dome of Rock, Jerusalem, Haram-a-Sharif, Mohammed), built mosque facing Church of Sepulcher, 83; do not allow use of bells to Christians, 117; hold keys to door of Church of Sepulcher, 79, 99, 116; in Jerusalem not a place truly sacred, 90; to recover strayed camel from misguided people, 62; sought to have graves dedicated as wakf, 95; 10,000 Muslim householders, 94; tradition Mohammed shall sit on pil-

Topical Index

lar (column) in judgment, 85, 123; we Saracens also count David as holy, 81

N

Nahmanides, heart with my children but loss compensated by joy, 98

Napoleon Bonaparte, inviting Jews to espouse reestablishing Jerusalem, 111

Nea Church, dedicated by Justinian, 34; God revealed natural supply of stone, 34; identical with Aksa Mosque or standing on site, 141; Israel's scholars redeemed, 202; Justinian sent Temple treasures to, 35; Justinian's builders dismantled porticoes of ruined Temple Mount to build, 202; 39 dexteri long and 35 wide, 42; thrown down by earthquake, 41; unquestionably al-Aksa, 138

Nebi Samuel, burial place of Samuel, 91; fine synagogue there, 91

Nehemiah, each builder had sword girded as he was building, 10; inspected the walls of Jerusalem, 10

O

Omar (Caliph), *Mihrab* of Omar, originally of David, 97; Patriarch said Church is David's Mosque, 97; this is not Mosque of David, 97

Ophel, cauliflowers grow to enormous size and in profusion, 185; Garden of King Solomon now a cauliflower bed, 160; the Hill of Ophel, 181

Oratory of David (see Tower of)

P

Pilgrimage (Christian) and Travelers (see also Indulgences), all temptation is here collected, 32; can make voyage through devout...meditations, 126; enthusiasm... wanting in travelers conveyed comfortably by steam, 158; if Divine grace more abundant in Jerusalem, sin would not be so much the fashion, 32; Greeks in particular stress it merits plenary indulgences, 133; heavenly sanctuary open from Britain, 32; here Pilgrims roam, that strayed so far to seek, 124; I admonish travelers not to make shipwreck of conscience, 110; interest of tourists...story vividly told, 206; most prevalent mode of apostasy, sacrilegious reverence for tombs and bones, 177; neither need Christian run hither... or thither...to be saved, 132; no one should think visiting to be light task, 81; now reduced...to a few monks, 133; pilgrimage to Jerusalem not included among good deeds, 32; rather than walk about holy places...examine our heart, 120; should undertake solely with intention of contemplating Holy Mysteries, 77; surrounded with perils, 68; that perfect, glorious pilgrimage/ Called the celestial, 80; Stations of the Cross...not to gain indulgences, 212; this book will make traveler of thee, 111; transformed republican citizen of America into "illustrissimus dominus," 174; which cannot be done without great fatigue, 81

pilgrims (Christian): all who come...to visit (Church of Sepulcher) pay tax, 88; arms marked with ensigns of Jerusalem, 121; carved on pillars and marble slabs, 85; did not believe guides, 110; guide gave name and history to every bank and boulder, 181; greatest expense...dues to Turks and Arabs, 146; Greek priests all over, selling candles, 154; here is stone where Christ leaned against, 161; I gathered up thorns... I picked up pebbles, 85; I turned to look at them...a living, moving mass of thousands, 174; most are Russians in long boots, 154; painted coats of arms, 85; pile up stones...to secure a place, 84; she had thrice been to Jerusalem, 79; should carry two bags, 78; suggested we...hire parties to visit for us and thus see by proxy, 182; touched the sacred pillar for plenary indulgences, 82

Pompey, first Roman to subdue the Jews, 20; seized Jerusalem on day of fasting, 20; went into Temple and saw what was unlawful, 16

Pools of Solomon, wisest of men looked into same pool, 171

Protestants (see Christians)

Richard Lion-Heart, the Cross, which is for you simply a piece of wood, 68; the

Topical Index

points at issue are Jerusalem, the Cross, and the land, 67; suffer me not to behold Thy Holy City, 68

Robinson's Arch, Dr. Robinson was mistaken...did not reach across valley, 185; proves incontestably antiquity of that portion of wall, 166

Rock (on Temple Mount), all rivers...clouds...winds come from under, 89; center of the world, 48; Christian altar erected on it, 118; detached on all sides, 97; first *kiblah* in Islam, 156; Franks built church and altar, 64; Franks cut pieces from, 64; footprint of the Prophet, 97; footsteps of Jesus, 69; *kiblah* for prophets, 90; Muslims turned faces to until Mecca became *kiblah*, 43; Noah presented his offering, 90; served in eyes of Muslims as ancient *kiblah* of Moses, 156; stone on which God commanded Moses to make *kiblah*, 43; where Abraham, Jacob, David prayed, all conveniently near each other, 166; who regards as *kiblah* is apostate, 90

S

St. Mary's Church (monastery) (in Valley of Jehoshaphat), not only her soul but also her body raised there, 65; where she was taken up, 27; where snatched up to heaven, 71

St. Savior Church (see also Franciscans; Mount Zion), called it St. Savior, 117; Franciscans acquire in 1559, 117; headquarters of all missions to Holy Land, 134; over past century perhaps 200 Catholic visitors, 146; very near Holy Sepulcher, 117;

Saladin, advised to demolish Church of Sepulcher, but majority opposed, 64; the city that David founded, 69; come, build your home, 60; if God gives us grace to drive His enemies, 69; God has rendered easy to recover strayed camel, 62; had bells in Church of Sepulcher broken, 117; Jerusalem has been in enemy hands, 69; Jerusalem is ours as much as yours, 70; ordered *mihrab* uncovered, 64; place where the people will assemble, 70; site of our Prophet's nocturnal journey, 70

Salem, is Jerusalem, 61; mockery sits on Salem's throne, 144

Sepulcher (Tomb) of Jesus (See also Calvary; Church of Sepulcher)
authenticity: authentic or not, no man can enter without breathless fear, 176; cannot be what it was then, 83; certain impious and godless persons had thought to remove, 31; exclaim, "This is not the place," and yet I must be wrong, 172; legendary localities were gradually accumulated, 141; no sound reason for supposing early Christians paid attention to site, 148; nothing to guide us but vague conjecture, 157; others assert not a piece as large as grain of millet left, 83; perhaps in gloomy vale of Kidron, 137; place of crucifixion and entombment must be sought elsewhere, 157; present site discarded by unprejudiced inquirer, 149; some say under marble slabs still exists entire, 83; testimony clearer than any voice, 31; tomb now shown not upon real place, 165; where had been statue of Aphrodite, 46

and Christianity: Constantine gave orders to purify, 31; disgusted with mummery yet indescribable emotion, 138; a frozen zeal that will not be warmed, 129; Greeks impede restoration, 116; Greeks unjustly claim absolute jurisdiction, 116; Heaven protect the Sepulcher when this tribe invades, 179; the Lord revealed his holy tomb, 46; the main fact abides there, 83; my gaze so firmly attached, could not tear away, 145; open from above, 55; at site of, was aware only of my own weakness, 145; on this very spot a new Jerusalem was constructed, 31; Wandering Jew comes once every century, 148; whether part be there matters very little, 83; whoever here will pray, all sins forgiven, 99; a witness of so much human ignorance, 148

and Muslims: allow to stand for three Our Fathers, 99; seals and keys held by Saracens, 99; Sultan has caused wall to be built round, 94

Siloam (Fountain of), above the water a hanging basilica, 34; flows forth only once in three days, 67; flows only

Topical Index

on certain days, 30; not a stream but a spring, 101; since it comes from Paradise, 96; a spring of Paradise, 90

Silwan, colony of ruffians inhabit the dismal place, 176; from eighth century BCE, cemeteries among houses of present village, 201; filthy in the extreme, 187; living persons dwelt in tombs, 161; a nest of stone huts and caves clinging to side-hill, 184; occupation of inhabitants begging and hunting for old copper coins, 184; troglodytes in caves and tenements of the dead, 138; villagers are notorious thieves, 187; well where the Jews hid fire from Temple, 104; where Blessed Virgin used to wash little clothes, 104

Simon (Maccabee), we have taken only inheritance of our ancestors, 11

Solomon, begins building Temple, (7); built underneath Temple to hide Ark, 66; stables built by him, 54, 85

Solomon's Stables (see Temple Mount)

Stations of the Cross (see also Via Dolorosa), first attempt to arrange as practiced in Europe, 109n; main purpose of, not indulgences but Passion of Christ, 212; mnemonic listing to recall, 105

Suleiman the Magnificent, expels Franciscans from church on Mount Zion, 131; sent officials who built Jerusalem's walls as in former times, 119

Templars (Knights), built living quarters against al-Aksa, 63; close to al-Aksa have many spacious buildings, 65; dwell in al-Aksa, 70; had their residence near Temple of the Lord, 73; kneeling on blood and necks of enemy, 53; most excellent soldiers, 53; sing in Chorus psalm of David, 53; three hundred in palace built by Solomon, 54; on the watch to guard and protect, 70

T

Temple, center of Jerusalem, 17; in first years of common era Western Wall of still existed, 200; site of not in doubt, 206

first Temple period: House of Lord burned by Nebuchadnezzar,

7; Nebuzaradan sent to pillage, 16; site lies beneath Muslim sanctuary, 207; Solomon begins building, 7; Titus expressed opinion to destroy, 36) Zerubbabel's work based on Solomon's foundations, 206

second Temple period: Antiochus ordered pollution of, 11; built in all its splendor, 7; Caligula ordered Jews to set up his statue, 21; the Lord has charged me with building Him a house, 10; never a statue of God there, 15; no representation of the gods within, 20; not a single statue there, 11; plowshare drawn over the consecrated ground, 114; Pompey saw what was unlawful, 16; Roman soldiers had such vast quantities of spoils, 16; who has not seen, 21n

and Christianity: all Solomon's sea of brass, 115; how long thy temples worshipless, 144; I will to thy house repair, 130; instruments of Jewish worship transferred from Rome to Carthage, 114; Jesus took the place of the Temple, 169; now called Templum Domini, 54; pride and glory of Israel is gone, 182; when Solomon's Temple stood, 114; which eyes are dry to look upon, 115

and Islam: ancient Holy of Holies has become shrine of Islam, 185; where Temple stood, Saracen house of prayer, 39

and Judaism: destroyed ninth of Av, 21; establish the House as of old, 87; even though in ruins, sanctity endures, 66; Foundation Stone is before Holy Ark, 17; fragrance of incense, 21; Gentile is master of the House, 87; like reflection of eye, 23; no other city where it could be built, 18; Solomon built underneath to hide Ark, 66

Temple Mount

traditions: Adam created from soil of, 18; chambers were Solomon's stables, 85; gate of Garden of Eden is near, 18; on ninth of Av all lamps go out, 94; stalling horses there irreverent, 85; two statues of Hadrian, 28; where Abraham bound Isaac, 95; where Abraham offered up Isaac, 66

and Christians: Christians built a church on this spot, 126; destruction vindication of Jesus' prophecy, 201; Justinian's builders dismantled porticoes to build (Nea) church, 202; most beautiful place in Jerusalem, 183; soil'd with gore and wet with lukewarm blood, 131

and Jews: blood-red banner of Mohammed waving over Jews' heads, 186; dare not set foot within its precincts, 186; delivered this day by you, 204; from House of Pilate could see whole Temple enclosure, 125; largest site of its kind in ancient world, 201; the Temple Mount is ours! 204; wakf knew Temple Mount built over foundations from Second Temple period, 200; where Adam was created, and offered sacrifice, 66; where Cain and Abel offered sacrifices, 66; where Noah built when he left the ark, 66

and Muslims: magnificent platform supports two mosques, 155

Titus, expressed opinion to destroy Temple, 36; to exterminate religion of Jews and Christians, 36; will endeavor to preserve Temple, 16

Tomb of David (see Mount Zion)

Tower (Citadel) of David, all around a moat, 99; built by David, 99; built by Solomon, 97; fortified stronghold, 64; house of David and Solomon, 64; never saw guard there, 79; not as when built by David, 99; ruin and rubbish everywhere, 187; small ill-fortified Castle, 129; still exists, 66; Sultan Isa transformed into mosque, 112; view from top embracing whole town, 187; in which he wrote the Psalter, 42, 56

and Bathsheba: spot where taking bath, 209; where David fell enamored of, 128; where David first saw her, 183

Travelers (see pilgrimage)

U

Urban II (Pope), enter upon the road to the Holy Sepulcher, 71; undertake this journey for remission of your sins, 71

V

Valley of Hinnom (Gehenna), I heard nothing, 43; is the Valley of Hell, 43; located east of Jerusalem, 31, 88, 90; Moloch, horrid king, besmeared with blood, 124; same as valley of Jehoshaphat, 30, 84; will be called Valley of Slaughter, 9

Valley of Jehoshaphat, dearest wish of Jew's heart to be laid to rest among long-buried ancestors, 172; is Gehenna, 30; Jewish burial ground most ghastly sight I have seen, 175; on ninth of Av mourn destruction, 95; pilgrims pile up stones to secure a place, 84; where Jews buried dead under shadow of Temple of Solomon, 172; where Virgin ascended into heaven, 84

as place of judgment: Christians: wherein world will be judged, 100; in which Lord will come to judge world, 54; world will congregate for judgment, 104; *Jews*: there will I sit in judgment, 9; *Muslims*: Mohammed will come to judge, 85, 181

Valley of Kidron, habitations of Jews in caves as wild beasts, 92; make vows in reference to shaving off hair, 177; sepulchers of frequented exclusively by Jews, 177

Vespasian, gave orders to demolish city and Temple, 17; "Judaea Capta," 23; why did you not destroy Western Wall, 17

Via Dolorosa (see also Stations of the Cross), Arab donkeys racing down the hill, 200; do not know how many times houses along it have been destroyed, but no obstacle, 183; faithful of Jerusalem do frequently, 117; by Imagination of mind conceive like way, 109; from St. Savior's Convent with very great devotion, 117; trod on that Friday far away, 160

Western Wall

appearance and condition: expect to see wall reminiscent of Herod and Solomon, 142; longest of Temple Mount's buttress walls, 200; men at one point, women at another, 183; a narrow passage, must use elbows, 142; only by permission dare Jews lift eyes toward, 150; on other side one of hovels of Magreb Quarter, 153; road leading to still in state of ruin, 163

and Christians: Jews endeavor to insinuate prayers through crevices, 173; leading our thoughts to self-invoked curse, 158; no site affected me more, 143; tradition which leads Jews to pray through this wall, 173; what a contrast these humbled people and proud Mohammedans, 159

Topical Index

and Jews: all approaching remove shoes, 162; all kinds of Jews there, 153; called the Gate of Mercy, 54; clung to the stones with lips framing the Shema, 210; exerted myself to have awning made, 163; experienced no deep emotion, 152; imagine standing on Second Temple pavement on Jerusalem Day, 201; with interlocking stones a guardian of Israel, 162; *ko* is God's name, *tel* means hill, 134; in Middle Ages begins to appear in Jewish sources, 200; once lived a moment there, you never go away, 205; to reach a wall where men stand weeping, 211; standing amongst the worshipers, at times amongst bewildered bystanders, 199; stones with human hearts, 193; stones witnesses to destruction of our land, 151; teardrops from mighty stones, 151; thin faces, strange motions fit terrible state of Wall, 151; we have returned to our holiest of holy places, 203

and Muslims: adjoins wall of Haram-a-Sharif where al-Burak was tethered, 168; importation of screen and attachment to pavement infraction of status quo, 192; Jews must be warned against raising voices and proclaiming doctrines, 168; paving inadmissable under Islamic law, 168; prevented from going too near lest I was a Jew, 209; Turk permits the tribes to creep…to lean or kneel, lament and weep, 160

and Roman period: why did you not destroy, 17

Z

Zion, Ah! See how Sion mourns, 130; dark'ned the renown with angry frown, 128; how long will there be weeping in, 40; not slightest ground for supposing not same as ancient, 139; the roads of in mourning, 86; if Sion hill delight thee more, 123; stronghold of Zion the *kiblah* of Christians, 185; Temple plundered, but sacred hills of Zion stand, 162; temporal Zion now in dust, but true Zion is rising, 176; walk about, count her towers, 9; by the waters of Babylon we sat and wept, 10; when shall I sing on Zion's hill, 120; when shall Zion's songs again seem sweet, 144; will you not ask peace of captives, 59

Bibliography of Works Cited

Adler, Elkan Nathan, ed. *Jewish Travellers: A Treasury of Travelogues from Nine Centuries*. 2nd ed. New York: Hermon Press, 1966.

Adrichomius, Christianus. *A Briefe Description of Hierusalem*. Translated by Thomas Tymme. London, 1595. Reprint, New York: Da Capo Press, 1969.

Anonymous Pilgrims I–VII (Eleventh and Twelfth Centuries). Translated by Aubrey Stewart. London: Palestine Pilgrims' Text Society, 1894.

Antoninus Martyr. *Of the Holy Places Visited*. Translated by Aubrey Stewart. London: Palestine Pilgrims' Text Society, 1890. Vol 2.

Aristeas. "The Letter of Aristeas." In *The Apocrypha and Pseudepigrapha of the Old Testament in English*. Vol. 2, *Pseudepigrapha*, edited by R.H. Charles. Oxford: Clarendon Press, 1913. Wesley Center Online. http://wesley.nnu.edu/biblical_studies/noncanon/ot/pseudo/aristeas.htm.

Armstrong, Karen. *Jerusalem: One City, Three Faiths*. New York: Ballantine Books, 1997.

Atwan, Robert, and Laurance Wieder, eds. *Chapters into Verse: Poetry in English Inspired by the Bible*. 2 vols. New York: Oxford University Press, 1993.

Augustine. *The Confessions of St. Augustine*. Translated by Edward B. Pusey. New York: Pocket Books, 1952.

Avigad, Nahman. *Discovering Jerusalem*. Nashville: T. Nelson, 1983.

Baedeker, Karl. *Palestine and Syria*. Leipzig: Karl Baedeker, 1912.

Barclay, J.T. *City of the Great King: Jerusalem as It Was, as It Is, and as It Is to Be*. Philadelphia: James Challen, 1857.

Bartlett, W. H. *Jerusalem Revisited*. London, 1855. Reprint, Jerusalem: Ariel Publishing, 1976.

———. *Walks about the City and Environs of Jerusalem*. London, 1844. Reprint, Jerusalem: Canaan Publishing, 1974.

Bellow, Saul. *To Jerusalem and Back*. London: Secker and Warburg, 1976.

Belon, Pierre. *Plurimarum singularium et memorabilium rerum in Graecia, Asia, Aegypto* (Antwerp, 1589). Translated for the author by S. Akielazek of St. John's University, NY.

Ben-Ami, Aharon. *Social Change in a Hostile Environment: The Crusaders' Kingdom in Jerusalem.* Princeton, NJ: Princeton University Press, 1969.

Ben-Arieh, Yehoshua. *Jerusalem in the Nineteenth Century: The Old City.* Jerusalem: Yad Izhak Ben-Zvi, 1984.

Ben-Dov, Meir. *Historical Atlas of Jerusalem.* New York: Continuum Publishing, 2002.

_____. *In the Shadow of the Temple: The Discovery of Ancient Jerusalem.* Translated by Ina Friedman. New York: Harper & Row, 1985.

_____. *Jerusalem: Man and Stone.* Tel Aviv: Modan Publishing, 1990.

_____. Mordechai Naor, and Zeev Avner. *The Western Wall.* Translated by Raphael Posner. Jerusalem: Ministry of Defense Publishing, 1985.

Benjamin of Tudela. *The Itinerary of Benjamin of Tudela.* Translated with commentary by Marcus N. Adler. First edition, London, 1907. Reprint, New York: Philipp Feldheim, n.d.

Benvenisti, Meron. *The Crusades in the Holy Land.* Jerusalem: Israel Universities Press, 1970.

Biddulph, William, in Purchas, *Purchas His Pilgrimes.* Glasgow, 1905. Vol. 8, ch. 9.

_____. *Travels into Africa, Asia, and to the Blacke Sea.* London: Printed by Th. Hauieland for W. Aspley, 1609. Reprint, New York: Da Capo Press, 1968.

_____. *The Travels of Four Englishmen and a Preacher into Africa...* (1611). In *Osborne Collection of Voyages and Travels*, edited by Thomas Osborne. London, 1747.

Blake, William. *The Portable Blake.* Edited by Alfred Kazin. New York: Viking, 1946.

Bordeaux Pilgrim. *The Anonymous Pilgrim of Bordeaux* (333 CE). Translated by Aubrey Stewart. London: Palestine Pilgrims' Text Society, 1887. Vol. 1. http://www.christusrex.org/www1/ofm/pilgr/bord/10Bord07aJerus.html.

The Breviary; or, Short Description of Jerusalem. Translated by Aubrey Stewart. London: Palestine Pilgrims' Text Society, 1890. Vol. 2.

Bibliography of Works Cited

Bunyan, John. *The Pilgrim's Progress* (1678). Edited by Roger Sharrock. New York: Penguin Books, 1984.

Burchard of Mount Zion. Translated by Aubrey Stewart. London: Palestine Pilgrims' Text Society, 1895. Vol. 12.

Byron, George Gordon. *Byron's Hebrew Melodies.* Edited by Thomas L. Ashton. Austin: University of Texas, 1972.

Calvin, John. "Traité des Reliques," Wikipedia encyclopedia. http://en.wikipedia.org/wiki/True_Cross.

Carmi. T., ed. *The Penguin Handbook of Hebrew Verse.* New York: Viking, 1982.

Casola. *Canon Pietro Casola's Pilgrimage to Jerusalem in the Year 1494.* Edited and translated by M. Margaret Newett. Manchester: University of Manchester Press, 1907.

Cattermole, C.R. *Sacred Poetry of the Seventeenth Century* (1835). New York: Burt Franklin, 1969.

Chateaubriand. *Itinéraire de Paris á Jerusalem.* Baltimore: Johns Hopkins Press, 1946. Vol. 2.

Chaucer, Geoffrey. *The Canterbury Tales.* Translated into modern English by Nevill Coghill. Rev. ed. Baltimore: Penguin Books, 1963.

Chesterton, G.K. *The New Jerusalem.* New York: George H. Doran, 1921.

Chronicon Paschale 284–628 AD [Easter chronicle 284–628 AD]. Translated by Michael Whitby and Mary Whitby. Liverpool: Liverpool University Press, 1990.

Cicero. Translated by Louis E. Lord. Cambridge: Loeb Classical Library, 1967. Vol 10.

The City of Jerusalem. Translated by Claude Reignier Conder. London: Palestine Pilgrims' Text Society, 1896. Vol. 6.

Conder, Claude Reignier. *Tent Work in Palestine: A Record of Discovery and Adventure.* London: Alexander Watt, 1889.

Daniel the Abbot. *The Pilgrimage of the Russian Abbot Daniel in the Holy Land 1106–1107.* Annotated by C.W. Wilson. London: Palestine Pilgrims' Text Society, 1895. Vol. 4.

Davis, John. *The Landscape of Belief: Encountering the Holy Land in Nineteenth-Century American Art and Culture.* Princeton, NJ: Princeton University Press, 1996.

The Deeds of the Franks (Gesta Francorum). Edited by Rosalind Hill. New York: Thomas Nelson, 1962.

A Dictionary of Hymnology. Edited by John Julian. London: John Murray, 1915.

Dio Cassius. *Dio's Roman History*. Translated by Earnest Cary. Cambridge: Loeb Classical Library, 1990.

Diodorus Siculus. *Diodorus of Sicily*. Translated by Francis R. Walton. Cambridge: Loeb Classical Library, 1967.

Eban, Abba. *My People: The Story of the Jews*. New York: Random House, 1968.

Egeria. *The Pilgrimage of Etheria [Egeria]*. Edited and translated by M.L. McClure and C.L. Feltoe. New York: Macmillan, 1919.

Eucherius. "The Epitome of Eucherius about Certain Holy Places." Translated by Aubrey Stewart. London: Palestine Pilgrims' Text Society, 1890. Vol. 2.

Eusebius. *The Life of the Blessed Emperor Constantine*. Revised translation by Ernest C. Richardson. *Nicene and Post-Nicene Fathers*, series 2, vol. 1. http://www.ccel.org/fathers2/NPNF2-01.

_____. *The History of the Church from Christ to Constantine*. Translated by G.A. Williamson. New York: Penguin Books, rev. ed., 1989.

_____. *The Onomasticon*. Translated by G.S.P. Freeman-Grenville; edited with an introduction by Joan E. Taylor. Jerusalem: Carta, 2003.

Eckardt, Alice, ed. *Jerusalem: City of the Ages*. Lanham, MD: University Press of America, 1987.

Fabri, Felix. *The Book of the Wanderings of Felix Fabri (Circa 1480–1483)*. Translated by Aubrey Stewart. 2 vols. London: Palestine Pilgrims' Text Society, 1897. Vols. 7–10.

Farhi, Estori. *Kaftor vaPerach* [Hebrew] (1549). 2 vols. Edited by A.M. Luncz. Jerusalem, 1897.

Fuller, Thomas. *A Pisgah-Sight of Palestine*. London, 1650.

Gabrieli, Francesco. *Arab Historians of the Crusades* (1969). First paperback edition. Berkeley: University of California Press, 1984.

Gibbon, Edward. *The Decline and Fall of the Roman Empire*. Edited by J.B. Bury. 7 vols. London: Methuen & Co., 1909.

Gilbert, Martin. *Jerusalem in the Twentieth Century*. New York: John Wiley, 1996.

Goldhill, Simon. *The Temple of Jerusalem*. Cambridge, MA: Harvard University Press, 2005.

Gregory of Nyssa. "On Pilgrimage." In *Ascetic and Moral Treatises. Nicene and Post-Nicene Fathers*, series 2, vol. 5, bk. 12. http://www.ccel.org/fathers2/NPNF2-01.

Halevi, Jehudah. *Selected Poems of Jehudah Halevi*. Translated by Nina Salaman. Philadelphia: Jewish Publication Society, 1928.

Hammer, Reuven. *The Jerusalem Anthology*. Philadelphia: Jewish Publication Society, 1995.

Al-Harizi, Judah. *The Book of Tahkemoni*. Translated by David Simha Segal. Portland, OR: The Littman Library of Jewish Civilization, 2003.

Heilman, Samuel. *A Walker in Jerusalem*. New York: Summit Books, 1986.

Heywood, Thomas. *Four Prentices of London*, 1615.

Hillenbrand, Carole. *The Crusades: Islamic Pespectives*. New York: Routledge, 2000.

Hoade, Eugene, ed. *Western Pilgrims (1322–1392): The Itineraries of Fr. Simon Fitzimmons (1322–23), a Certain Englishman (1344–45), Thomas Brygg (1392), and Notes on Other Authors and Pilgrims*. First impression 1952, reprinted 1970. Publication of the Studium Biblicum Franciscanum. No. 18. Reprint, Jerusalem: Franciscan Printing Press, 1993.

Holtz, Avraham, ed. *The Holy City: Jews on Jerusalem*. New York: Norton & Co., 1971.

Horn, Elzear. *Ichnographiae Monumentorum Terrae Sanctae, 1724–1744*. Translated by Eugene Hoade, preface and notes by B. Bagatti. Jerusalem: Franciscan Printing Press, 1962.

Ibn Battuta. *Travels in Asia and Africa, 1325–1354*. Translated by H.A.R. Gibb, 1929. Reprint, New Delhi: Manohar, 2001.

Ibn al-Firkah al-Fazari. *The Book of Arousing Souls to Visit Jerusalem's Holy Walls*. Translated by Charles D. Matthews, in *Palestine: Mohammedan Holy Land*. New Haven, CT: Yale University Press, 1949.

Ibn Ishaq. *Sirat Rasoul Allah*. Translated by Edward Rehatsek. London: Royal Asiatic Society of Great Britain and Ireland, 1898. http: www.faithfreedom.org/Articles/sira/index.htm.

Ibn Khusru [Khusraw], Nasir. *An Account of Jerusalem*. Translated by A.R. Fuller. London: Royal Asiatic Society of Great Britain and Ireland, 1872.

Ibn al-Qalanisi. *The Damascus Chronicle of the Crusades*. Translated by H.A.R. Gibb, 1932. Reprint, New York: Dover, 2002.

Jacobus de Voragine. *The Golden Legend of Jacobus de Voragine*. Translated by Granger Ryan and Helmut Ripperger, 1941. Reprint, New York: Arno Press, 1969.

St. Jerome. Epistle [Letter] 46: to Marcella. "Jerome," *Catholic Encyclopedia on CD-Rom*. http://www.newadvent.org/fathers/3001046.htm.

_____. Epistle 58: to Paulinus. *The Principal Works of St. Jerome*. Translated by Wm. Henry Freemantle. Oxford, 1893. The Saint Pachomius Library. http://www.voskrese.info/spl/jerome058.html.

_____. Epistle 127: to Marcella. *Select Letters of St. Jerome*. Translated by F.A. Wright. London: William Heinemann, 1933.

John of Wurzburg. *Description of the Holy Land*. Translated by Aubrey Stewart. London: Palestine Pilgrims' Text Society, 1896. Vol. 5.

Joinville, Jean de. *Joinville's Chronicles*. In *Memoirs of the Crusades*. Translated by Frank Marzials. New York: E.P. Dutton (Everyman's Library), 1957.

Josephus. *The Life and Works of Flavius Josephus*. Translated by William Whiston. New York: Holt, Reinhart & Winston, 1961.

Karo, Joseph. *Shulhan Aruch*.

Kenyon, Kathleen. *Archeology in the Holy Land*. 4th ed. London: Ernest Benn, 1979.

_____. *Digging up Jerusalem*. London: Ernest Benn, 1974.

Kernohan, R.D. *The Road to Zion: Travelers to Palestine and the Land of Israel*. Edinburgh: Handsel Press, 1995.

Khalidi, Walid. *From Haven to Conquest: Readings in Zionism and the Palestine Problem until 1948*. Washington: Institute for Palestine Studies, 1971.

Kollek, Teddy. "Jerusalem." *Foreign Affairs* (July 1977): 701–16.

_____. and Moshe Pearlman. *Pilgrims to the Holy Land*. New York: Harper & Row, 1970.

The Koran (*Al-Qur'an: A Contemporary Translation by Ahmed Ali*). 2nd revised ed. Princeton: Princeton University Press, 1990.

Le Strange, Guy. *History of Jerusalem under the Moslems from 650–1500*. Originally published 1890. Reprinted from *Palestine under the Moslems* (Beirut: Khayats, 1965). Jerusalem: Ariel Publishing, 1975.

Lewis, Bernard. "The Revolt of Islam." *New Yorker* (November 19, 2001).

Lithgow, William. *The Totall Discourse...* (1632). Reprinted as *Travels and Voyages...* Edinburgh, 1770.

Ludolph von Suchem. *Description of the Holy Land*. Translated by Aubrey Stewart. London: Palestine Pilgrims' Text Society, 1895. Vol. 12.

Maccabees, Book of. In *Seforim haHitzonim* (*Books of the Apocrypha*). Edited by Avraham Kahana. Tel Aviv: Massada, 1959. Vol 2.

Maimonides. "Hilchot Bet HaBechira" [Laws of the Temple]. In *Mishneh Torah (Sefer Avodah)*. Rambam L'Am edition. Jerusalem: Mossad HaRav Kook, 1987. Vol. 6.

Manning, Samuel. *Those Holy Fields* (1874). Reprint, Jerusalem: Ariel Publishing, 1976.

Margoliouth, David Samuel. *Cairo, Jerusalem, and Damascus*. New York: Dodd, Mead, 1907.

Martineau, Harriet. *Eastern Life, Present and Past* (1848). Reprint, London, 1875.

Marx, Karl, and Frederick Engels. *Collected Works*. New York: International Publishers, 1975. Vol. 13.

Maundrell, Henry. *A Journey from Aleppo to Jerusalem in 1697*. Beirut: Khayats Oriental Reprints, 1963.

Mazar, Benjamin. *The Mountain of the Lord*. New York: Doubleday & Co., 1975.

Melville, Herman. *Clarel*. Edited by Walter E. Bezanson. New York: Hendrick's House, 1960.

Miller, Perry, and Thomas H. Johnson, eds. *The Puritans: A Sourcebook of Their Writings*. New York: Harper Torchbooks, 1938. Reprinted 1968. Vol. 1.

Millgram, Abraham E. *Jerusalem Curiosities*. Philadelphia: Jewish Publication Society, 1990.

Milton, Giles. *The Riddle and the Knight*. New York: Farrar, Straus & Giroux, 2001.

Milton, John. *Paradise Lost*, bk. 1.

Moryson, Fynes. *An Itinerary*, 1627. New York: Benjamin Blom, 1967. Vol 2.

Muqaddasi, al-. *Description of Syria and Palestine*. Translated by Guy Le Strange. London: Palestine Pilgrims' Text Society, 1897. Vol. 3.

Naor, Mordecai. *City of Hope: Jerusalem from Biblical to Modern Times*. Jerusalem: Yad Izhak Ben-Zvi, 1997.

Netanyahu, Benjamin. *A Place among the Nations*. New York: Bantam Books, 1993.

The New Testament. In Hebrew and English. London: Trinitarian Bible Society, n.d.

Niccolo, Fra, of Poggibonsi. *A Voyage Beyond the Seas (1346–1350)*. Translated by T. Bellorini and E. Hoade, 1945. Reprint, Jerusalem: Franciscan Printing Press, 1993.

Obenzinger, Hilton. *American Palestine: Melville, Twain, and the Holy Land Mania*. Princeton, NJ: Princeton University Press, 1999.

Oesterreicher, John M., and Anne Sinai, eds. *Jerusalem*. New York: John Day, 1974.

Ogier. *The Holy Jerusalem Voyage of Ogier VIII, Seigneur of Anglure (1395–96)*. Translated by Roland A. Browne. Gainesville: University Presses of Florida, 1975.

Oliphant, Laurence. *Haifa: Life in the Holy Land 1882–1885*. New edition, with introduction by Rechavam Zeevy. Jerusalem: Canaan Publishing, 1976.

Oren, Michael B. *Power, Faith and Fantasy*. New York: Norton & Co., 2007.

Origen. *Contra Celsum*. Translated by Henry Chadwick. Cambridge: Loeb Classical Library, 1953.

Osband, Linda, ed. *Famous Travellers to the Holy Land*. London: Prion, 1989.

Peters, Edward, ed. *The First Crusade: The Chronicle of Fulcher of Chartres and Other Source Materials*. 2nd ed. Philadelphia: University of Pennsylvania Press, 1998.

Peters, F.E. *Jerusalem*. Princeton, NJ: Princeton University Press, 1985.

Petrarch, Francesco. *Itinerary to the Sepulcher of Our Lord Jesus Christ*. Translated by Theodore J. Cachey, Jr. Notre Dame, IN: University of Notre Dame Press, 2002.

Pliny. *Natural History*. Translated by H. Rackham. Cambridge: Loeb Classical Library. Vol. 2.

Pococke, Richard. *A Description of the East and Some Other Countries.* London, 1745. Vol. 2.

Prawer, Joshua. *The World of the Crusaders.* New York: Quadrangle Books, 1972.

———. and Haggai Ben-Shammai, eds. *The History of Jerusalem: The Early Muslim Period, 638–1099.* Jerusalem: Yad Izhak Ben-Zvi, 1996.

Prescott, H.F.M. *Jerusalem Journey: Pilgrimage to the Holy Land in the Fifteenth Century.* London: Eyre & Spottiswoode, 1954.

Procopius. *Buildings.* Translated by H.B. Dewing, 1940. Reprint, Cambridge: Loeb Classical Library, 2002. Vol. 7.

———. *History of the Wars.* Translated by H.B. Dewing. Cambridge: Loeb Classical Library, 1916. Vol. 2.

Pryce-Jones, David. "Jews, Arabs, and French Diplomacy." *Commentary Magazine* (May 2005).

Purchas, Samuel. *Hakluytus Posthumus: or, Purchas His Pilgrimes; Contayning a History of the World in Sea Voyages and Lande Travells, by Englishmen and Others,* 1625. Reprint, Glasgow, 1905. Vol. 2.

Roosevelt, Theodore. *Theodore Roosevelt's Diaries of Boyhood and Youth.* New York: Scribner's, 1928.

Rosovsky, Nitza, ed. *City of the Great King: Jerusalem from David to the Present.* Cambridge, MA: Harvard University Press, 1996.

Runciman, Steven. *A History of the Crusades.* Cambridge, MA: Harvard University Press, 1953. Vol. 1.

Sanderson, John. *The Travels of John Sanderson in the Levant, 1584–1602.* London: The Hakluyt Society, 1931.

Sandys, George. *A Relation of a Journey Begun 1610.* London, 1615. References are to the 1621 edition.

Schappes, Morris U., ed. *A Documentary History of the Jews in the U.S. 1654–1875.* New York: The Citadel Press, 1950.

Schur, Nathan. *Twenty Centuries of Christian Pilgrimage to the Holy Land.* Tel Aviv: Dvir Publishing, 1992.

The Seventh Day: Soldiers Talk about the Six-Day War. Edited by Avraham Shapira. New York: Charles Scribner's Sons, 1970.

Shadur, Joseph, ed. *Young Travelers to Jerusalem: An Annotated Survey of American and English Juvenile Literature on the Holy Land 1785–1940.* Ramat Gan: Bar-Ilan University, 1999.

Shipler, David K. *Arab and Jew: Wounded Spirits in a Promised Land.* New York: Random House, 1986.

Silberman, Neil Asher. *Digging for God and Country: Exploration, Archeology and the Secret Struggle for the Holy Land, 1799–1917.* New York: Knopf, 1982.

Silk, Dennis. *Retrievements: A Jerusalem Anthology.* Jerusalem: Israel Universities Press, 1968.

Slonim, Shlomo. *Jerusalem in America's Foreign Policy.* The Hague: Kluwer Law International, 1998.

Smith, George Adam. *Historical Geography of Jerusalem.* 2 vols. Reprinted from the 1907 edition. Jerusalem: Ariel Publishing, 1974.

Stanley, Arthur P. *Sinai and Palestine.* London, 1889.

Stephens, John Lloyd. *Incidents of Travel in Egypt, Arabia Petraea, and the Holy Land,* 1837. Edited by Victor von Hagen. Norman: University of Oklahoma Press, 1970.

Stern, Menahem, ed. *Greek and Latin Authors on Jews and Judaism.* 3 vols. Jerusalem: Israel Academy of Sciences and Humanities, 1974.

Storme, Albert. *The Way of the Cross: A Historical Sketch.* Translated by Kieran Dunlop. 2nd rev. ed. Jerusalem: Franciscan Printing Press, 1976.

Strabo. *The Geography of Strabo.* Translated by Horace L. Jones. Cambridge: Loeb Classical Library, 1917. Vol. 7.

Suriano, Francesco. *Treatise on the Holy Land,* 1516. Translated by T. Bellorini and E. Hoade, 1949. Reprint, Jerusalem: Franciscan Printing Press, 1983.

Tacitus. *The Histories.* Translated by Clifford H. Moore. Cambridge: Loeb Classical Library. Vol. 3.

Tal, Eliyahu. *Whose Jerusalem.* Jerusalem: International Forum for a United Jerusalem, 1994.

Tanakh: The Holy Scriptures; The New JPS Translation According to the Traditional Hebrew Text. Philadelphia: Jewish Publication Society, 1985.

Tasso, Torquato. *Jerusalem Delivered.* Translated by Edward Fairfax. New York: G.P. Putnam's Sons, 1963.

Bibliography of Works Cited

Thackeray, William Makepeace. *Notes of a Journey from Cornhill to Grand Cairo.* In *Sketch Books.* New York: Harper & Brothers, 1903.

Theoderich. *Guide to the Holy Land*, ca. 1172. Translated by Aubrey Stewart, 1897. 2nd ed., with introduction by Ronald G. Musto. New York: Italica Press, 1986.

Theodosius. *On the Topography of the Holy Land.* Translated by J.H. Bernard. London: Palestine Pilgrims' Text Society, 1890. Vol. 2.

Thomson, W.M. *The Land and the Book.* London, 1887.

Timberlake, Henry. *A True and Strange Discourse of the Travels of Two English Pilgrims.* London, 1616. In *The Harleian Miscellany*, by William Oldys, et al. London: Robert Dutton, 1808. Vol. 1.

Tuchman, Barbara W. *Bible and Sword*, 1956. Reprint, New York: Minerva Press, 1968.

Tyndale, William. *Doctrinal Treatises and Introductions to Different Portions of the Holy Scriptures.* Edited for the Parker Society by Henry Walter. Cambridge: Cambridge University Press, 1848.

Twain, Mark. *The Innocents Abroad.* 2 vols. New York: Harper & Brothers, 1911.

Vilnay, Zev. *Aggadot Eretz Yisrael* [Legends of the land of Israel]. 7th ed. Jerusalem: Kiryat Sefer, 1970.

_____. *Yerushalayim birat Yisrael: Ha'ir ha'atika* [Jerusalem the capital of Israel: The Old City]. Jerusalem: Ahiezer, 1970.

Vogel, Lester I. *To See a Promised Land: Americans and the Holy Land in the Nineteenth Century.* University Park: Pennsylvania State University Press, 1993.

Volney, C.F., *Travels through Syria and Egypt in the years 1783, 1784 and 1785.* 2 vols. Translated from the French. London, 1788.

Walker, Franklin. *Irreverent Pilgrims: Melville, Browne and Twain in the Holy Land.* Seattle: University of Washington Press, 1974.

Warburton, Eliot. *The Crescent and the Cross.* London, 1886.

Warner, Charles Dudley. *In the Levant*, 1876. Reprint, New York: Houghton Mifflin, 1893. Vol. 1.

Warren, Charles. *Underground Jerusalem.* London, 1876.

Wiesel, Elie. *A Beggar in Jerusalem.* New York: Random House, 1970.

_____. *Souls on Fire: Portraits and Legends of Hasidic Masters.* New York: Random House, 1972.

Weizmann, Chaim. *Trial and Error: The Autobiography of Chaim Weizmann.* New York: Shocken Books, 1966.

Werblowsky, R.J. Zvi. "The Meaning of Jerusalem to Jews, Christians, and Muslims." Revised ed. Jerusalem: Israel Universities Study Group for Middle Eastern Affairs, 1978.

Wey, William. *The Itineraries of William Wey...1458 and 1462.* London: Roxburghe Club, 1857.

Wilhelm, Kurt, ed. *Roads to Zion: Four Centuries of Travelers' Reports.* Translated by A.M. Lask. New York: Schocken Books, 1948.

Wilken, Robert L. *The Land Called Holy: Palestine in Christian History and Thought.* New Haven: Yale University Press, 1992.

Wilkinson, John. *Jerusalem Pilgrims Before the Crusades.* Jerusalem: Ariel Publishing, 1977.

William of Tyre. *A History of Deeds Done Beyond the Sea.* Translated by Emily Atwater Babcock and A.C. Krey. New York: Columbia University Press, 1943. Vol. 1.

Wilson, Charles W. *Jerusalem: The Holy City.* Reprinted from *Pictureseque Palestine,* 1880. Jerusalem: Ariel Publishing, 1975.

Wright, Thomas, ed. *Early Travels in Palestine,* 1848. Reprint, New York: Ktav Publishing House, 1968.

Yaari, Avraham. *Igrot Eretz Yisrael* [Letters about the land of Israel]. Ramat Gan: Masada, 1971.

_____. *Masa'ot Eretz Yisrael* [Travels to the land of Israel]. Ramat Gan: Masada, 1976.